Web and New Media Pricing Guide

Web and New Media Pricing Guide

JP Frenza & Michelle Szabo

Hayden
Books

Web and New Media Pricing Guide

Warning and Disclaimer

Associate Publisher	John Pierce
Publishing Manager	Laurie Petrycki
Managing Editor	Lisa Wilson
Development Editor	Bront Davis
Publishing Coordinator	Karen Flowers
Book Designer	Michelle Szabo
Manufacturing Coordinator	Brook Farling
Production Team Supervisor	Laurie Casey
Production Team	Kim Cofer, Janelle Herber, Mary Hunt, William Huys Jr., Joe Millay, Rowena Rappaport, Christy Wagner
Indexer	Bront Davis

Trademark Acknowledgments

Hayden Books

The staff of Hayden Books is committed to bringing you the best computer books. What our readers think of Hayden is important to our ability to serve our customers. If you have any comments, no matter how great or how small, we'd appreciate your taking the time to send us a note.

America Online: Hayden Bks

Internet: hayden@hayden.com

Visit the Hayden Books Web site at http://www.hayden.com

Contents at a Glance

*Dedicated to all of the hard-working people
involved in new media developement.*

Foreword

The title of this book, *Web and New Media Pricing Guide*, doesn't do it justice. Most people will think the book covers the pricing of new media—what a Duh-ism. The problem is that this book covers much more than the limited confines of pricing. Properly named by an evangelist, this book would be called *Web and New Media Business Guide* or some such generalized marketing drivel.

Alas, I come not to name this book, but to foreword it, and I shall fulfill my function. The purpose of a foreword is twofold: first, to help differentiate this book from the other 5,000 tree-killers in the computer section of your local bookstore; second, to ingratiate the others so that they will return a favor someday.

Re: differentiation.

I'm a big believer in art for art's sake and doing the right thing—for crying out loud, I work for Apple, not Microsoft. The problem with art—and creating web pages and new media projects is art—designers (and clients) often forget that there is also a business side of things.

If more than Bill Gates and Marc Andreessen are going to make money on the Internet, then this book is what we Romans call "sine qua non." Both designers and clients have to understand proposals, pricing, budgets, and legal agreements in addition to the "cool" factor for the Internet to move forward at a rapid pace. This is the ONLY book that I know of that fills this need, and thus, I will sleep better at night knowing that Web and New Media Pricing Guide exists for the benefit of my digi-friends. (No matter what the title.)

Re: ingratiation.

This book is what I call DICE: Deep, Indulgent, Complete, and Elegant. Deep refers to the way the book provides both high-level concepts and implementable minutiae. Indulgent refers to the fact that you think you're buying a book about pricing but in fact you get much more. Complete refers to the rich variety of information from pricing charts to case studies to interviews. Elegant refers to the writing style and layout: Clean, crisp, and to the point.

Finally, do the authors and the book justice: Don't buy it only if you are a new media creator or designer. Buy it also if you're a client, so that you can learn about the baseline professionalism that you should expect from your prospective vendors. In a perfect world, creators and designers would buy it to give to clients, and clients would buy it to give to creators and designers.

It's that kind of fog-clearing book.

Guy Kawasaki

Apple Fellow

author of the upcoming book *Rules for Revolutionaries*

About the Authors

JP Frenza is the Director of Business Development for the Earth Pledge Foundation, a full-service Internet agency dedicated to building Web sites for non-profit organizations and socially aware businesses. He can be reached by email at jpfrenza@earthpledge.org.

Michelle Szabo is a designer and educator with over 16 years experience. Her company, New Media Designs, specializes in 3D and interface design for the Web and new media. She has worked directly for corporate clients, as well as consulted for agencies attempting to offer these services to their current client base. Ms. Szabo can be reached at mszabo@newmedia designs.com.

Acknowledgments

"Few things are harder to put up with than the annoyance of a good example," wrote Mark Twain. If he was right, I have had the pleasure of being "annoyed" by a great group of people, each in their own way representing a "good example"—personally and professionally.

They include: George Zieguelmueller, Mike "Bear" Bryant, "the gang" (Dan Hintz, Jeff LaFave, and James Lucas), Susan Meadow, Vince O'Brien, and Greg Varley.

On a special note, I would like to thank: My family for doing what families do by "pulling together"; Edward Potter for his energy and enthusiasm, which got me so jazzed I had no choice but to jump mouse first into the digital realm; Peter Frishauf and all of the staff at SCP Communications; Nancy Carr and all of the folks at Apple Computer; Heather Sommerfield for being a great friend and willing digital guinea pig; and John Belmonte for reviewing the manuscript of this book to see if it really made any sense at all:

Without the following people, this book would not have been possible:

- Kris Kiger for understanding that we couldn't go to see our favorite opera because I had deadlines to meet and also for reading what I wrote and helping me shape it so that it might have some sense of value to graphic designers trying to grapple with new media and the Web.

- Theodore W. Kheel, noted mediator and the President and founder of the Earth Pledge Foundation, the organization for which I am priviledged to work.

- Leslie Hoffman, a friend and colleague, whom I respect perhaps more than any person I know.

Special thanks are in order to my co-author, Michelle Szabo, who had faith in the idea for this book and simply never gave up. I would also like to thank the folks at Hayden Books for their "win-win" mentality, in particular Bront Davis and Melanie Rigney.

Finally, I would like to extend my sincerest gratitude to all of the developers, colleagues, and friends who agreed to be in this book and those that were the inspiration for it.

JP

Faith and encouragement—two of the most important ingredients to success and growth. I have been surrounded by many different types of people in my life. Few of them have encouraged me and had as much faith in me as these—

- JP Frenza with whom I have had the great pleasure to work with once again. Thank you from the bottom of my heart for all of your faith, encouragement, honesty, and trust.

- My mom who put up with missing receipts for months—it will probably never change.

- My children for remembering they love me even when I was fused to my computer.

- David Teich for understanding that I had to concentrate more on this book than our project for a few months—I'll make it up to you.

- Jennifer Begelman for listening to all my mumblings day in and day out. I forgive you for going to Maine.

- Kevin Kall for understanding my insanity and telling me it was OK.

- Bruce Wands for giving me the chance to grow and trusting me to do it well.

- Barbara Lieberwitz for her well-timed phone calls and encouragement.

- Justin Maguire for his wonderful letters just when I needed them— handwritten and beautifully crafted.

- Beth Baldwin for always being there, even when we didn't talk for months.

Special thanks to Bront Davis and Melanie Rigney for believing in this project and having a great sense of humor along the way. And, to all the other colleagues at Hayden—Thank You!

Thanks also to all those who agreed to be interviewed for this book and trusted us to use their names, work and information.

Michelle

Introduction

There are many excellent books available that tell you how to design and produce various new media, but none of them concentrates so clearly on the business side of proposal writing and budgeting as the one in front of you. Because of a lack of standards, most professionals tend to perform these important aspects of a project with little or no guidance. What's more, newcomers to the industry have nowhere to turn to understand the important fiscal matters of running a profitable business, and buyers of new media have little or no concept of what it takes, in both time and resources, for their designers and producers to prepare a successful Web site, CD-ROM, kiosk, or other interactive project.

From Tokyo to San Francisco to New York, the Web and other new media continue to grow as communication mediums. Anywhere in the world, the questions are the same—What do we need to communicate? How can we communicate our (our client's) message? The concept of sound business practices and organizational skills are similar in all cultures and creating new media content and presenting that content requires both.

What This Book is *NOT*

This book is *not* about how to design or produce Web sites and CD-ROMs or what platform or software to use for development.

What This Book *IS*

This book is about working with clients to create Web sites and other new media projects, writing the proposals to solicit business, developing pricing structures and budgets, and most importantly, learning from the experience of others in the form of elaborate, no-holds-barred case studies, proposals, budgets, and interviews, which detail real-world concepts.

Why Did We Write this Book?

With the explosion in popularity of the World Wide Web and other new media over the past several years, we have increasingly realized that there are little or no standards on which to base business and budgeting rationale. Over and over, until it rings in our ears as we sleep, we have heard people ask—How do you price this stuff? What do you give the client in your proposal? Even the respected Graphic Artists Guild has not yet wrapped their arms around this issue. We decided—enough. We started asking questions, a lot of questions. The answers follow in the form of this book.

And, just in case you were wondering, we separated the Web from new media in the title of this book because the Web is currently the fastest growing area of new media that has taken on a life all its own.

Who is This Book For?

This book is for:

- Every individual designer who has a client they want to move into new media

- Every design studio and graphics department that is pitching and purchasing new media and Web development services

- Every company involved with the World Wide Web or other new media

- Everyone who needs to purchase these services

Your level of design or production ability doesn't matter. This book will help you understand the scope of a Web site or other new media project in terms of planning, proposals, and budgeting. Additionally, it touches on the design aspects as they relate to the business and pricing of these projects.

How Big is the Market for the Web and Other New Media? Is there Enough Room for Me?

In 1995, U.S. spending on new media was $7.2 billion and by 1999, it will be around $14.2 billion—outpacing cable, radio, and broadcast TV networks and ranking behind recorded music, magazine publishing, books, and film. So the good news is that the new media business is booming! The CD-ROM marketplace is huge and almost mature. The World Wide Web is a nuclear blast of the largest proportions with numbers growing so fast that it is impossible to keep up. It is estimated that by the year 2000, 35 million households will be online and most computers sold today are equipped with a CD-ROM drive, which allows CD-ROMs to be an easy-to-use, inexpensive media for storing large amounts of information. Other technology such as CD-i (Compact Disk-interactive), DVD (Digital Video Disk), and interactive kiosks also play a role. The numbers are endless.

The question for each of us becomes—where do we fit in?

The New Media Marketplace

The growth over the past several years of the Web and new media has created a booming new business for the graphics industry as well as others. CD-ROM production continues a steady growth. The growth of the World Wide Web is astounding. And businesses are finding more ways to utilize interactive diskettes and kiosks than ever before.

EMedia Professional (formerly CD-ROM Professional) reports regulary from various sources on the state of new media's growth. Here are some of the facts, figures, and findings they have reported in the last half of 1996:

- At the end of 1995, 38.5% of American households owned a PC.

- Television is getting some major competition from new media. Computer users are at their PCs an average of 11.4 hours per week, with CD-ROM drives and subscribers to online services the most likely to take away from traditional commercial television.

- The installed base of CD-ROM drives worldwide has topped 65 million.

- Average CD-ROM drive prices have fallen rapidly in 1996 and the appearance of 12X drives promises to push the numbers down further.

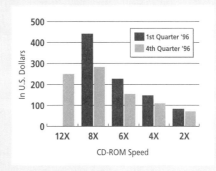

- Online transactions are expected to double in 1997.

- The estimated $300,000 to $3.4 million launch and year-long maintenance Web costs are expected to double by the end of 1997.

- Advertising revenues from online services and the Web are expected to reach $1.97 billion by the year 2000.

- 51% of large companies have Internet access and another 15% had planned to connect by the end of 1996.

Business Basics

Business Management

Many new media and Web development companies are born of the spirit of one or two talented entrepreneurs with a certain expertise—the proverbial two guys or girls in the garage who don't get much sleep. They know how to design a CD-ROM, they understand the intricacies of programming, or they are adept at building Web sites. Others are traditional design studios that build a Web site for a client, then another, and another. Their membership in the new media and Web development community is a part of the studios' development as they seek to offer their clients a full range of graphic services. In either case, success is defined by the notion that after the bills are paid, "There's still some money left in the bank."

Building on its success, the company lands additional projects. Staff needs increase. Full-time employees are added. A network of available freelancers specializing in new media or Web develoment is established. Business, as one new media developer said, "becomes a runaway train." Another developer explained, "I used to stay up all night working, sleeping until noon," only to be chided by his partner, "You had it good, at least you got to sleep." But the same development team admits, "You can't continue with that approach. Not only does it take a physical toll, you also realize that you now have 12 people for whom you are responsible. You have to be in the office to deal with them. And they not only prefer sleep, they actually sort of demand it."

In most cases, younger companies focus on the right elements: satisfying their clients and producing excellent work. But sooner or later, a company without infrastructure starts to suffer from inefficiency. Inevitably systems have to be put into place.

There is a tendency for many new media and Web developers to perceive that because they are operating with a new set of tools—digital—they must be guided by completely new management and business principles.

An attitude best summed up by one Web developer who commented at a trade show, "We aren't widget makers and this is not the Industrial Age."

Indeed, such claims are true and this is not a book focused on how to manage a company in the "nanosecond nineties." There are plenty of books that cover that subject in detail with great success (for example, anything written by Tom Peters). Magazines and newspapers shed much light on the subject—just check out the *New York Times*, *The Wall Street Journal*, *Business Week*, or the energetic and insightful newcomer, *Fast Company*.

Whatever business you choose, there are simple questions that must be addressed—questions that affect every business. Questions such as:

- How do I sell my products and services? And, more importantly, how much does it cost to sell my products and services?

- How much does it cost to produce my products and services? What are my labor costs? What are my expenses?

- How much capital do I need to produce my products and services?

- How much can I make in doing so?

- What is my break even per project? How much must I make before I agree to take on a piece of work?

- How much do I need to bring in annually to cover my expenses (fixed and variable)?

- How much do I need to meet my bills from one period to the next pay period (known as cash flow)?

These are the elements that every business—from widgets to the Web—needs to know.

There are two basic building blocks of any business—the timesheet and the accounting system. This chapter offers a look at each and discusses how these two all important building blocks not only make writing proposals, determining pay scales, and building budgets easier, they serve as key business management tools as well.

Time Sheets

How important is a time sheet? Well, it might seem obvious, but without a time sheet you can't track the most important resource you have: time.

Without a time sheet, you have no real idea what you do on a daily basis. How many hours do you spend reading and answering email? How many hours did you spend on your client's interface design? How many hours writing a CGI script? How many hours troubleshooting your computer network?

Try a simple and effective experiment. Write down how you spend every hour of your day for one full week. If you have dinner, and it takes an hour, write it down. Write down that you were stuck in traffic for one hour. Write down that your machine crashed and you had to reinstall a certain piece of software. Write down everything you do! Don't show your boss you spend a total of three hours in one day surfing the Web—but be honest with yourself.

At the end of one week, look at your list. How many of the things that you are doing, and the hours that you spent doing them, are actual billable hours that you could charge a client for? If you are like most people, you will be shocked. In most cases we have done this little experiment (and people were honest!) and less than 50% of the time spent was related to helping the company sell new projects or work on projects that were already sold.

A certain amount of administration and maintenance is necessary, and in many cases, such as when it comes to system backups, critical. But it is almost undeniable that too much time is spent in most companies focusing on the wrong things. As author Steven Covey says "The main thing is to keep the main thing the main thing." Without a time sheet, you have no idea if you are following Covey's excellent advice.

If you are a one-person company, a design shop, for example, your time sheet is simple and straightforward. It might look like the one shown in Figure 1.1.

While we are on the subject of time and money, one of the most difficult aspects of a business seems to be associated with determining hourly rates. Certainly, the community as a whole establishes benchmarks over time. For example, creative development and design might range in the $100 to $200 an hour from a small- to mid-size studio. That rate range becomes what is referred to as a generally accepted price for a particular practice. Price yourself too low in comparison to the industry average and you risk the perceived value of your services. Price yourself too high in comparison to the industry average and you are likely to loose the work.

Week of: October 1 through 5						
Categories	Monday	Tuesday	Wednesday	Thursday	Friday	Total
Clients						
Insurance Company	4				2	6
Local Bank					2	2
Contract with Joanna's Design Firm		6				6
Mutual Fund Company		0.5				0.5
Newsletter for Local Hospital	2.5		10	10		22.5
General and Administrative						
Organizational/Office		2			3	5
Computers (Back Up, Training)	1.5	1			4	6.5
Accounting/Financial					1	1
Total	8	9.5	10	10	12	49.5

Figure 1.1
A Simple Time Sheet

In figuring out an hourly rate, it is best to figure out how much you need to cover your expenses...and then some. How much do you pay in rent? What is your monthly phone bill? How much do you need to spend on hardware? Software? Healthcare? How much for entertainment? How much for books and magazines to stay on top of developments in the industry? How much for memberships to professional organizations? While you are at it, how much for the vacations you plan to take? How much for retirement savings?

For the purposes of illustration, let's make the following assumptions:

- This is a one-person graphic design studio.

- It has $4,166 in expenses per month (approximately $50,000 in expenses per year).

- It has included everything from pocket change for the movies, to cash reserves for the slow months of July and August.

- It knows it needs to make $50,000 a year to break even. (Of course, the studio might want to grow, take on bigger clients, and hire additional staff, but we are simply focused on the break even.)

- It wants to have a normal life—we know that's a big assumption for the new media and Internet industry!

- There are 5 days working days a week and 52 weeks in one year (260 workdays per year).

- It wants to take three weeks vacation a year (21 days) and five sick or personal days (by now we are all really jealous!)—that leaves 234 workdays per year (260–21–5=234).

- It wants to work eight hours a day (where do we sign up?).

That means for the one-person design studio, there are 1,872 potentially billable hours a year (234 days × 8 hours). If we divide our break even salary per year by the number of potentially billable hours (1,872), we see that the one-person design studio needs to generate approximately $26 per hour to break even. Of course, we all want to do better than break even. However, we now know that for any piece of business to be worth it to the one-person design studio, it must at least pay $26 per hour—a reasonable sum. This is not to say that you shouldn't charge your clients more. We are only illustrating the point that you can make a decent living (a lifestyle choice) working at a reasonable pace. Sometimes you might have a problem finding work, thus, you won't be able to bill that many hours (1,872) and your break even rate will rise. Sometimes you will be able to bill your client twice your break even ($52), and you will be ahead of the game. In either case, having this information is helpful not only for your annual planning process, but also for evaluating your clients on a project-by-project basis.

Suppose you told your client you would do the job for $3,000 and that you estimated the job would take you 30 hours at $100 per hour. Suppose that on the second day of the project, after only two-ten hour days, you finish the project. You spent 20 hours to earn $3,000—or you earned $150 per hour, well ahead of your break even!

Over time, as you use your time sheet to manage your business strategy, or at least provide you the appropriate information with which to manage your business strategy, you will set up minimum, maximum, and average project requirements. For example, you will know that you absolutely will not take a job that pays less than $26 per hour. You might find your industry accepted average is $70 per hour, and you will know that each project averages somewhere in between these two numbers. You now have some of the most important answers with which to run your business.

While we are on the subject of running a business, perhaps another important point to consider is how much do you really need? That's an especially tough question given that the tools with which we work are constantly changing, and the culture of the industry urges us to buy more, faster, and cheaper.

What Are You Worth?

One wise accountant advised his client to live his life by three simple principles:

1. Figure out what you need in life.

2. Figure how much what you need in life costs.

3. Work only enough to get what you need.

In their excellent book, *Your Money or Your Life: Transforming Your Relationship with Money and Achieving Financial Independence,*

Joe Dominiguez and Vicki Robin offer an interesting perspective. According to the authors; if you are 20 years old, you have, on the average, 56.3 years, or 493,526 hours, to live. If you are 30 years old, 46.9, or 411,125. Are you 40? You have, statistically speaking, 37.6 years, or 329,601 hours remaining on planet Earth. "Now that you know that money is something you trade life energy for, you have the opportunity to set new priorities for your use of that valuable commodity. After all, is there any "thing" more vital to you than your life energy? An important perspective to be sure.

Back to Time Sheets

Suppose you are working on a Web project and you have a three-person Web development team—a common "configuration" for this type of work. There's one team member who serves as the designer and production artist, one person who is the programmer, and one person who is the project manager and the client contact.

Each person would fill out a timesheet tracking his or her own hours and the totals by the type of activity that they were working on. For example, the designer would separately track the amount of time spent on creative and design activities and the amount of time spent on production for the Web site. Totals would then be added to a summary sheet for the whole project.

For example, the designer's weekly time sheet might look like the one shown in Figure 1.2. Notice that sometimes the designer records time doing design work, while on other occasions, the designer is recording time as both the production member of the team as well as client management.

The fact that every team member is called upon to perhaps pitch in on several project functions is a good reason to make sure that each person's time sheet lists the full range of potential job functions.

Timesheet for Jane Doe, Designer						
Week of November 1 through 5						
Web Site for Client X						
Categories	Monday	Tuesday	Wednesday	Thursday	Friday	Total
Design	12	4	3	1	2	22
Production			6	9.5	7	22.5
Programming						0
Project Management						0
Client Management		4			2	6
						0
Total	12	8	9	10.5	11	50.5

Figure 1.2
A Designer's Individual Time Sheet

At the end of the week, each team member turns in his or her time sheet and the results are summarized into weekly project totals. Depending on the length of the project, a new total sheet could be produced weekly. When the project is completed, a final summary sheet for the project is produced (see Figure 1.3). That way, the entire team knows exactly how much time is actually spent on the project—valuable information for a business to use when determining the project's fiscal success and also key information in producing future business proposals and budgets.

Timesheet Totals						
Week of November 1 through 5						
Web Site for Client X						
Categories	Monday	Tuesday	Wednesday	Thursday	Friday	Total
Design	12	4	3	1	2	22
Production			6	9.5	7	22.5
Programming	2	6	18	12	20	58
Project Management	6	2	9	6	8	31
Client Management	4	13	4	6	2	29
Total	24	25	40	34.5	39	162.5

Figure 1.3
Weekly Time Sheet Totals

The issue of time sheets starts to get fairly complicated with larger developers. Say a company that has five employees, working on three projects, for more than one client. And, on each project, each employee is working on multiple parts of the project—design, programming, project management, production, testing, and so on.

A time sheet for one person at such a company might look like that in Figure 1.4. Notice that each project has a job number. Even the time spent developing new business proposals is being tracked.

Name: John Doe
Date: August 1 through 5

Project Number/Activity	Mon	Tue	Wed	Thurs	Fri	Total
New Business (00):						
00 Business Proposal 1 for Company A	2					2
00 Business Proposal 2 for Company A						0
00 Business Proposal 1 for Company B		2				2
00 Business Proposal 1 for Company C						0
00 Business Proposal 1 for Company D			1			1
00 Business Proposal 1 for Company E						0
Web Sites						
Project 1: DNS						0
Project 1: Server Set Up						0
Project 1: Content Development	4	2				6
Project 1: Design						0
Project 1: Production						0
Project 1: Marketing						0
Project 1: Site Maintenance & Management						0
Project 1: Client Management	2					2
Project 1: Hardware & Software Development						0
Project 1: Reports						0
Project 2: DNS						0
Project 2: Server Set Up						0
Project 2: Content Development	2					2
Project 2: Design						0
Project 2: Production						0
Project 2: Marketing						0
Project 2: Site Maintenance & Management						0
Project 2: Client Management	2	8		2		12
Project 2: Hardware & Software Development						0
Project 2: Reports						0
Project 3: DNS						0
Project 3: Server Set Up						0
Project 3: Content Development			4			4
Project 3: Design						0
Project 3: Production						0
Project 3: Marketing			3			3
Project 3: Site Maintenance & Management		4				4
Project 3: Client Management				2		2
Project 3: Hardware & Software Development						0
Project 3: Reports						0
General & Administrative Tasks						
GA (50:P2): Computers/System Maintenance						0
GA (50:P3): Administrative/Organizational				4		4
GA (50:P4): Financial				2		2
GA (50:P5): Sick/Personal Time						0
GA (50:P6): Vacation					8	8
GA (50:P7): Conferences						0
Total	12	16	8	10	8	54

Figure 1.4
Individual Employee's Weekly Time Sheet Totals by Project

At the end of the week, a total sheet is compiled for all five people at the company by week as shown in Figure 1.5.

Company X Time Totals						
Date: August 1 through 5						
Project Number/Activity	Mon	Tue	Wed	Thurs	Fri	Total
New Business (00):						
00 Business Proposal 1 for Company A	2					2
00 Business Proposal 2 for Company A					6	6
00 Business Proposal 1 for Company B		2				2
00 Business Proposal 1 for Company C						0
Web Sites						
Project 1: DNS	2.5					2.5
Project 1: Server Set Up/Programming	2					2
Project 1: Content Development	4	2				6
Project 1: Design	2					2
Project 1: Production	5	7		6		18
Project 1: Marketing						0
Project 1: Site Maintenance & Management					7	7
Project 1: Client Management	2					2
Project 1: Hardware & Software Development	4					4
Project 1: Reports						0
Project 2: DNS						0
Project 2: Server Set Up/Programming			6			6
Project 2: Content Development	2		7			9
Project 2: Design						0
Project 2: Production	3		9			12
Project 2: Marketing						0
Project 2: Site Maintenance & Management					6	6
Project 2: Client Management	2	8		2		12
Project 2: Hardware & Software Development						0
Project 2: Reports						0
Project 3: DNS						0
Project 3: Server Set Up/Programming						0
Project 3: Content Development			4	5		9
Project 3: Design	2					2
Project 3: Production	5					5
Project 3: Marketing			3			3
Project 3: Site Maintenance & Management		4				4
Project 3: Client Management				2		2
Project 3: Hardware & Software Development						0
Project 3: Reports						0
General & Administrative Tasks						
GA (50:P2): Computers/System Maintenance	2	5				7
GA (50:P3): Administrative/Organizational	9			11		20
GA (50:P4): Financial		12	9	12		33
GA (50:P5): Sick/Personal Time						0
GA (50:P6): Vacation					8	8
GA (50:P7): Conferences						0
Total	48.5	40	38	38	27	191.5

Figure 1.5
Company's Weekly Time Sheet Summary

You now have a summary of how much time the company spent for the entire week. To have information that you can use to evaluate your business better, let's take a look at how that time looks when you summarize it by project, as shown in Figure 1.6.

Company X Project Totals	
Date: August 1 through 5	
Project Number/Activity	Total
New Business (00):	
00 Business Proposal 1 for Company A	2
00 Business Proposal 2 for Company A	6
00 Business Proposal 1 for Company B	2
00 Business Proposal 1 for Company C	0
Web Sites	
Project 1: DNS	2.5
Project 1: Server Set Up/Programming	2
Project 1: Content Development	6
Project 1: Design	2
Project 1: Production	18
Project 1: Marketing	0
Project 1: Site Maintenance & Management	7
Project 1: Client Management	2
Project 1: Hardware & Software Development	4
Project 1: Reports	0
Project 2: DNS	0
Project 2: Server Set Up/Programming	6
Project 2: Content Development	9
Project 2: Design	0
Project 2: Production	12
Project 2: Marketing	0
Project 2: Site Maintenance & Management	6
Project 2: Client Management	12
Project 2: Hardware & Software Development	0
Project 2: Reports	0
Project 3: DNS	0
Project 3: Server Set Up/Programing	0
Project 3: Content Development	9
Project 3: Design	2
Project 3: Production	5
Project 3: Marketing	3
Project 3: Site Maintenance & Management	4
Project 3: Client Management	2
Project 3: Hardware & Software Development	0
Project 3: Reports	0
General & Administrative Tasks	
GA (50:P2): Computers/System Maintenance	7
GA (50:P3): Administrative/Organizational	20
GA (50:P4): Financial	33
GA (50:P5): Sick/Personal Time	0
GA (50:P6): Vacation	8
GA (50:P7): Conferences	0
Total	191.5

Figure 1.6
Company's Weekly Time Sheet Totals by Project

Looking at the total amount of time spent by project, you can now use your time sheets as a tool to help manage your company and make decisions on how you run your business.

For example, you can see that the company spent 10 hours, or more than one full day, preparing proposals for prospective new business. Is this too much? Should it spend more? Does the company actually need more work at this point? If that prospective business is sold, can the projects be produced given the current workload? Will additional staff need to be hired? Can the company afford to hire new staff? Does the business proposal and budget for the new business reflect the cost of hiring additional staff?

On Project 1, the company spent 18 hours on production. How does that 18-hour figure relate to the estimated budget? Is the production for the project finished? Or is there more production work to be done? Is the company currently within budget? Is the company over budget? If so, what happened? If the company is over budget, can it recoup costs on other aspects of the projects? More importantly, is the company revising its production estimates to more adequately reflect higher production costs?

Additional questions might be asked of the amount of time spent on financial for the week. Was it necessary to spend a total of 33 hours on accounting work for the week? Was this because corporate financials were being produced? Is it tax time or is the company implementing an accounting system?

It is certainly true that not all Web sites are alike, nor are all CD-ROMs. When you start to use time sheets to analyze not only how each project you produce fares, but also how your businesses work, you start to build data upon which you can make better informed judgements about your business as a whole. Developing this type of history will enable you to make more intelligent decisions in responding to the sea of changes that you are likely to encounter. It truly is the Information Age. Shouldn't you then have as much information as possible upon which to navigate your businesses?

The Accounting System

The accounting system is the second critical building block of our business. There's much to say about an accounting system, but in this section we will touch on some basic key elements a good accounting system should include and the functions that such a system should enable you to perform.

"Accounting," an old accounting instructor used to shout to his classes, "for better or for worse, is the language of business. I say this despite the fact that most people feel it is for the worse."

Accounting is also an important feedback mechanism for a business. It let's a company know whether the company is in the black or in the red, by how much and by how far. But numbers don't mean anything if you don't do anything with them, and that is why accounting can become an important tool in managing your business.

Recently, a number of excellent accounting programs performing powerful accounting functions have been released on both the Macintosh and Windows platforms. Some simply serve as electronic checkbooks, whereas other, more robust programs include everything from inventory managment to timeslips and tax estimation.

Job costing

Although the specific program your company might need varies according the the type of business you are in, there is no question that one invaluable feature that your accounting system *must* include is job costing. Job costing is a term that refers to the capability or function of tracking income and expenses in an accounting system to specific projects produced, whether those projects are widgets, Web sites, or CD-ROMs. With job costing, every project in your company has a specific job number, usually a number that identifies the name of the project. In an effective job costing–based accounting system, all income and expenses are tracked to their respective job numbers. For example, a corporate CD-ROM might have CD-01 as a job number. That number appears on a time sheet as CD-01, and time spent on the specific job is identified as labor costs directly associated and "billed" to CD-01.

Most companies that have job costing systems include labor sub-categories, so that, for example, time spent on sales is allocated to CD-01: Sales. In cases where one employee performs many roles, such as designer, production, and project manager, the employee tracks time by function.

In this example, one person might spend hours on a project such as this:

CD-01: Design: 9 hours

CD-01: Production: 12 hours

CD-01: Project Management: 4 hours

These companies generally acknowledge that it is impossible to track every minute by job and function, but that the clearer the picture of reality, the more intelligent the company is in assessing its true costs.

Expenses are also tracked in the company accounting system by job number so that Federal Express shipments to and from the client are billed to the same job—CD-01, for example.

In a job costing based–accounting system, all income for a particular project is allocated to the specific job number for which it was earned.

Why is this important? Let's look at the numbers of a real job from a real company.

Labor	
Design:	$7,500
Production:	$3,000
Programming:	$6,000
Project Management/Sales:	$4,000
Expenses	
Shipping:	$375
Extra Equipment and Software:	$1,275
Overhead allocation:	$5,500
Total Expenses:	**$27,650**
Income	
Payment 1:	$15,000
Payment 2:	$15,000
Payment 3:	$15,000
Payment 4:	$15,000
Total Income:	**$60,000**
Difference:	**$32,350 (total income minus total expenses)**

This is a simple example. How detailed can job costing get? Very. Some companies not only track shipping expenses, they also detail sales expenses such as client luncheons, long-distance calls, even staff parties in which the company celebrates over beer and pizza because the project was a success.

The key in this case is to use your accounting system as a tool to evaluate each project and be certain that each job pays for as many of the expenses directly associated with the project as possible.

The Big Picture

Now that we have had a look at the two most important foundations for a business, let's take a look at the big picture and examine how those tools can help manage the overall business.

The first and most important part of the big picture, is the sales process. If you don't have business coming in, you don't have a business.

The Sales Process

The goal of the sales process is simple: to generate business. This generally means getting a client to ask your firm to respond to a Request for Proposal (RFP). A Request for Proposal is a document that identifies a need and asks for strategies to fulfill that need. RFPs can be short—a fax saying "I would like a Web site for our company, and we are willing to commit $55,000 for the project"—to much longer requests with very intricate details specified.

In many cases, the RFP is a verbal one, a need that the client asks for on the phone or in person ("Tom, thanks for doing our annual report; what do you suppose it would cost to put this on the Web?"). The danger with verbal RFPs is that they come from a client, go to a sales person, and then, at some point, are translated to a business development executive who then has to try to interpret from the sales person what the client actually wanted in the first place.

Whether the RFP is casual, formal, or verbal, it makes good business sense to spend a few minutes with the client in the beginning to answer basic questions about what he really wants—the client's expectations. The more refined the RFP, the better the business proposal. The better the business proposal, the better the business.

Once the client has asked for the RFP, what happens next in the sales process depends on the type of client and your relationship with them, the size of the project, or a host of other factors.

In most cases, your company will prepare a business proposal and budget for the project based on the RFP. On other occasions, the client might retain your firm to develop a design document, specifications, and a prototype for the project. If the client hires you to develop a design document, specifications, or a prototype, your company will want to draw up a letter of agreement, or contract, specifying the terms of the arrangement. At that time, it will be important to define who owns the preliminary work, whether your company has the exclusive and final right to produce the project, or whether for a fee, the client can hire someone else to produce the final project.

If you are preparing a business proposal, the same issues should be addressed. Who owns the copyright on the material presented in the proposal? It needs to be stated up front so that the client doesn't merely read your business proposal and benefit from your efforts, and then "borrow" your creative ideas to produce the projects himself, or worse, with your competitors. This is where working with your attorney, and solid business contracts, is invaluable. See Chapter 6, "Legal Landmines," for more information.

This entire process is generally referred to as new business development, the goal of which is to get the client to say "Yes."

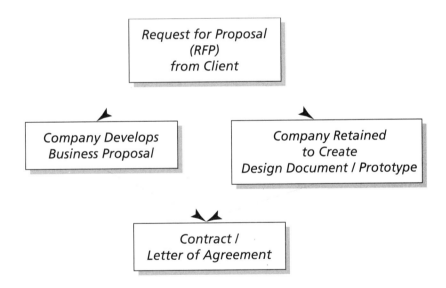

Figure 1.7
From Sales to Contract

Important business basics at this point include tracking the time and expense associated with developing each prospective piece of new business. If the project is sold, the cost of the business development is allocated as a specific expense associated with the project. If the company does not sell the project, the total cost is most likely labeled an overhead expense and recognized simply as a "cost of doing business."

After the contract is signed, the company begins the project development phase. Along the way, time sheets are used to track the amount of time spent on the project. Expenses are input into the accounting system and allocated to the specific job. At regular intervals, the project manager, team leaders, and everyone working on the project, review their budgeted expenses (both in terms of labor and other expenses) and compare them to the actual expenses being incurred on the project. This makes it possible for everyone working on the project to answer the proverbial question: "How are we doing?"

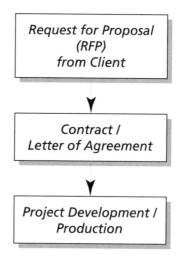

Figure 1.8
From Sales to Production

After the Project is Done

After all the client changes had been made, and all the nightmarish glitches ironed out, most companies are tempted never to look back at the project again. It's done. It's finished. What ever happened, happened. You can't change history. It's best to look forward. On to the next project.

Although it is very tempting to not want to review a project very carefully, good business practices mandate such an examination. Project reviews, or "post mortems" are invaluable in signaling to a company what it is doing right, and equally as important, where it needs improvement. Due to the fact that they tend to be sensitive (you are really looking at whether the project, and the people who produced it, were successful), project reviews can be risky. The staff that worked on the project might be defensive about the decisions they made while finishing the project. There is a tendency for the people initiating the project review to be perceived as critical, rather than constructive. Despite these dangers, and they are dangers in that they strike right at the heart of employee morale, the benefits to be obtained far outweigh the potential risks.

Project reviews enable a company to refine how it operates every aspect of its business. Were the business proposal's estimates too high or too low? Where did you go over budget? Why? Did you simply understimate the amount of time needed to do the work? Did you agree to do more work for the client as the project went on—work that you didn't charge for? Do you need more staff? Were the freelancers too expensive? Is there something about the way in which you work that makes you less efficient? Can you change your workflow to make you more productive? These are the all important questions that can be answered in a successful project review.

In addition, the more open and communicative the type of company you are running, the less likely people are to fear the project review ("Gee, I wonder if it makes me look like I didn't work hard enough?") and the less likely they are to be defensive about the process ("It's easy now to say I should have done this, but I had been working 18-hour days for two weeks; how could I have done what they are asking?").

The most important thing to remember when it comes to the project review is that the purpose is not to blame anyone, but instead to make the company function better—in short, to give people the information they need to be more successful. A successful project review is as important as a scoreboard in a baseball game. Without it, the game continues, but it's hard to tell who is ahead.

Budgets versus Actual Costs

Figure 1.9 is an example of a spreadsheet that was actually used by one company during a project review. (CPU refers to Cost Per Unit.)

Looking at this analysis, which was for a very small Web site, we now have some insight as to how the company performed on the design and production aspect of the project.

You can see that the company did not budget any time to meet and work with the freelance designer on the design concept development for the project. Yet, on the actual project, 16 hours of time, whether it was billed from the freelancer directly, or from someone at the company who had to allocate the time associated with working with the freelancer, was actually associated with the cost of the project.

To use the project review process to improve the business process, the project manager should look into this number. Was there a miscommunication between the company and the freelancer? Was the freelancer billing for time when it was not appropriate? Is this an important process that needs to be added to the general charges included in the development of creative concepts?

Budget Category	Description	Unit Type	Budgeted # of Units	CPU	Total	Actual # of Units	CPU	Total	Variance
Design/ Production	Initial consultation with	Hour	12	0.00	0	16	50	800	-800
Design/ Production	Create initial sketches	Hour	8	100.00	800	8	100	800	0
Design/ Production	Create assets (logos, icons)	Hour	24	100.00	2400	8	100	800	1600
Design/ Production	Create final designs	Hour	16	100.00	1600	8	100	800	800
Design/ Production	Client approval	Hour	4	100.00	400	1	100	100	300
Design/ Production	Conversion of artwork	Hour	8	100.00	800	16	100	1600	-800
Production	HTML; creation of final page code	Hour	12	50.00	600	4	50	200	400
Production	HTML; creation of all links, navigation, etc.	Hour	8	50.00	400	2	50	100	300
Production	HTML; Testing in browser and on server	Hour	4	50.00	200	8	50	400	-200
Sub Totals					$7,200			$5,600	$1,600

Figure 1.9
Company's Weekly Time Sheet Totals by Project

You can also see that the estimated time to create initial sketches (8 hours) was right on target.

The company also learned that it took less time to create logos and icons for the Web site than actually estimated—24 hours budgeted, 8 actual. This is important information. Why is this the case? Was it that people worked faster than they anticipated? What was it about the specific aspect of the job that enabled the company to complete this process more quickly? Were the estimates simply too high? Are congratulations in order for the design team? How can this information be used to reinforce the positive contribution of the design team that came in under budget?

Finally, you can see that the conversion of artwork, which was estimated to take 8 hours of time, actually took 16 hours. Again, this is critical information. What happened? Was the estimate simply too low? Was the work harder than it first appeared? Is the process more involved? Are more people required to complete this part of the budget?

These and other questions are the types of issues that sound management and effective business leaders ask. These are the kinds of questions that, if evaluated correctly, make the difference between expanding a company's office space, or closing its office doors.

Now that you have some insight into the basic building blocks of a successful business—the time sheet and an accounting system—you have a better vision in regard to the overall financial picture of a particular project and our business as a whole. You have a greater understanding as to how these two building blocks can be used to improve the business operations of your company.

Whether you are a one-person company with a few freelancers, a 10-person company, or a 100-person corporation, it is important to examine the process of how your company works and how much it costs to produce the products that your company sells—both in terms of labor and other expenses. In the end, you will be able to answer the following questions:

- How much do I need to spend in terms of sales and business development, for my company to win new business?

  The answer can be found by adding the sales and business development expenses associated with each project sold to the amount of time

spent on projects that haven't sold, which is in our overhead alloca-
tion under sales and business development.

• What does it take my company to actually produce a Web site or
CD-ROM?

The answer can be found on the project totals in our time sheet summary and by evaluating the job costing expense and income statement
for a particular job number.

• What is my break even per project?

Again, you can find this important information on the job costing
reports of your accounting system.

The same information will also tell you how much money you need to make
to cover all of our expenses, how much money you made as a company,
your margins, and more—important information for any age in any kind of
business.

The Nuts and Bolts of Producing

Philippe Stessel
VP, Executive Producer
Kaufman Patrcof Enterprises
http://www.kpe.com

The goal at Kaufman Patricof Enterprises (KPE) is to produce its own content, which it intends to make available through a network of Web-based programming, primarily entertainment (along the model of HBO).

Philippe Stessel graduated from Columbia University with an English major and a minor in Classical Latin. He worked for Holt, Reinhardt, Winston in the college art textbook division and later at American Express' *Travel and Leisure Magazine* as an assistant editor before going on to spend seven years in film production.

He landed at The Voyager Company, where in two years, he produced seven CD-ROM titles, including the first Voyager preview disc, Laurie Anderson's highly acclaimed *Puppet Motel*, the political *Live From Death Row: Mumia Abu-Jamal*, and the well-received *New Voices and New Visions* among others.

After leaving Voyager in June of 1996, Stessel went on to produce the Web site for President Clinton's re-election campaign (Clinton-Gore 96). After that project wrapped up, he went on to work on a Web site about the Royal Family for a London publisher, "I'm making the rounds, Presidents and Kings and Queens," he says smiling.

You are one of the few people who has produced very successful projects in both new media and on the Internet. Which do you find harder?

There's no question that CD-ROM is harder.

How so?

With a CD-ROM you are traditionally dealing with much more content—up to 650 megabytes. That's a lot of material! But I would also say that producing a CD-ROM is a very technical endeavor. Not that the Web isn't technical, but I clearly find myself relying less on a programmer than I used to. The Web as a medium is something that a non-programmer can be successful with given that the bandwidth limits the kinds of things that can be delivered—like video and audio on CD-ROM. It seems as though I am moving backwards in terms of bandwidth—from film, to CD-ROM, to the Web!

What are the challenges you find that are unique to the Web?

On the Web, you see the results of your work immediately. When you are making a CD-ROM, there's a huge testing cycle where many things can go wrong, and the final results of your work can be delayed for months.

Also, when a CD-ROM product is finished it's "in the can." But you are never done with a Web site. You have to stay on top of it. There's a dynamic nature to it and change has to occur constantly in order to drive viewers back to the site—if not daily, certainly weekly.

When we were working in the Clinton-Gore Web site, we had two or three major revisions to the site where we rebuilt it from scratch.

What skills did you develop in producing CD-ROMs that transferred to the Web?

Being at Voyager, I had solid training, working for the best CD-ROM publisher ever and with some of the best people in the industry. The formality of working in that media forces you set up a rigid production schedule if you are going to get a product to market. It also forces you think extensively about the interface—how people will use the product, how they will navigate it, how to keep people from getting lost, how to make it visually interesting. When it comes to the Web, that approach is an enormous advantage.

How do you define the role of the producer?

The producer is the person responsible for the quality, shape, direction, look and feel of a project as well as the overall responsibility for the budget.

How hands-on do you get as a producer?

Very, very, very hands-on. My philosophy has been that as a producer, you need to know every single piece of the project as well as every tool used in the creation of the project. I realize that many other producers might disagree with that but as far as I am concerned, a producer that doesn't use all of the tools does the team and the project a disservice.

For example?

When I worked on CD-ROMs, I used Photoshop, Illustrator, DeBabelizer, Director, Quark, SoundEdit-16—the whole suite. On the Web, I have coded Real Audio, built Web Maps, and have worked in Java. Granted, I didn't program the whole CD, but I did program parts. On the Web, I didn't write every PERL script, but I did write several.

Ultimately, my thought has always been that if you are going to produce, you have to use the tools. How can you produce and not know the tools?

As a producer, what do you find is the most challenging task?

Mapping out the project. It's great to develop the design from the outset and structure that design so that it flows, and the user can easily interact with it. Everything else is the execution of that idea, which can be difficult, but not really impossible.

You mentioned that one of the key responsibilities of a producer is to manage the budget. Any thoughts on how?

Well, I came from the film industry where budgeting is a serious matter. Every activity in the film industry is broken down line by line.

When you have a start-up company where everyone is working crazy hours and contributing to a project in many ways, it is virtually impossible to track time and come up with real numbers. But you can take everyone who worked on the project's salary, calculate the percentage that they worked on the project, and add in hard expenses to get some sense for the business success of the project. It's not an extremely accurate picture, but it will give you a general idea as to how profitable the project was or wasn't.

Any final words on the keys to sound project management?

No matter who you are and no matter how hard you work, something always comes up that you could have never in a million years predicted. It could be anything, from a software bug to something that is incompatible with a certain machine, and it is generally not your fault. The key to being a good producer is to anticipate so that when the inevitable happens, you can react effectively and move on. The way you do that is through sound organization. More than anything else, sound organization is crucial. At the beginning of a project, setting up the right system for everything and moving forward in an orderly way is the core of good project management.

There's only two ways you learn this stuff...the hard way...or through intelligence. I am not going to comment on which approach I took.

Business Philosophies

**Greg Deocampo
AVX Design, Inc.
http://www.avx.com**

When AVX was established by Greg Deocampo and Michael Rothbard in the summer of 1994, it marked what Deocampo says "represented the next iteration in a series of organizational experiments that I had been conducting." His first such organizational engineering was the Company of Science & Art, or CoSA, which had, as its mission, "To create science and art that maximized the use of computing and communications technologies."

CoSA's first project was what Deocampo describes as "an early expression of a suite of technologies that other companies have subsequently developed and made famous—Netscape Navigator, Adobe Premiere, Adobe Photoshop, Macromedia Director, and Adobe After Effects (remember CoSA After Effects?)." He says, "My personal goals were not to be acquired. I had formed CoSA in reaction to the large corporate environment, which I respect, but feel is not the place to actually create new technologies, much less art."

His interests led him to a collaboration with Gardner Post and Josh Pearson who had recently formed what became the critically acclaimed, avant garde Emergency Broadcast Network (EBN), a multimedia art and production group. One of EBN's principle art projects was a video sampler based on the concept of expressing in video the musical ideas enabled by audio sampling, sequencing, and scratching. Deocampo says the project represented "a technologically interesting problem, requiring real-time interactive media playback which focused my attention on real-time interactive computing."

Deocampo persuaded a select group of other digital artists from CCI to come to his home in Providence, Rhode Island, and start making things using the newly developed video technology. "From the beginning, I wanted to establish a culture that was art-centric rather than technology-centric. The idea was to form a personal ensemble that would have more of the qualities of an improvisational band than a corporation," he says. The goal: to create paying jobs that enabled team members to create digital art—as opposed to becoming millionaires.

"We called the company AVX Design, Inc.," he says. "AVX for Audio/Visual/Whatever, Design to remind everyone of the importance of this thought process to the culture of art making, and Inc. to remind everyone that, unlike EBN, we would at least attempt to make some money." The mission of AVX is a difficult one—to build a business that builds art.

What is the philosophy behind that?

Our corporate mission at AVX Design, Inc. is to profitably create products, services, and businesses that satisfy demand for computing and communications media and technology, biomolecular nanotechnology applications, and education.

We know that you have given a lot of thought to the idea that science and technology have the power to transform society in both an artistic and spiritual sense. How do you reconcile those ideas in the context of a business?

I believe in the idea that a "business" in a participatory, democratic, global industrial society, can offer a way to co-opt, or transcend traditional capitalistic notions of agression and dominance by materially rewarding personal and collective effort and service.

How can that be possible in the current and highly competitive environment we have today?

I think that this system creates an incentive in the individual to identify a social need and to satisfy it. I believe that this can contribute in a positive way to the fulfillment of human potential and that this notion is especially relevant in the domains of computing and communications, biomedicine, and "big science." While motivated by typical primate concerns, in the course of building a business and dominating a market, people will nonetheless be fundamentally changing the nature of their environment and themselves.

What role does new media and the Internet—a key part of the information revolution—play?

In a future world where global information is universally accessible, where the ability to understand and evaluate that information is technologically augmented beyond current capabilities, and where business practice causes vast wealth to be concentrated in these domains, I believe that at least a small portion of that humanity will transcend their personal perspectives and make manifest a collective conscious. This will open all of humanity to a "Singularity," to use a term used by Vernor Vinge, beyond which it's impossible to speculate, but which represents the next step in human evolution.

An interesting philosophy but in terms of running a business, how does it translate?

Personally, I believe we're rushing towards a fundamental change in human awareness comparable to the initial rise of self-awareness, when humans first made a thoughtful distinction between themselves and 'animals.'

Within this context, which we hope is an upward spiral, we try to create and concentrate wealth in the form of intellectual property that can be physicalized by solving relevant problems at the leading edge of science and technology, and by reacting to that environment as artists.

I believe that this process leads to the development of products along with the creation of business units to support the products. That is what we are doing at AVX.

In doing so, what is your biggest challenge?

Without a doubt—people. People are our biggest challenge; finding ones that fit into the work ethic and company culture. It's also tremendously challenging to keep everyone productively employed as well as serving their best interests for personal growth.

Our business is essentially about successfully transforming personal creativity into some kind of physical product that can be sold. Preserving an intimate culture that encourages creativity, freedom of thought, freedom to experiment, freedom to fail, while still bringing in our projects on time and on budget, that's a huge challenge. That and keeping the payroll flowing.

What's the management strategy for staying on budget and on time?

It's personal. Management at AVX is intensely personal. All the dynamic elements in a person's life are relevant, from the personal to the professional. It can be difficult to understand those elements, and direct people to do specific things in such a way that is in their best interest and the company's best interest. It can be difficult to subsume one's personal best interests to that of

the company's, but it is essential to creating com-munity. Somebody's got to do it (That's why entrepreneurial founders should be well-rewarded). As makers of digital media, it has been challenging to successfully blend the cultural needs of good engineering with the cultural needs of good art, and get good synthesis.

Lately we've been adding professional scientific researchers into the mix, increasing the challenge. Although everyone speaks separate languages, a common culture is necessary to facilitate communication. This common culture is based on an aspiring idealism practiced by imperfect humans: serve others; use your powers for good, not evil; help where you can; live by the golden rule; act out of love. Living as a company this way can be tough when competing for jobs or product dollars or whatever with people and companies who are trying to express a more ruthless and less compassionate (and in my opinion, short-term and less successfull approach to creating long-term wealth) form of capitalism.

What strategy do you employ to overcome those challenges?

At first, I tried to overcome these challenges by using a personal-leadership model combined with specific knowledge as to what specific things actually need to get done, when, and for how much money.

I invested heavily in personal relationships with the key players in the company to establish a basis for trust that gave me enormous flexibility in directing people to what needed to be done without having to explicitly build group consensus. We have weekly meetings where everyone's professional problems get articulated and everyone suggests ways of dealing with it. Then we try and articulate a short to-do list and assign someone to make sure it gets done.

Recently, I have expanded upon this personal base to build an organizational structure. We have a Board of Directors composed of many points of view, from the esthetic to the technological to the financial; a subset of the Board is the Executive Committee, responsible for articulating a strategic business plan and directing it to Ops, the group responsible for implementation. Ops then directs project leaders as appropriate.

Project leaders direct the individuals best suited to the project.

This approach lacks some of the intimacy of the original, personal-leadership approach, but it scales better and enables more. The lack can be made up by strong community culture. We're about to try and expand the scope of our business in terms of number of people and diversity of projects; we expect to this model to be successful. If it is, it will represent our strategy for the next stage of growth, essentially seeding start-up companies within the parent.

Client and Project Management

It can be very difficult sometimes to understand what your client really wants. You meet with them, ask a lot of questions and then go back to write your business proposal and find you have more questions. You go around and around several times and realize that your client really doesn't know exactly what they want. Not only that, but they are not willing to tell you what they want to spend. This might sound as though we think clients are stupid. Well, they are not. They are simply trying to understand a very confusing business.

There are two very important items to consider when beginning a relationship with a client: *education* and *trust*. Let's look at what is meant by each of these.

Education

If your client is not educated in the media they are trying to purchase from you, it is your job to educate them—especially since many clients are not familiar with the process of Web site or new media development. Some of you might say—"Right, like I have time for that!" Well, make the time. The more you educate your client, the more she will know and the faster you can gain her trust. The proposal you write for her will be better understood if she is educated. Your client may be asking different things of several companies, and you never know whether she will be comparing proposals and budgets accurately. If you can get her to understand as much as possible, she can make a more informed and intelligent decision. It is your job to show her how to make that decision and why you are the best person (or company) for the job.

Trust

Now comes the trust part. A Web site or other new media project is generally a fairly large, if not huge, undertaking. That means you and your client are going to get to know each other very quickly and very intimately. It is a team effort in every sense of the word. And, unless your client asks to be excluded from particular areas, you can assume he should be involved. Where you have expertise, in the Web or other new media business, you should guide your client in the choices to be made. Let's face it, you're spending *his* money. You have to let him be involved with how that money is spent. In the areas that he is an expert, for example, his business, listen to what he is trying to accomplish and what his market tells him. Work as a team.

Understanding Your Client and the Project

It is imperative that you understand several things about your client before thinking about the proposal for the project:

- Who is the client? Is it an established company? Can you trust them? Get references.

- What do they do? How do they currently do it? Get to know their products and services.

- Why do they want to do it differently? What is their motivation behind their request?

- What type of support they are looking for from you? Are you creating the entire project or just doing a piece of it?

- Who are the key players?

- Who will have final sign-off on the project?

- Does the president of the company have any major dislikes? As ridiculous as this sounds, if you design something in green and the president hates green, you may have a difficult time selling the work. Fortunately, intelligent people (and you hope you are dealing with intelligent people) don't have these types of phobias, but they are out there.

- Get a copy of the corporate ID manual, if one exists, to be sure you do not use their logo incorrectly.

- What is there budget? Many clients are reluctant to give bugets because they think that you will then spend it all. Well, that is probably true, but if they are not honest with you about money up front, it is very difficult to give a budget that will be comparable to other proposals they may be asking for from other vendors. If you are not in a multiple bid situation, then this is not as much of an issue.

- What type of new media will you be using?

- Why are you using that particular media?

- Is this truly the right media for the message?

- What does the client hope to gain with this project?

- How long do you have to produce the project?

- What is the primary message to be conveyed?

- What are the secondary messages to be conveyed?

- What are the givens—for example, art that already exists, logos, copy, and so on?

- What is the benefit of this product or service to the audience?

You must answer these questions before you proceed with any proposal and pricing. You can get some of the information from the client's annual report or promotional materials. If they don't exist, you will have to ask more detailed questions.

On the other hand, some clients simply do not know what they want. In that case, it is your job to try and narrow down the needs and wants in as much detail as possible. Take them out to lunch, play a round of golf, something to get them to loosen up and tell you what they are after. Breakfast meetings are often good for brainstorming. Everyone is usually fresh and alert. Get the team together and talk about what is needed.

Understanding the Audience

It is vitally important to the success of any project that you understand the user of your product. You may want to look at the following:

- Age range

- Gender

- Ethnic background

- Average income

- Likes and dislikes

- What they do for a living

- What they do for fun

- What types of purchases they make

The more of these questions you answer, the better you will know your audience. Then you can create a product that is interesting to the user. If the client already has the answers to these questions, then she probably have some kind of marketing plan—ask to see it. If it is well written, it will give you great insights into their needs.

A Word from Marketing

Christopher Matthews
Vice President of Marketing,
Rewards Programs
MasterCard International

Matthews holds a BA in both History and English from Boston University. He got his start in the publishing industry working for Simon and Schuster. His move to advertising proved to be the start of a very successful career in marketing. He has worked for several large advertising agencies, including J. Walter Thompson and Grey, and has also worked on the client side for Coca-Cola and now MasterCard International.

At MasterCard, Matthews is responsible for rewards programs for retail merchants, travel, and entertainment. He forges long-term alliances with people who accept the card and uses media such as television, radio, print, in-store kiosks, Web sites, and direct mail to support those relationships.

You have worked both sides of the marketing fence—for the agency side and the client side. What do you find the differences to be?

On the agency side, it is generally less structured and more creative.

On the client side, you have more responsibility and accountability. But, you also have more access to other marketing disciplines—advertising, sales promotion, point of sale, direct mail, and so on. You also get a deeper understanding of the value of market research. Market research doesn't give you all the answers, but it is important to direct you in what you are trying to acheive and it minimizes the risks. It's part science, part art. For example, launching a new product is more fact-based than launching a new marketing initiative.

You see a lot of people both internally and externally who offer you services. What things do you look for when they come in to present project ideas to you?

I look for a base knowledge of the discipline they are involved with and more importantly what they have learned in the process of their work experiences.

They need to be able to create programs out of the norm. For example, if we are doing a kiosk, I'd like to see them think beyond the design of the kiosk—take the kiosk out of the normal context. Creativity comes in a number of ways. Creative taste is one, but make the kiosk work with something else and get people to react a certain way— that's also creativity. I like to see work break through the rest of the media—be different.

Do you find most of them to be "buttoned up?" Why or why not?

It really varies. Most of the people are faking it. By that I mean, they come in with a presentation that looks great, but when you start asking them questions about how the program works, they don't have the answers. They haven't thought through the entire content. Also, I find that many times, people are not focused. They come in with a bunch of ideas and none of them really stand for anything.

So you think content is important?

Yes. Content is very important. People should spend more time thinking. The best presentations I've seen are thought through, focused, and simple. If the idea is right, the presentation will work.

What mistakes do you see people make most often?

People take their ideas and make them too complicated. They don't give you a complete story. They don't understand the business they are going after. If the idea is not relevant to the business and the consumer, then it is useless. A lot of people try to fit a square peg into a round hole. Convenience, price, and service is what people look for.

What advice would you give companies that present their work?

Understand the business, how your idea helps the business, and how it benefits the consumer.

What advice would you give companies?

Often times, it is very difficult, sometimes impossible, to coax information out of your client. If you have asked every question in every conceivable way and still do not have the answers you need, you will have to make some assumptions. These assumptions should be outlined in your proposal in detail, so that it is clear exactly what you are assuming in order to complete the project. You also need to make your client understand the reason you are asking these questions. Designing their new media project is based on solid information and the more of it you have, the more successful the end result wil be. There are excellent classes in marketing available all over the place. Take one. It will open a whole new world of information to you.

Raising Your Price After the Proposal is Accepted

The two worst things to do to a client are: lie and tell them the price is going up after they have accepted your proposal. The first is self-explanatory— simply don't do it because it will come back to bite you.

Sometimes it is impossible to anticipate every little detail a client may ask for in the course of a project, so raising the price mid-stream may be unavoidable. You can, however, help your client to understand what they are asking for if his request increases the price of the project and what the impact is in time. This comes back to education and trust. Be sure that you understand exactly what your client wants to achieve. Then, show the client the alternatives to help educate him and help him make the right decision. His choices should be at least:

- The original specification

- The requested change

- At least one other alternative that meets their needs, but costs less if appropriate

This will show the client several things:

- That you are thinking

- That you have their best interest in mind

- That you are being careful with their money

- That you care

All of this adds up to that trust quotient again. Be careful to balance your client's needs against time constraints and dollars. If it is going to take extra time to come back to her with alternatives, you must allow your client the courtesy to refuse this extra time spent and just do as they ask, but make sure she is aware of the financial and time implications—no surprises after the fact. Sometimes, time is the only dictator. Learn to read your client. If you cannot, then be blunt and straightforward.

In Summary

The bottom line is that it is important to carefully manage your business both internally and externally. If you find you do not have enough hours in a day, consider hiring a person to do some of the leg work for you. It will free your time to do things that really need your attention. If you cannot afford to do this, you should revisit the way you are conducting business and what you are charging.

The Business Proposal

Perhaps no other facet of the new media and Web industry is as important as the business proposal. And no other aspect instills as much fear and trepidation.

Many companies prepare business proposals not unlike one World Wide Web developer who described the process as, "We write a concept, we attach some numbers, and we send it out the door. It's like playing Russian roulette."

Other companies take a different tact. They submit an idea in the form of a concept paper, and when selling the project to the client, they never say no. Price is determined by asking what the client is willing to pay. Reality, in this case, is what happens after the client says yes.

Despite the perceived difficulty, preparing a well thought out, fiscally responsible business proposal is a remarkably straightforward and simple process. It doesn't have to be a game of chance, nor does it have to be a solicitation of charity. After reading this chapter, you'll gain insight into developing a business proposal, become more comfortable in creating business proposals of your own, and, hopefully, make your company more profitable in the process.

In This Chapter, We:

- Define what a business proposal is and discuss why business proposals are important.

- Look at how a business proposal can provide key insights into the operation of a company. This is an important consideration in that every business proposal you write has a big impact on the profitability of your company.

- Hear from the experts who write and review business proposals.

- Talk about the relationship between you, your business proposal, and your client.

- Examine the difference between a business proposal and a business plan (the design document is dealt with in Chapter 3, "Designing for New Media").

- Prepare a business proposal step-by-step.

What Is a Business Proposal and Why Is It Important?

At its most basic level, a business proposal is a *specific plan of action presented by one party to another party in reference to the potential sale of goods or services to that party.* In some cases, a large company seeking to solicit business proposals (bids) from subcontractors will issue a formal Request for Proposal (RFP), or a document that defines a project or product that the company is seeking contractors to produce.

Business proposals are important because they define the parameters between the client and the contractor. Suppose a multimedia developer specializing in producing interactive press kits on diskette and CD-ROM is talking on the phone to an insurance company about producing an interactive sales and marketing program. At this point, the conversation is theoretical. Although there is a cost associated with the phone call, it is minimal. As soon as the potential client asks to see a business proposal, the "costs of goods sold" increases. The multimedia developer now has to think about the content, the design, and the technical aspect of producing the project. At best, this is a first step to selling a project and winning new business. At worst, it is a cost that fails to provide a return on investment if the project does not sell.

*As soon as you put words and numbers on paper
in the form of a business proposal,
you have shaped and defined more fully
the relationship between you and your client.*

Although your client might have formed an impression of you based on a personal meeting, *nothing* more formally defines the relationship between you and your client than your business proposal. This is especially true given that, in many cases, your contact with the client is not with the person who signs the final project. Your business proposal is then the only evidence the "higher-ups" have in front of them upon which to base their decisions.

A Business Proposal Is Not a Business Plan

A business plan (which is a subject for another book) presents a road map for the entire business—the mission statement, key staff members, the market it is striving to compete in, prospective revenues, projected expenses, and financial statements. The business plan provides the big picture in terms of what the company is, where it is going, and how it is going to get there.

A business proposal focuses on one project—not the entire company. It defines a specific project—its objectives and its terms.

Think of a business plan as a compass, indicating what direction the business is going—North, South, East, or West. Think of a business proposal as a specific map that defines how to get there.

It is always a good idea to ask yourself how each business proposal relates to your business plan. If, for example, your business plan says you are a company that designs, produces, and distributes CD-ROMs and the last 10 proposals you have prepared are for Web projects, you need to step back and re-evaluate the direction your company is going.

Should you take the Web work and forgo the CD-ROM business? Some people would say yes, immediately. Writing a solid business proposal with a fiscally sound budget would be one way to answer the question for certain. After the business proposal answered the question on whether or not you should take the specific job outlined in the business proposal, you need to re-evaluate the general business plan. Should you redirect your attention to the Web? More important, what expenses are you incurring to develop your CD-ROM business that might be better allocated as you shift your corporate mission from CD-ROMs to building Web sites?

This is an industry in which it is best to act swiftly. It is also an industry in which you must act prudently as well.

Defining Goals

Business proposals also define the goal that each party in the process is striving to obtain.

For the insurance company, the goal might be to produce an interactive sales and marketing kit that helps its regional offices understand the company's newest product line. The kit might also help the regional offices by enabling them to print sales specification sheets and other important information helpful in the sales process. For the client, the goal is simple: create a product that improves company sales by presenting vital information in an easy, interactive format. The insurance company wants to increase sales by enhancing communication.

For the multimedia developer (and most companies involved in this type of work) producing the product, the goal is generally two-fold: to perform her best work and showcase her company's talents and to make a profit. The multimedia developer wants to increase sales by enhancing communication.

The business proposal is the document in which both parties first state their intentions and define their goals (of course, it is up to you to spell out the client's goals, in this case). Business proposals also sketch out the approximate terms each party is willing to accept to reach those goals.

Every company handles its business development process in its own way, arrived at by years of hard-earned experience. For some people, the client signs off on the business proposal and that business proposal becomes the final contract between the company and the client. In business proposals where this is the case, issues such as the number of designs presented to the client, terms of payment, liabilities, and so on are all spelled out. In instances where the project is small, or the company has built a long-term relationship with the client, having the business proposal serve as the contract is acceptable and appropriate.

The approach that we favor, however, and the one that appears to have the most success, is to separate the business proposal from the contract, or Letter of Agreement, between the company and the client. This way, the business proposal focuses on the relationship between the two parties, the definition of the project, and the budget. Contractual terms are included in a separate contract (and are perhaps best handled by a lawyer). In either case, it is the business proposal where these terms are identified.

Solid business proposals have an impact on a project far beyond the initial terms of agreement. Business proposals are key to well-articulated projects. They form the basis for external communication (between the company and the client) and internal communication (between the members working at the company).

A great deal of business literature has been published recently discussing how highly successful businesses should be restructured to open the channels of communication between all of their employees, subcontractors, and clients. In fact, many large companies, such as AT&T, are reorganizing around the principle of having teams in which communication lines are open and employees are closer to "the decision-making process."

If you are producing a Web site for a client, an interactive floppy, or a CD-ROM, chances are that no other document in your company communicates the goal of the project more clearly than the business proposal.

In fact, how a company produces and handles its business proposals provides insight into how the company operates its business. It's a subject that we feel is so important, the entire next section is devoted to it.

What Business Proposals Teach Us About Our Business

Preparing straightforward and fiscally responsible business proposals requires more than writing a good sentence. It means relying on open communication and sound business practices.

Consider two possible scenarios.

Scenario One: The 20th Century Company

The 20th Century Company, a very large publisher, is divided along strict departmental lines: a sales department, a creative department, a production department, an editorial department, and an accounting department.

In this company, business proposals are created by a sales team with the goal of selling a project. That's it, period. Never mind what happens to the project after it is sold (that reality is "not the sales department's problem"). In preparing the business proposal, the sales department never asks the creative department for its ideas on how the project might take shape. It never asks the editorial department for input into the business proposal—it just recycles the same ideas over and over again ("The last client liked it, let's stay with it," is the reasoning). The production department is never consulted on how much work it will take to produce the project—let alone how much it will cost. No one ever bothers to ask the accounting department how much, if any, money was made on the last project. The sales department has no idea if the business proposal is fiscally responsible.

The project is sold. A quick meeting is called. Management tells all the groups they have no choice but to take on the project, because the company needs the business. The creative department has no budget (or time) to shape an appealing product. The editorial department has to try to figure out what the project will do. Half the production department quits, because they are tired of working 14-hour days without overtime, a break, or any thanks. The accounting department is frustrated, because it knows the company has lost money on the last three projects and this one looks like a sure loser.

The project comes in over budget and late. The 20th Century Company loses the client (not to mention its $250,000 worth of business).

Scenario Two: The 21st Century Company

The 21st Century Company considers itself an information organization that, on occasion, is a publisher of traditional print products, and on other occasions, a new media creator. This company is divided into groups. What's more, people are free (and encouraged!) to move from one group to another.

There's a sales team, a creative team, a production team, an editorial team, and an accounting team. There's also a project management team, which consists of members pulled from all the other teams.

When a piece of new business comes in, the company calls a lunch meeting (the company buys!). Members from each team sit down and discuss concepts to present to the client. Everyone participates. The sales manager and the project manager assigned to the project write everything down. Meeting notes are typed and distributed throughout the company via electronic mail. People who couldn't attend the meeting are given the opportunity to offer their input for a specified period of time.

After collecting comments and feedback, the sales manager and project manager work together to create a rough draft of the business proposal. The rough draft is then routed to the creative team, which develops a few design ideas, creates a few comps, and even puts together a few slides to be used during the sales presentation. The production team gets the proposal, evaluates how much it will cost to produce, and contacts a few outside vendors to collect actual estimates based on the ideas presented by the creative team.

One person on the editorial team, it turns out, is an expert on the subject and points out to the sales team that new regulations are going to change the potential client's business environment. The editorial team comes up with a new concept for the client based on positioning in that new regulatory climate.

The accounting team reviews the budget and finds that in a similar project, the company took far longer than expected to get the project approved from the client's three regional offices. It relays that information to the sales and project managers who build into the business proposal language that protects the company from client delays.

In preparing the business proposal, every group at the company has input. The client understands the concept, thinks the proposal is fair, and likes the design. The project is sold.

The 21st Century Company throws a party—this time with wine and cheese (yes, the company pays again). The project begins, and the entire company is involved and excited. The project has its problems, but all of the teams pull together.

Halfway through the project the accounting team calls a meeting. It seems that the editorial team underestimated the time needed to research the project. It is running behind and labor costs are over budget. The production team says it can lean on the vendors to speed the printing of the packaging that the product will ship in, making up for the lost time. The creative team scales back some of the designs. The project finishes on time and within budget.

The client likes the final project and as a result the company wins two additional, and larger, projects—$650,000 in new business!

Both of these scenarios actually did happen. The 20th Century Company is now out of business (although some of the people who worked at the company now work at the 21st Century Company). The 21st Century Company is still in business. In fact, the president of The 21st Century Company verified business couldn't be better—profits have soared and the number of employees has doubled.

Truly the business proposal can tell you a great deal about the type of company you work for and how effective its operational structure might be. Sure, the business proposal is not the only factor to consider—but these scenarios, and others like them, demonstrate that the business proposal is often the best litmus test.

Look around your company. Are you responsible for writing the business proposals your company sends out? Are you a small company using freelancers? Do you ever ask your freelancers for their help in preparing a business proposal? Do you show your proposals to other groups in your company? Do you allow input from others? Does everyone have access to the business proposals after your company has sold the project? Or are they locked in a filing cabinet in the boss's office?

Why Do We Have Business Proposal Insecurity?
How We Can Overcome It?

We guard our business proposals more than any other document our company produces. Think about it. You can, without too much trouble, call any Fortune 500 company in the United States and have them send you financial documents that present highly detailed, audited information about the company, including its gross and net earnings. It's called an annual report (see the example in Figure 2.1), and the Securities and Exchange Commission (SEC) requires all publicly owned corporations to report this information.

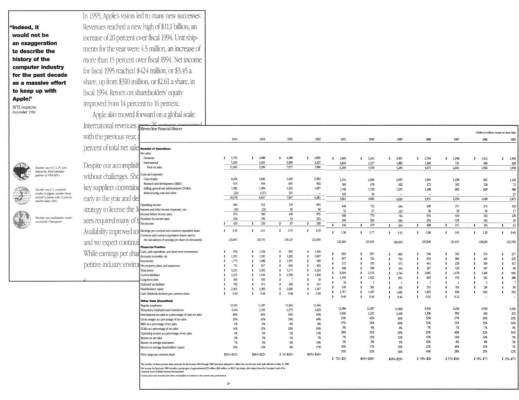

Figure 2.1
Apple Computer's Annual Report Shows
Detailed Financial Information about the
Company's Expenses, Profits, Losses, and So Forth

The United States Post Office requires magazine publishers to provide detailed circulation information for everyone—readers and competitors alike—to see. The Post Office even requires that the publisher *print* this information in the magazine once a year (see Figure 2.2.)

Figure 2.2
Every Periodical Must Print
Detailed Circulation Information
Due to Postal Regulations

In both cases, the information presented (the annual report and the circulation audit) offers important data on the inner workings of a company's business. When is the last time you saw a business proposal from another company? Chances are, you might never have seen one because, business proposals are guarded as if they are secret covenants. Whereas other information (such as financial statements) tells us what a company did, a business proposal sheds light on specifically how the company accomplished its goal. And, in a competitive business environment, *how* is far more important than *what*.

Whereas the privileged few might enjoy the services of a wizard proposal writer, most of us lack the knowledge or the confidence to compose what is arguably the most important of all business documents.

Don't Fear Your Business Proposal

We fear our proposals are too short or too long. We fear our proposals are priced too high or too low. We fear the layout is too simple or too complex. We fear how our proposal presents us in the eyes of current or potential clients as well as our relationship to our competitors. So what's the best way to overcome these fears? Or, a more appropriate question: *who is* in the best position to help us overcome our fears? Answer: Our clients!

If you are presenting a business proposal to a client for the first time, it makes sense to present "the works"—a comprehensive document that includes:

- Table of contents

- Robust summary and objective

- Detailed project development and production steps

- Complete background and justification about the subject matter (regarding the history and marketing potential of the Internet, for example)

- Complete background, mission statement, and project list from your company (more on these topics later in this chapter)

After you have had the time to interact with the client and proven your company's capability to deliver quality products and services at fair prices, take the time to ask your clients what works for them. Don't be afraid to ask: What do they like in their business proposals? What don't they like? What do they need to see? What don't they want, or have the time, to see? Many companies offering business proposals tend to be afraid of their clients. Don't fall into this trap!

Most clients (sure, we grant not all) want you to succeed. Let's face it. Most clients are very busy—if they weren't, they wouldn't have the capital to have you produce their interactive CD-ROM or Java-packed Web site. If they weren't busy, they would sit down, learn HTML, and do it themselves. More important, given much of the down-sizing in our present economy, your clients don't have the internal resources to produce their own product. They, in short, rely on you.

We know of a situation in which a client invited his account executive over for Thanksgiving dinner. In another, a client asked an art director for help in picking out a Christmas gift for her husband.

What does this mean? It means that the client considers the contractor part of the family—almost as if the subcontractor were an employee. Sure this has its risks, but it proves that clients rely on their vendors. How many graphic designers have been saved by the immortal words to their printer, "I don't have time to deal with this, can you save the file and do your *normal, fantastic* job?"

Because of their need for reliable, affordable, and quality-driven contractors, many clients are delighted when they find a vendor with whom they are comfortable working.

So why not talk to them? If you are afraid to talk to and be frank with your clients, you do not have the kind of relationship with your clients that you need to grow your business either. Chances are, you have the wrong clients. You know the type—you do one or two jobs for them and they nickel-and-dime you along the way. You make a little money and get a big headache. They don't understand the value and expertise you offer them. They figure they don't need you, and they go their merry way. They are the clients who take the logo you designed for them, and they buy a desktop package of page layouts and prepare their brochure themselves. Is this how to grow your business?

One very wise marketing executive once pointed out, "It takes time and money to *chase* bad clients, time and money that takes away from *servicing* better clients." He added, "Exemplary service sells."

If you send a business proposal to a client, don't sweat it out waiting for them to make a decision. If you prepared a sound business proposal your chances are as good as they are going to get. Move on! Service your current clients and prepare another business proposal for another job. After a week to two weeks, call the client. If they don't return your calls, consider yourself lucky. If it takes 10 calls to get a client on the phone about a business proposal you sent them, how many do you think it will take to get a client on the phone about your check?

Too many of us are familiar with the client who needs that business proposal overnight—complete with accurate price estimates. He is the same client who is never heard from again and there is no discussion about what ever happened to the "life and death" project or the business proposal you dropped everything and worked for three days to complete.

When you talk to the client, be frank. Ask him how he liked the concept for the business proposal. Ask him about the prices. Ask if you were too high. Ask if the business proposal represents what he had in mind.

If You Don't Get the Job, Ask Why!

In one case, AI, a small and newly established Web design shop was called in to pitch redoing a Web site for a large telecommunications company. The client contact at the company was honest with the firm (which they had seen speaking at a national Internet seminar) and told them they were up against three other companies. AI made an initial presentation to the client contact and was one of two companies asked back for the final round of evaluation. AI made an additional presentation to a group of five people—executives from the telecommunication company's home office in London. The presentation went well, but AI did not get the job. The client contact told AI not to worry because there was other work that the company needed done and that the firm had impressed the company, even though, in the end, it wasn't awarded the job.

The head of AI candidly asked why his company didn't get the job. The client contact was honest: "Even though you are a new firm, based on your past work at Company X, there was no question about your ability, or the quality of your work. In the end, I was pulling for you and the board liked you, but they are not too bright. Your ideas were excellent, but the other company had done large (20" × 30") poster boards of their concept. While I feel their designs were not as good as yours, the board, which tends not to be design-oriented, was impressed by those boards."

The client contact concluded: "Next month I want you to pitch a job for our West Coast office. Keep your proposal the same, your price range was fine—in fact, it was a little low. Do some storyboards, maybe a few slides, and you will be in good shape. Presentation matters to these people. We aren't going to spend the time to search for design firms all over again. If you present the board with a more visual approach, you will get the job." And AI did.

Have any of your clients given you feedback like that? If you never ask, how could they? Are you as frank with your clients? Can you afford not to be?

In another case, an interactive company lost a job to a competitor. The account executive, Kathy, had done work for the client for several years, but her main contact had retired. A new contact on the job, though capable, was in a new position and was in a little over his head. Robert awarded the job to another vendor based exclusively on price. Kathy called Robert and said, "I want to take you to lunch."

During lunch, Kathy was frank. "I know we lost the bid based on price. I want you to know that I have done this type of work for your company for four years. My prices are 15% higher for a reason. We have overhead that our competition does not. It's a fact. It also enables us to deliver very complicated projects on a long-term basis. Be careful with this project. It has a few quagmires that the company you hired is not capable of handling. I don't mean to speak ill of them, but I know that they have over promised." Kathy concluded, "I want you to succeed in your new job, because if you fail, I lose your business on more than this project."

Robert was impressed. But he did not change his agreement with the company he selected. Halfway through the project, however, it became clear that Kathy was right. The project had missed its first three deadlines. Robert's contact at the company producing the project had changed twice. The company did *not* have the expertise to produce the job.

Eight months later, after losing the initial bid, Kathy got a call from Robert. The project was in trouble and the company needed help. "We can help you," said Kathy. "Let's get together as soon as possible. And this time, Robert, you're buying lunch." Kathy still does work for that client today.

Pitching the Client

Many companies are not sure whether business proposals should be presented in an interactive format. That is, if the business proposal should contain slides, touch screens, video, animation, and so on.

The question confuses two very different processes. The first is "pitching" a client—that is making a sales presentation to the client. The second concerns presenting on paper the goals and terms of the project being pitched—the business proposal.

As far as "pitching" a client, the level of multimedia incorporated into the sales process depends largely on the type of client and the project. If you are pitching an interactive kiosk to a company that is technically sophisticated, you may need to create a high-powered presentation. If your client is afraid of computers, but knows she needs to be on the Internet tomorrow, you might be okay showing her a few Web basics. In short, how you present your information depends on circumstances in which it is nearly impossible to develop a foolproof rule.

No matter how you present your sales pitch in person, you still have to document that pitch for the company to evaluate and you do that in the business proposal. The situation is analogous to the job interview—no matter how well it goes in person, you still need a résumé.

It's amazing that, despite all the overhead projectors, Powerbooks, flat panel displays, CD-I players, CD-ROMs, slide shows, and Macromedia Director presentations, what sells a project for the most part are paragraphs of simple words and numbers on 10 (or so) sheets of good old-fashioned paper.

Business Proposal Dos & Don'ts

Deanna Vincent
VP, Market Development
iVillage, Inc.
New York, NY
http://www.ivillage.com

Vincent graduated a Journalism major with a magazine focus from Temple University. She spent three and half years at *Home Office Computing* magazine as Senior Reviews Editor, specializing in telecommunications for small businesses; 10 months at iVillage, a start-up online content studio backed by America Online (AOL), TCI Interactive, Tribune Company, and Kleiner Perkins Caufield & Byers. iVillage, which launched three sites specifically for America Online and others for the Web, sells products and advertising, as well as develops "mini-sites" for its clients.

iVillage's clients include: Polaroid, MGM/UA Home Entertainment, Starbucks Coffee Co., Nissan, Toyota, Microsoft, Prudential, Hewlett-Packard, Sandoz (Triaminic), Fisher-Price, Compaq, PBS, Procter & Gamble, IBM, UPS, and Chase Bank.

How many proposals do you write a year?
Fifty or more...

On the average, how long does each one take?
From two days to two weeks, including meetings and brainstorming sessions, as well as the review process.

How long are they?
Our proposals range from 5 to 20 pages.

What are the price ranges?
$60,000 to $170,000.

What's the biggest challenge you face in writing a proposal?
Not having enough information from the salesperson on the client's specific goals in sponsoring a Web site. For example, what is the client really looking to accomplish?

Another challenge is trying to estimate a price for a project when the client has no idea what they want. Often they'll ask "How much does it cost to create an online site?" This is like asking, "How much does it cost to create a print ad?" It depends on whether or not you hire Cindy Crawford to model for your ad or you create a black-and-white ad using only type. Clients tend to understand this analogy.

Any favorite section/element you like to include in your proposals?

Understanding. We could write proposals simply selling banner spaces on our sites, but we don't.

We strive to provide our clients with proposals that demonstrate the idea that we have a crystal-clear understanding of our client's business—the objective of their sales and marketing campaigns. We provide a few pages of content ideas—sometimes unsolicited—that are geared to meet our client's objectives. We try to prove we are not simply in love with the medium, but that we have solid, real-world suggestions on how the medium can work for our clients. Our proposals also show that sponsorship buys a lot of hand-holding from our company.

Any guiding philosophy for proposal writing?

Absolutely—solid planning! Sometimes we role-play, so that we can imagine any potential hesitation on the behalf of our client. I work on creating a bulletproof proposal that addresses any and every potential objection that the client might raise. In doing so, we use the client's own language, so that they know we are not just *selling* to them...we are *listening* to them.

As a former editor, I tend to be really strict about good writing in proposals, and I try to pass this on to people I'm training. I don't understand why writing standards tend to be lower on the marketing side of the business. At my former magazine, *Home Office Computing*, we would strive for editorial excellence, but our media kits were an embarrassment—they didn't live up to the same standards the editorial group had set. At iVillage, our proposals read well, and I think clients assume this level of intelligence will be carried through in the work we do for them.

I also tend to present information using short paragraphs. Some people think that terse, "bullet-point" summaries work best. My experience has been that clients can't make sense of them when they re-read the proposals. Something's missing. Well-written sentences have more depth than lists of items.

Any final thoughts?

People shouldn't be afraid to exhibit a passion for what they are selling in their proposal.

When my boss and I started working on Parent Soup, neither of us had ever sold advertising. We didn't have a formal model, so we wrote proposals that simply explained Parent Soup's goal—bringing parents together to help raise their children.

I think our honesty—and that we really believe in what we were selling—attracted top-rate sponsors who shared our viewpoint and our passion.

And it worked?

We sold a million dollars' worth of advertising in a matter of months.

Business Proposal Dos and Don'ts

Richard Adams
Producer and Business Development
Executive
EarthWeb, Inc.
New York, New York
http://www.earthweb.com

Adams holds an undergraduate degree from the University of Rochester (Liberal Arts; English) and a Masters in Communications from the University of Southern California-Annenberg School of Communications Technology. He has spent one year at a major online service and one year at EarthWeb, a start-up Internet software company and high-end Web developer.

How many proposals do you write a year?

Five.

On the average, how long does each one take?

Two weeks.

How long are they?

Twenty pages.

What are the price ranges?

$50,000 to $3,000,000.

What's the biggest challenge you face when writing a proposal?

Giving a price quotation and drawing up a contract based on a Request for Proposal (RFP) rather than a solid specifications which provide exact details about what the project requires. RFPs are often written by committees and are typically very vague.

Any favorite section/element you like to include in your proposals?

I like to propose a two-week consulting period in which we deliver a functional spec based on the RFP. The client can evaluate our work during this period while we develop a better document to base a development contract on.

Anything you try to avoid?

I try to avoid including hourly estimates.

Any guiding philosophy for writing a proposal?

Quote the questions posed in the RFP and answer them. Don't ad-lib or deviate. Your clients will appreciate and admire your precision.

Any final thoughts?

Consult your technical and artistic production staff first. They are the stars of the show, and they will have to live with the client after you get the job.

To be fair, it is often difficult to solicit information from a production staff during the early stages of business development because they are generally very busy. But you have to make sure the production staff appreciates the importance of their participation. Remind them that they will have to live with the client should you win the business. That typically gets their attention, since the reason they are so busy is that they are living with the client you won last month. Ask lots of questions and make sure that you listen to their concerns.

Also remember that programmers and artists are reluctant to render judgment or opinions based on incomplete information. More often than not, RFPs do not provide enough precise information and production teams have trouble giving you exact time or cost estimates. When possible, initiate communication between the potential client's technical staff and yours.

When this is impossible, you must fill in the blanks as best you can. That is your job.

Business Proposal Dos and Don'ts

Kevin Howat
VP, Education Technology Group
Simon & Schuster

How long have you been at Simon & Schuster?

Two years. Formerly, I was with Macmillan Digital USA.

What does your division do at Simon & Schuster?

We publish high-quality, interactive reference titles for consumer markets. The Education Technology Group is in start-up mode, but will publish multiple media education products for the home market.

And your role?

I have been responsible for all product development, including building a staff of producers and developers capable of taking products from conception to market.

So, you've seen a few business proposals?

You can say that. I review well over 50 business proposals a year.

What are the kinds of things you like to see in a business proposal?

To me, a good proposal should always have a succinct statement of product objectives. It should also clearly define the intended audience, offer competitive positioning of the product being proposed, and contain a statement of the team's qualifications to take on the project.

The business proposal should also include a budget, schedule, technology strategy, and requirements (including type and amount of media). Additionally, it should contain an assessment of rights issues and some analysis of the project's fit with the strategies of our company.

Anything else you find helpful?

I like to see samples of a company's related work.

What is the biggest business proposal faux pas?

Making claims that the project can and will be all things to all markets while addressing the specific needs of none.

Optimal length?

Five to eight pages.

Optimal format?

I like to see text and a spreadsheet; perhaps a pert chart as well as any interactive or media elements that may be available.

What is it about your favorite kind of business proposal that makes you want to read it on the beach, or late at night in bed?

I really enjoy reading business proposals for products that include thoughtful market analysis, where I learn something about the market that either confirms or challenges an assumption I have made.

What kinds of business proposals make it into the "recycling bin?"

Business proposals that are for projects that lack a strong point of view or competitive positioning will likely not find a market. Too often I see claims that, "No other product like this one exists."

Writing a Business Proposal: Step-By-Step

In this section, we walk through the step-by-step creation of an actual business proposal. Later, in Chapter 5, "Building a Budget," we will create a budget estimate for this proposal.

Before we begin, it is important to recognize that every company has their own way of preparing a business proposal. In truth, there really is no one correct way to present a business proposal to a client.

The true measure of success of any good business proposal are:

- The client buys it

- You make money on it

Creating a business proposal generally begins by developing a *client profile* and *needs assessment*.

Client Profile. The company preparing the business proposal tries to identify the client. What does the client make or do? What is it about how or what the client does that makes it stand out among its competitors? In short, what is it about the company that *matters* to potential consumers?

Needs Assessment. The company preparing the business proposal identifies what it is the client actually *needs*. For example, why does the client need to be on the Internet? What is the specific need and how will the company help the client meet that need?

Developing a client profile and a client needs assessment goes a long way toward developing an effective business proposal.

The best way to create a client profile is to interview your client. Ask him or her the following types of questions:

- What is the history of the company?

- What products does the company make?

- What is the philosophy of the company? What is its mission?

- If the company produces a specific product, by all means, check it out! Get the product.

- Does the company have a media kit? Look at its press clippings.

- Does the company have a video? If so, make sure you watch it.

- Ask to speak to experts on the company's products. Ask them what they think.

- Ask to speak to people who purchased the company's product. Most companies have references, or people who are avowed loyalists, who are available to offer testimonials about the company's product.

Ask yourself, how is this company's product positioned in the marketplace? Why? Has the company's positioning been successful? If so, why? If not, why not?

In short, if you are going to produce a product for your client, you need to understand your client. This is where good old-fashioned journalism can make the difference between working *for* your clients and working *with* your clients.

Let's start by looking at an actual business proposal that was presented to Joe Breeze, President and Founder of Joe Breeze Cycles, makers of high-performance bicycles. We think this case study is applicable to the small to mid-level size Web sites that most small to mid-level size design studios are likely to encounter as prospective clients. Sure IBM subcontracts out Web development, but those sites are more difficult to obtain. The majority of the Web work for small to mid-size design studios will involve working with current clients and ushering them into the digital age.

Profile: Joe Breeze Cycles

In the late 1970s, a group of gnarly young Californians was interested in riding bikes and playing hard. Their downhill rides on bikes adapted from the old balloon-tire Schwinn's we all knew as kids created an entirely new sport—mountain biking.

Today, mountain bikes have practically become synonymous with bicycling in the United States and have developed into a billion dollar industry. More and more cities are creating car free paths for the burgeoning numbers of bike riders. Mountain biking debuted as a sport event at the Atlanta Summer Olympic Games and Volkswagen now "bundles" a mountain bike with the sale of one of its cars. From the winding back roads of Marin County, to the big business of the recreation industry, mountain biking, it might be said, has arrived.

Those original downhill daredevils—Tom Ritchey, Gary Fischer, and Joe Breeze—are not only creators of the sport. The companies that bear their name are also responsible for creating some of the sport's finest bicycles.

Since their initial downhill days, each of the sport's pioneers have gone their separate ways. Although he still makes a limited number of performance bicycles, Tom Ritchey specializes in making quality oriented components such as clipless pedals, tires, and so on. Gary Fisher has expanded his product line, which is manufactured and distributed by Trek, one of the largest and most respected names in the industry.

Then there is Joe Breeze, who is known for having a philosophy unto himself. His line of bikes, which he calls "Breezers," are awe inspiring. In the words of one mountain bike magazine editor, "When the Breezer rolled into our office, our jaws hit the floor. It was simply the most beautiful mountain bike we had ever seen."

While he keeps current with cutting edge bike technology, the real engineering marvel in a Breezer is the fact that Joe, himself an avid rider, focuses on mechanically efficient designs that year in and year out get stronger, faster, lighter, and more comfortable.

We know because one of us rides a Breezer. That's how we got his business. We liked our Breezer so much we called Joe and asked him if we could design and develop his Web site. He said yes.

Assessment: Joe Breeze Cycles

We approached Joe Breeze to build a Web site that would communicate the philosophy of his company, let bike riders check out his newest bicycle models, and let bike enthusiasts keep up to date on how Team Breezer, the company sponsored racing team was doing in mountain bike races across the nation.

The Web site also needed to inform potential customers where they could go to buy a Breezer. Since Joe Breeze does not sell his bicycles directly to consumers, there is no reason to have online transactions on his Web site. More important, the way the bicycling industry works is that the bicycle maker creates his product, and that product is sold to large bicycle distributors that might carry more than one line of bikes and other bike-related products. The distributor sells the bike directly to the bike stores you are likely to walk into when you decide to purchase a bike. Therefore, the bike maker has a vested interest in directing calls to his or her distributor. That way, the distributor can direct calls to the bike retailer of their choice.

The Title Page

The title page should contain the following basic information:

- Title for the business proposal being presented
- Name of the person to which the business proposal is being presented
- Name of the person from which the business proposal came
- Date
- Copyright and a declaration of confidentiality

The Title Page: Joe Breeze Cycles

"It's a Breezer":
A Proposal to Design and Develop a World Wide Web (WWW) Site for Joe Breeze Cycles

Prepared for:
Joe Breeze
President
Joe Breeze Cycles
Mt. Tam, California

Prepared by:
JP Frenza
Earth Pledge Foundation's
Division for Sustainable Media
New York, NY

Date: September 1, 1996

© 1996 The Earth Pledge Foundation's Division for Sustainable Media

This proposal has been specifically prepared for limited distribution Joe Breeze Cycles. This document contains materials and information which the Earth Pledge Foundation's Division for Sustainable Media considers confidential, proprietary, and significant for the protection of its business. The distribution of this document is limited solely to those full-time Joe Breeze Cycles employees, either actively involved in the evaluation and selection of the Earth Pledge Foundation's Division for Sustainable Media as the firm to conduct this assignment, or those that will be involved with the program described herein.

The Table of Contents

If your proposal is short, there probably isn't much need for a Table of Contents. Even if your proposal is longer, many people feel that there is no real need to add a Table of Contents. It's entirely up to you.

We feel that every business proposal should have one because it makes the proposal more organized, and it is particularly helpful if you are talking on the phone with your client and you need them to navigate your proposal quickly and efficiently. That is, unless your client says they don't need one.

The Table of Contents: Joe Breeze Cycles

The Summary and Objective

The purpose of the summary and objective is to succinctly state what it is your company is going to do for the client and how it will be accomplished.

In many business proposals, the summary and objective is the most read page. Clients tend to refer to it again and again. In fact, most clients really only read the summary and objective and the budget—and they flip back and forth between them, ignoring practically everything else!

It's a good idea to write the summary and objective before you write any other part of the business proposal. That way you force yourself to focus. As you write every other section of the business proposal, ask yourself, "How does this relate to, strengthen, and help clarify the summary and objective of the project?"

Here are the kind of questions that you might want to answer in your summary and objective.

- State what you are proposing to do for the client. For example: "Our Company proposes to do A, B, and C, for Company X, Y, Z."
- Why does Company X, Y, Z need this done?
- What is likely to happen if they do this?

The Summary and Objective: Joe Breeze Cycles

The Earth Pledge Foundation's (EPF) Division for Sustainable Media proposes to design, produce, and maintain a World Wide Web (WWW) site for Joe Breeze Cycles.

Joe Breeze promotes the bicycle as an energy efficient, environmentally friendly form of transportation. The Earth Pledge Foundation promotes sustainable development—the balance between economic growth and environmental preservation.

Based on this appropriate intersection, the Joe Breeze site will be hosted in the Mall section of EPF's Web site, enabling the company to market its products to the more than 1,000 weekly visitors hitting http://www.earthpledge.org.

The primary objective of the Joe Breeze Cycles site is to showcase the company's 1997 product and direct interested customers to Breezer distributors where they can locate the nearest bicycle retailer that sells Breezer products.

The Web site will also provide a forum to provide updates on Team Breezer, the racing team the company sponsors, as well as provide visitors with background information about Joe Breeze Cycles.

The Project

The project section of the business proposal is where you identify the specific structure of the project proposed in the summary.

If you are developing a CD-ROM, this is where you identify the project's editorial and design concept, the opening screen (the interface), the sections the CD-ROM will contain, and as much detail about the subsections as possible.

This project definition (some people refer to this as the "Design Document" and it may be a separate document) is important because it tells the client the basic goals and components of the project. The more specific the goals and components are identified, the better.

For example, it is in this section that you have to tell the client you are producing an interface that contains three buttons. Button one will contain three elements. Button two will contain a video. Button three will contain two elements. Here, you state what each button is and where it leads.

It is important to review this project definition with the client. If he is not comfortable with it, have him suggest alternatives—additional buttons, sections, subsections, and so on. This should all be discussed before the client signs the Letter of Agreement and before work on the project begins. This project definition serves as the basis for your contractual agreement with your client. It is spelled out in detail in the business proposal (which is signed off by the client) or in the Letter of Agreement.

That way, when the client comes up with an entirely new section of the CD-ROM that he absolutely must include, you can state clearly to him that the business proposal (and its prices) were not based on the new section and that adding a new section will result in additional charges. In this case, an addendum to the business proposal or Letter of Agreement is created and the client signs off on it.

We know of one particularly successful company that often adds material to its clients projects without charging them. They still, however, go through the motions of creating an addendum to the proposal and having the client sign it. "The client gets a good feeling out of seeing a piece of paper saying we are going to do X more work on the project than we agreed to, and we will do it at no charge. It makes it easier when we really do need to charge them more," explained the business manager.

Creating a CD-ROM, an interactive diskette, or a Web site, can be a tumultuous proposition at best. Client changes can come fast and furious to the point where it is almost impossible to keep up with the work itself, let alone the business component of the work. There have been a number of long-term projects where these changes were not accurately tracked, record keeping relaxed, and the project became an ongoing cycle of client changes, corrections, more changes, and more corrections. All the while, the project became less profitable.

Design studios traditionally agree to present more than one concept to their clients. For example, in the process of design and pitching annual reports, it is a common practice to offer the client several design themes from which to choose.

New media is no different. Whether you are designing a CD-ROM or a Web site, if you are presenting multiple design concepts to your client, state exactly how many you agree to present in the project section of your proposal.

The project section of the business proposal is enhanced by a diagram of the project as well as any design concepts. The diagram and the design concept enable your client to be better visualize the project and the more they can visualize the project, the more likely they are to help you shape the project in a way that is clearly defined (communicated). The more clearly defined the project, the better it is, and the more profitable it is, to produce. Of course, seeing is believing and presenting the look and feel of a concept goes a long way toward getting the client to say yes.

On the next three pages, you will see the project description for the Joe Breeze Web site in the form of editorial and pictorial representations.

The Project: The Joe Breeze Cycles Web Site

The home page for the Joe Breeze Cycles Web site (accessible by clicking on the Joe Breeze Cycles icon in the EPF Mall) ties together the Breezer concept in short, sharp terms which all highlight the product name—Breezer. The page takes viewers into the following sections (a description of each follows):

Why Breezer?

This section is where mountain biking enthusiasts tap into the Breezer background—the origins of mountain biking, Joe Breeze's involvement in the creation of the sport, as well as his views on bicycling as an environmentally friendly technology. Sub-level pages include:

1. Breezer History. The history of mountain biking and background on Joe Breeze Cycles.

2. Breezer Philosophy. What makes a Breezer a Breezer? Straight talk on designing and engineering Breezer products.

3. Breeze on Biking. Where is the sport heading? Where should it be heading? A pioneer on the sport he helped invent.

Ride Breezer.

Here they are...the Breezer designs for 1997. This section will contain seven pages: one for each of the company's five mountain bike offerings, one for its road bike, and another for the company's special tribute to the inspiration that started it all—the balloon tire Schwinn bike.

Wear Breezer.

A one-page scroll down look at Breezer's 1997 clothing, including shirts, shorts, gloves, and so on. Each product is presented with one-line description and sizes.

Team Breezer.

This section outlines the individuals that are Team Breezer. Sub-level pages include:

1. The Team Breezer Philosophy. Unlike other bike racing teams, this team does not accept sponsorship from automotive companies. Isn't being on a bike supposed to mean you are not in your car?

2. Team Members. Short bios of Team Breezer riders.

3. Race Results. A scroll-down page which identifies the race, the location, the date, and information on how Team Breezer finishes in the standings. This page will be updated regularly.

4. Up and Coming. A one-page listing of races (including location and dates) where Team Breezer riders will be competing.

Buy Breezer.

A one-page listing of distributors in the United States and around the world, where interested riders can call to find the nearest bike shop that carries Breezer bikes and accessories.

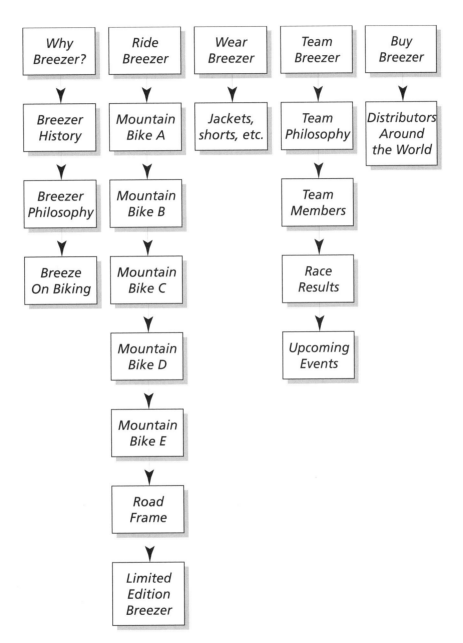

Figure 2.3
Site Architecture for the Joe Breeze Web Site

57

Figure 2.3
Sample Pages from the Site Design

58

Program Development

It is a good idea to communicate the development process of the project in the business proposal. For the most part, the more communication you have with your client about a particular project, the better off you will be.

On the other hand, some clients want to sign the proposal and hear from you when the project is finished. Even in these cases it is a good business practice to send the client a status report every two weeks or so and let them know how you are progressing. This can take the form of a short fax or e-mail or a more elaborate status report.

After you have worked with a client, and both parties have reached a communication comfort level, the frequency of the status reports can be adjusted accordingly.

It is a good idea, however, to always inform the client when major project milestones are coming up, so that they can prepare to respond appropriately. For example, if they need to be available to sign off on a design.

In addition to documenting the actual steps in the development of a project, the business proposal should also sketch out basic time frames for each. These deadlines should be written into the proposal so that both parties are aware of their responsibilities. That way, if a project falls behind because the client did not approve the design concept within the amount of time specified, the reason for the delay is clear.

The following page shows the program development for the Joe Breeze Web site:

Program Development: Joe Breeze Cycles Web Site

Program Development for the Joe Breeze Cycles Web Site will include the following basic processes. We estimate that this project can be completed from start to finish in four weeks (assuming client approval).

- **Editorial Development.** Review all of the editorial material available regarding Joe Breeze Cycles (including history and background, catalogs, product reviews, information on Team Breezer, and so on) and work with Joe Breeze to determine what material will be included on the site. This proposal assumes all content is provided on disc by Joe Breeze Cycles.

- **Site Architecture.** Categorize all of the available content into sections for the Web site, create hierarchies of information, and structure each section on the site. In addition to defining the site's structure, this step includes creating a site blueprint, presenting the diagram to Joe Breeze Cycles for approval, and incorporating client changes.

- **Design.** Create initial site sketches based on one design concept, incorporate client approval and receive final sign off on initial sketches, create final page designs and all site assets (including photographs, illustrations, navigation buttons, icons, and so on), and manage revisions and final approval with Joe Breeze.

- **Production: Graphics.** Optimize all design elements and site assets for the Web, including conversion of artwork from Illustrator to Photoshop, indexing, reviewing graphics in multiple browsers, and making final adjustments of graphics after indexing.

- **Production: HTML.** Create page templates and combine all design elements and site assets into final Web page creation.

- **Site Review and Testing.** Proof and review final HTML files for content accuracy, check design consistency, and verify all links and navigation. This also includes final client approval.

- **Uploading to Server.** Place files on the server, test all links, as well as incorporating any last-minute changes and additions from the client.

- **Marketing.** Register the site with various search engines as well as surfing the Web for online bicycle magazines, and mountain biking related Web sites, and notifying them that Joe Breeze Cycles is on the Web! This step is important since the bicycling community has a strong presence on the Internet, including bike manufacturers, riding clubs, retailers, catalogs, and more.

About Your Company

This section of the business proposal should include a mission statement from your company as well as a company background, bios from key members of the team, projects produced, and previous clients.

In some cases, when the client doesn't know your company, it makes perfect sense to put the About the Company section of the business proposal directly after the Summary and Objective. We have seen both approaches function well.

About the Company

Earth Pledge's Division for Sustainable Media recognizes that computers and communications technology can convert information into knowledge and connectivity into cooperation promoting sustainable solutions to the challenges we face.

A full-service Internet agency, the Division for Sustainable Media raises funds from the private sector to support the development of World Wide Web (WWW) sites for non-profit organizations and businesses practicing the principles of sustainable development.

The Division believes sustainable media uses technology to promote sustainable development by:

- Focusing on programs that minimize the impact of the communications process on the environment

- Fostering greater dialog on environmental, social, and economic needs

- Showcasing innovative solutions and fostering relationships that integrate economic growth, equity, and the environment in public policy

Division for Sustainable Media clients include Apple Computer, AT&T, the Open Text Corporation, the Foundation for the Prevention and Early Resolution of Conflict (PERC), the law firm of Tremont & Sheldon, and more.

The Budget

The budget for this case study is presented in step-by-step detail in Chapter 5.

Additional Project Considerations

It is a good idea to present a few additional options that your client might want to consider. These options include "room to grow" suggestions that set the groundwork for "add on" or "follow up" business.

Additional Project Considerations: Joe Breeze Cycles

After establishing the initial Joe Breeze Web site, the Division for Sustainable Media suggests the company consider establishing its own Internet presence by moving the site to http://www.breezer.com (although Earth Pledge would continue to provide market pull to site by featuring it in its Mall).

Depending on the interests of the company at that time, Joe Breeze Cycles might want to consider sponsoring "Mountain Bike Quiz" in conjunction with the Mountain Bike Hall of Fame and offer Breezer clothing and accessories to the winners. The ultimate goal might be to start to sell Breezer clothing and accessories directly on the Web site.

The Appendix

We have found that background information on the industry, for example, why the Internet is important, is not an essential component of a business proposal. Most, although not all, companies do not need to be sold on new media or the Internet—they are already privy to all the hype!

In the event that you feel your client needs to be educated on the specific justification, it is not a bad idea to print a few Web pages from their competitor or a couple screen shots of how her crosstown rival is sending out interactive floppies with their latest product line. That, combined with a few solid paragraphs of analysis, should be sufficient. Remember, most clients rarely read this stuff anyway—they already read it everyday in the *Wall Street Journal*, or their local newspaper.

Here's a small sample of what we presented to Joe Breeze in terms of background on the Internet. Even Joe admits he never read this. But, if you have a client you feel needs the background, by all means, feel free. Again, in some instances, in particular, where the client lacks an understanding of the Internet, this section might even go before the Summary. As we said, there is no one correct way. The key is to have the right elements and present them in the most appropriate order.

Since the information in the Appendix has been repeated everywhere, we only include a partial summary.

The Appendix: Background on the World Wide Web

The following bike companies are on the Web: Cannondale, Trek, Specialized.

Why?

The Web is unrivaled as an advertising and marketing medium.

Estimates suggest that the Web is the fastest growing marketplace in the world with more than 100,000 business currently involved in marketing and electronic commerce.

The Web is unrivaled as an advertising and marketing medium.

Where a one-time, printed advertisement could cost as much as $10,000 (and prices up to $30,000 are common), a full presence on the Internet for a whole year could, reaching far more potential clients, cost only two or three times the total of one page of its printed counterpart.

Marketing economics such as that have all led Sony, General Motors, Levis, and a host of other marketing and advertising savvy firms to the Internet with great success. Internet marketing is also interactive—customers respond to surveys, request more information, and so on—and changes and updates are done at little or no cost.

In Summary

There are many ways to present a business proposal. But the important thing to focus on is the *process*—the development that goes into the creation of the business proposal. By gaining insight into the mechanics of this process, you can learn what works for you, what you want to borrow in the preparation of your own business proposals, what you don't need, and more important, what you can do better!

Designing for New Media

"The biggest challenge designers face in working with the computer medium is not mastering the various technologies that are its constant companions, but introducing meaning and life into the products and services on the human side of the screen."

Clement Mok
Designing Business, Adobe Press

The Design Document

In the previous chapter, you saw a simple example of a business proposal for a small Web site. It includes many elements: the assessment, summary and objectives, project description, and so on. In the project description, we mentioned a design document. When creating a separate business proposal and design document, be sure to include detailed assumptions in the text. In the business proposal, you can make a more general statement such as, "We plan to include simple 3D animations of no more than one per page." In the design document, you will want to be more specific—"The simple animations on each page will draw attention to special offers, new information, etc. There will be no more than one per page as this will become overly distracting for the viewer. The objectives of the animations are to…" This gives the client a general idea of where you are headed and avoids confusion down the road. Of course, the more specific you can be in the design document, the better. See the sidebar "What is a Design Document?" in this chapter.

In the Joe Breeze site, the design document was small and simple and easily included in the business proposal. However, often times, a design document can take up many pages and be quite complex. In that case, you would want to supplement the business proposal with a separate, detailed design document. It would include the following:

- General outline of the project
- List of team players
- Navigation map

- Storyboards or screen roughs
- List of existing content
- Deliverables
- Detailed production schedule

Let's look at each of these in more detail.

General Outline

The general outline will summarize the general purpose of the project.

- Why it is being done—a general statement of purpose
- What is being created—a general description of the project elements
- Who is doing what—the expectations of client and supplier involvement
- Where is it being done—this depends on the clients involvement in the production—it may not be appropriate
- When is the expected delivery date

Each of these items should be expanded upon in the rest of the document. The general outline can be easily copied from the business proposal.

The Team Players

Certainly, to keep communication smooth, there will be two key people, one on the client side and one on the vendor side, who will be the focal points of communication. But it is important that everyone understand who the other players are and what they do. It often doesn't make sense for the two primary people to get involved in every single detail. It is important, however, that everyone have access to the other members of the team so that design and production can move along as scheduled. When an issue arises that cannot be easily solved, then the two primary players get involved. It is also important to have regular meetings with your client to apprise them of developments as appropriate.

Navigation Maps

These maps describe how the Web site or CD-ROM is organized—how each page or screen relates to the others. You saw a simple navigational map example on page 57. These maps can get very complex and ultimately confusing. Flushing out the details will help you arrive at the organizational model appropriate for your new media project. Clement Mok's, *Designing Business* (Adobe Press) discusses these organizational models and is well worth reading, especially if this is a new concept to you.

Storyboards or Screen Roughs

Sometimes, a navigation map is not enough to show how pages or screens relate to each other. Or, maybe you have an animation or video sequence that needs more explanation. This is where storyboards and screen roughs come into play. They are vehicles to describe your ideas in more detail.

Existing Content

There are often existing elements that will be required for inclusion in your project—logos, tag lines, animations, illustrations, and so on. All of these should be listed in detail.

Deliverables

This is probably the largest part of the document and is often combined with the navigation map, storyboards, and screen designs. It should list every single deliverable item in the project. This should include the contents of the new media project, any packaging needs, replication needs, maintenance needs, and so on.

> For example, the home page will include:
>
> One header illustration that is an image map of four elements: services, products, contact us, and technical support. Each element will have a text alternative.
>
> Four image links—one for each of the company's products. Each element will have a text alternative.
>
> Three text links—one for each service offered by the company.

These may be described further if the information is known at the time. This list also doubles as a checklist for items as they are completed.

Production Schedule

This is a detailed production schedule for all parties that lists key item delivery and approval dates. If a delivery is not met or an approval is delayed, the schedule should be revised. The client must understand that it is vital to the production process that approvals be timely or the schedule will not hold.

Just because an approval is delayed only 12 hours, does not mean that the schedule will only be delayed 12 hours. Often times, schedules can be impacted disproportionately. Be sure to get your clients input on approval cycles in their company. It may be more complicated than you think and will keep you from running too ragged when critical dates draw near.

What is a Design Document?

Matthew Winston & Kathy Migliozzi
Founders of Synesthesia™
Brattleboro, Vermont
(802) 254-4313

Background

Worked at the legendary Kodak Center for Creative Imaging (CCI) as well as contributed to projects for Gillette, Duracell, the Sharper Image Company, Simon & Schuster, American Signature Graphics, and the Vermont Web Project, a national educational program to bring technology to teachers and their students.

How would you describe Synesthesia's business philosophy?

We try to employ two basic principles to every project that we get involved with.

First, we recognize that there is a distinction between the business aspect of a new media project and the multimedia, or technology aspect, of a new media project. It's important to keep those two very different objectives separate—the business and the creative.

Many projects we are offered present a wonderful opportunity artistically and creatively, but the business side of the project might not justify our involvement.

We tend to take only those projects that appeal to our creative sense while also fulfilling our business needs.

And your second philosophy?

We approach each project as a team, where each member has equal say in the outcome of the project. It's important that every member of the multimedia team—from the creative side, to the business side, to the technical side—feel their input is appreciated, accepted, and incorporated into the project.

What's a design document?

For us it is the critical step after you have sent the client the business proposal. The business proposal is the front end. Someone who picks up the business proposal can find out what the goal of the project is and why it is being done. The design document is what actual work will be accomplished and how. For example, "We agree to do X for Y." Without a design document, X is never specific and Y is always a variable.

How does the design document work in conjunction with the business proposal?

While they work together, they do very different things. When you send a client a business proposal it is meant to conceptualize a project. Business proposals are marketing documents. You are trying to attract the client to sign on to the project and choose your company to produce the work. Business proposals are written in suggestive terms, they are meant to be evocative and "advertise" the projects key figures. The design document takes the concepts presented in the proposal and translates those concepts into detailed production specifications.

So, it's a production-oriented document?

Exactly. It's a "production bible."

Can you provide a broad picture showing how the design document fits into the business proposal process?

Sure. First, there is the Request for Proposal (RFP) in which the client says, "We are interested in having you bid on a project."

Second, you write a business proposal. Here you demonstrate why the project should be done, why your company is uniquely qualified to do it, and what features you would include in the project. The goal is to sell your company and your ideas. What you are really saying at this point is "retain us" to create a look and feel for your project. A contract is then signed for the next phase, and depending on the agreement, for the final project as well.

Third, the client signs an agreement, or a contract, and the project moves into the design phase. For example, you present the client with one, two, or three interface options to review. Of course, at this point, you are under contract, so you are being paid for your work. There's also the issue of who owns the designs at this point, but that is another matter altogether.

Finally, if the client approves the design you present, you submit a design document and define the specific specifications for the project. Depending on how you have drawn up the contract, the client signs off on design document and

you move into the production phase at this point. If the client doesn't like it, you go back to the design phase and revisit the goal of the project.

Often, the company managing the design phase and the creation of the design document is the same company that produces the project. Do you have any insight on that?

Yes. That's a good point. We know some consultants who only make design documents. Then they hand the design document to their client who manages, oversees, or subcontracts the production. In other cases, the consultant manages the subcontractors.

How do you think the design document benefits other aspects of the business process?

First, since the design document contains the clearest definition of the project, it becomes an addendum to the contract.

Second, because it is the best definition of the project, it creates the specific line items that need to be addressed in the budget.

Any final comments?

Guy Kawasaki always says "Under promise. Over deliver." Without a design document there is no hope to "over deliver."

Design documents should be incredibly detailed. They should cover every detail of the project from how many minutes of digital video to precise production schedules. We like to think of it like this: Suppose the entire design team was abducted after finishing the design document and rescued a week after the project was completed. All the production team had to guide them was the design document. The rescued design team should look at the final project and say "Yep. This is exactly what we envisioned."

Pricing Issues

It is important to detail any additional pricing issues if they have changed from the original proposal. At this point, the client has hired you to create a project, and you need to be sure that they understand exactly what they are buying. If this has been already completed, you should refer to the document that contains the information. In a small project, it is appropriate to include this information in the business proposal. For larger projects, it is often better to include it in a separate document with reference to them in the design document.

Page Design and Pricing HTML

Larry Aronson
laronson@acm.org

Larry Aronson is a consultant, popular lecturer and seminar speaker, and self-described "Webscape architect." One of the first students to enter the Computer Science Department at the University of Illinois, where he graduated, Aronson plied his programming skills at IBM, Columbia University, Boeing, CBS, Mobil, and Merrill Lynch, among others.

In 1993, he got interested in the Web and two years later wrote the first book on Web publishing, the *HTML Manual of Style* (Ziff-Davis Press), which sold more than 65,000 copies. Referred to as the "Strunk and White" of HTML, the *Manual of Style* provides a "clear and concise reference" for HTML 2.0. His follow-up, second edition covered HTML 3.0, and he is currently working on a third edition that covers the soon-to-be-approved HTML 3.2.

If you had to define a set of HTML core competency skills what would they include?

First, I would say that a person should be able to work with text files on any operating system. For example, if you are working with a client, the specific HTML tools you use are largely irrelevant because by design, HTML is a cross-platform standard. I think it is important for an individual to be able to edit and fix what ever simple changes need to be made, whether the document is on Windows, Macintosh, or even Unix. I am not saying that you need to know the intricate details of every operating system, but you should be able to make simple changes. It is important for people to have cross-platform competence.

Second, there needs to be an understanding of preparing graphics. You should be able to get an image in any format and convert those graphics so that they are "Web viewable." That includes an understanding of transparent GIFs, interlacing graphics, and the difference between JPEG and GIF formats.

I also think that people should know tables, be able to flow text competently around graphics, and have a basic understanding of using color on a Web page.

What about frames?

I don't think that people need to know frames—although that is a plus. The fact of the matter is that HTML is so simple that if you learn what you need to know when you need it. For example, if you need to know frames, you go a site that uses frames, look at that HTML, and adapt it to suit your own purposes.

As someone who does a lot of consulting and is pretty known in the industry, what kinds of salaries are you finding that people are getting for HTML?

I hear about people getting paid in the range of $25 an hour for HTML.

Although my experience has been that if you have good skills, have produced several Web sites, and can demonstrate an understanding of design and navigation, you can expect an hourly salary in the $40 range.

Recently, there have been a number of HTML tools released that assist in creating HTML. Do you have a preference for any particular product?

Yes. On the Macintosh, my favorite is BBEdit 4.0, hands down. On Windows, I use Webber (http://www.csdcorp.com). Most people use Hot Dog Pro, but Webber is more like BBEdit and it's half the price of Hot Dog.

As far as HTML 3.2, what are the most important features?

I think you will see HTML 3.2 as more of a scaling back, a more manageable version of HTML. HTML 3.0 fell apart—it was too ambitious. With 3.2, what you will see is a more generalized

standard that is more compatible with both Netscape's Navigator and Microsoft's Internet Explorer. In the process, there's been some stuff thrown out.

What's new that got put in?

Stylesheets. The whole secret to the Web is that content is separate from the presentation. A page can be viewed on any display device. Style sheets reintroduce the element of presentation into the the HTML—they provide a separate way to tell the computer how to present the HTML. For example, to assign attributes to the HTML such as fonts, leading, margins, etc.

And in the future?

I think that 1997 will be the year of Internet retailing. While there are programs and solutions that currently make selling merchandise on the Internet a reality, each of those solutions has been expensive. They are generally custom solutions that cost in the $75,000 to $100,000 range to implement and are time-consuming. We are now starting to see standards being set that will make Internet retailing more cost-effective. For example, Microsoft's soon-to-be-released Merchant server will reduce the cost of setting up systems to sell merchandise on the Internet to $20,000 to $25,000 and will cut implementation time from a full year to a few months. At that point, marketing and sales are a Web-based reality for many, many players.

Design Basics

Designing the look and feel (interface design) of a Web site, CD-ROM, or other interactive project includes many things and is tightly wrapped to the business and ultimately profit of the project. Designing an interface without marketing objectives and a business proposal is akin to suicide by lethal injection at low doses. It is imperative that you know the objectives of a project and work closely with your client and other team members to be sure you are always on target. It is very easy to lose sight of the needs of the project when you have found the greatest, coolest new Java capability or super-cool video technique that you just have to use. To keep you on track, think about these things throughout the project's development:

- Layout of pages or screens in relation to one another—in other words, the navigation

- Flavor and feeling of the project (is it scary, hard-edged, Spanish, sporty, professional, rustic, and so on)

- What is the client trying to communicate (primarily and secondarily)

- Are we within budget?

If you can keep sight of these things, you have a much better chance of pleasing your client and making a profit.

Adding the Dazzle

In any Web or other new media project, there is the possibility of clients wanting illustrations, animations, video, or other additional "cool" things included. This is where your budget can go right down the proverbial toilet if you are not careful—for example, a Web site that has no animation versus one that does can change the price depending on the complexity. Usually these items are budgeted in the original estimate and are not very complex. But what if your client decides she wants to re-create her product in 3D and show it in full color as a QuickTime movie. Then you've got a problem. To re-create a simple product is not a big deal, but if the product is complex and takes you a couple of days to model, that's another story.

If your client wants an illustrative rendition of her CEO, it may cost you quite a bit of money to get an illustrator to create this piece of art. Some clients will like a Photoshop filter version, and others will balk at it on sight, so be sure to ask just how much they want to spend. This will tell you what you can do. If they don't know, give them their options—A, B, C—that reflect three differently priced versions.

Adding specialized illustration, animation, video, chat, Shockwave, Java, and other capabilities to Web sites or new media projects, as appropriate, can be important to your clients message as well as can add some "wow" value to the project to keep viewers interest. There are two major things to consider:

- Is it important to the message? Does it clarify and communicate the message better?

- Does art, video, footage, and so on exist or will it have to be created?

The first item is pretty self-explanatory. If the message is sent more clearly with this type of addition, it may be worth including it in the site or CD, but there are many hidden costs that cannot be ignored. And that comes to my second consideration. Does the art, video footage, or 3D models exist? If it does not, it can add some significant costs to your project. So, before promising anything, find out what is available and what you have to create.

Generally, the pricing for these additions to a Web site or other new media project are based on how long it will take the designer or production artist to create and edit it. But, usage rights and size can come into play as well.

Video

Video can add great energy and impact to your CD-ROM or kiosk project, but is often not appropriate for Web sites or disk-sized projects due to bandwidth and space limitations. There are simply not enough high-speed modems in place at a consumer level yet to make video a wide-spread option at this time. Video should be limited to the audiences that are known to have higher-end equipment. As for diskettes, you can only squeeze so much into 1.4 megabytes of space.

It can take quite some time to download video over the Internet, even in small formats, for playback on a computer. Until everyone has super-powered Internet connections, video is either a download and play option or is reserved for intranets (which are generally faster). There are technologies being developed that will bring video more immediately into Web use, but it is not realistic in broad terms at this time—give it a year or two.

On a floppy disk, there is simply not enough room for video to be a consideration except in the smallest and most crude formats.

Pricing for video clips can vary greatly. If you are simply taking existing content and editing it, pricing can be very reasonable—in the $300 – 400 range for about a 10-second clip. However, this can also depend on how much time you need to plow through the existing footage, whether it has been digitized, the size of the frames, and frame rates for the final clip.

Animation

Animation can come in two flavors—2D or 3D—and can be anything from simple to complex. Animation for film and broadcast television has always carried a high price tag, to the tune of about $1,500–$5,000 per second and more. Animation for CD-ROMs, kiosks, and Web sites have lowered the price in many instances—the quality demanded is not as high, frames rates are lower, frame sizes are smaller, and they generally take less time to create. Also, the budgets are simply not as high as for film and television. Kiosks can often have higher frame rates because developers have control over the equipment being used for playback, but it is not always necessary to have full-frame, full-motion video in a kiosk either.

2D Animation
Animated GIFs or ShockWave Files
A simple 2D animation is generally priced at about $150–$200 each and, as they get increasingly complex, may go as high as $600.

3D Animation
3D animation is generally priced per second at about $250–$350 on the simple end and up to $1,200 on the more complex end.

Of course, depending on how detailed the modeling needs to be, the complexity of illustrations, size of frames, and number of frames per second, these numbers can be higher.

Custom Programming

Custom programming, such as Java applets, CGI scripts, and chat areas are very specialized and cost anywhere from a few hundred dollars to many thousands of dollars. There is simply no way to nail this down in one example or statement. Whenever a client asks for something that will require some special programming, be sure to talk with a programmer before making a commitment in either time or money. What seems very simple at first may be more complex than you realize or vice versa. A simple CGI script can be as little as $200, but if a programmer has to work for two weeks programming on your location, you can bet it will cost you several thousand dollars. Programming is very specific and very detailed. It is difficult to estimate programming costs except by the hour. So, you have to have a solid understanding of what you want the Web site or CD-ROM to do. Additionally, see the sidebar interview with Larry Aronson, on page 70, and the Web Pricing Index on pages 144 and 145.

Kristen Kiger
Art Director, Designer, Illustrator
New York, NY

What type of new media projects do you produce?

Mostly Web design—everything from architecture and structure to design and illustration of the site. I have also worked on CD-ROMs.

How long have you been involved in designing these types of projects?

About two years.

Why did you become involved in designing new media projects?

I was personally interested in new media—specifically animation and video. The Web itself seemed like such a great way to broaden my reach, and the interactivity seems to be a great way to allow the end-user to personalize his experience.

Clients were also definitely interested. Trying to get them to use the Internet, educate them, and help them to realize how its potential might help their particular line of business was more the challenge.

Were you a print designer before that?

Yes. I was trained in graphic design and primarily did print. I had some experience with television and video. The switch to Web design and interactive media was not too difficult for me because of my exposure to video. I had a hard time realizing the limitations in the realm of 72 ppi. When you go from designing or illustrating a piece that you are accustomed to seeing at 600 ppi (having really clean edges and curves) to 72 ppi, the attention to detail still needs to be there, because you find that the few pixels you do have

to work with are just as, or more, important in creating the visual effect.

In print design, it is customary to give three different design approaches. Do you do that with Web and other new media projects?

Yes, I do usually give the client a few different choices. You are still dealing with the client in a very similar way. Presenting a few different design strategies allows the client to relate to one or another by seeing the differences and which one really best suits their needs. The best client relations, I find, are those where you are able to get them on board with an idea, and together you can create a really dynamic team.

Do you ever do spec work for Web or new media projects?

I have been put in positions where I have had to do spec work for Web design. I find it to be very difficult, and not very effective. Spec work is difficult because it creates a disadvantage for the creation of the piece itself. It seems that the ideas generated are usually done so under a very tight deadline, and with little or no in-depth knowledge of the project or the company. Each studio or designer pulls together ideas that they think might fit the bill or catch the decision-maker's eye, with little or no thought to what is behind it. When the decision is made and all is said and done, the design of the project is ahead of where it should be in the process of creating effective communication. This seems to promote and reinforce the surface quality of the work over the substance. Especially in Web design, the architecture, structure, and function of the site is just as important as the look of the piece.

How do you find the interactive design process to be different from the print design process?

The storyboarding and flow of a piece is a lot harder to deal with. When you think of all the different ways an individual can interact and relate to a piece compared to the print model, it's not like any other medium. The control over your viewer isn't there as in a linear type of experience.

Do you think preliminary planning is important to the interactive design process?

Absolutely. Like any other project, the more thought and planning that can go into a project up front, the better the piece will be in the end, and there will usually be a lot less wasted time and energy.

In the case of Web sites, designing and planning for the growth of the site, as well as laying out a very organized and well-mapped directory structure, will save a lot of time and frustration when it comes to putting together your final pages, as well as any changes that might, and often do, occur along the way.

What is the biggest design mistake you see in interactive pieces?

One of the biggest design mistakes is the designing of sites that are not functional. I have seen beautifully designed pieces that don't function well in real-time on the network. The artwork is sometimes too big to be downloaded in a reasonable amount of time, or they haven't taken into consideration the limitations of the color palette, monitor size, or the browsers, their settings, and how they interpret the information.

The other common mistakes I've seen are in structure. The jumps sometimes take you to a place from which you can't easily return. The links are not thought out from the viewpoint of the potential user who would be interested in trying to retrieve information from the site.

There are also those Web pages that were thrown online to mirror the information from a print piece, with little or no regard for the power of the new and different medium.

Why do you think these mistakes are made?

In most cases these mistakes are made because of a lack of knowledge, understanding, and experience of the new medium. It seems logical that if you came from a print background, you would naturally approach this new medium from that familiar paradigm. Sometimes it just doesn't work in the same way.

Can these types of mistakes be avoided?

Sure. The more you work within the restrictions of a medium, the more mistakes can be avoided from the outset. The design can be approached in a way that takes full advantage of the form of communication. It helps to read as many articles and books and to talk to a lot of people within the field and find out how they have dealt with similar problems.

How early in the development process are designers involved in a project?

Designers should be involved from the very beginning of the development process. It adds to the strength of the piece overall.

Unfortunately, designers tend to be viewed as the people who are responsible only for the beautification or ornamentation of the page and add very little to the content. I think that it is the responsibility of the designer to add to the content, by amplifying and reinforcing the message the client wants to send. It's important that the designer is included from the beginning, but should also continue to be involved throughout the project—over-seeing its implementation from beginning to end.

Do you find it difficult to estimate design pricing for them?

I think it's very difficult to price jobs for the Web. Everything is so new. Everyone is scrambling to find out what the market will bear and what methods for pricing works. Usually a job is estimated at a certain overall price, based on the hours estimated to complete the work.

There is currently a wide range of prices for Web sites. I'm sure that this will level out in the near future as people gain more experience with production and it's costs.

In a few cases, I have been involved in very successful relationships with clients who are looking to buy illustrations for their sites. We collaborate with in-house creative teams on what the site should look like, discuss the needed pieces, and I deliver the illustration in the form of GIFs for them to place in a template *we've* designed. It was a pricing structure based more on an illustration model. Usage and placement of the pieces figured in what their end cost was to be. However, it can be very hard to control the usage of artwork placed on such a free medium as the Web.

What is the main piece of design advice you would give designers of Web and new media?

Remember your main focus and purpose. As a designer it is important to remember that you are helping the client clearly communicate and articulate a particular message in a captivating way. It's easy to get caught up in the newest technology to come along. There is nothing worse than design that is created to service a designer's ego at the expense of the client's message.

What is the main piece of design advice you would give buyers of Web and new media?

As a buyer, you are in fact creating an effective collaboration between yourself and the producers of your Web site or CD-ROM. It's important that you select team members who will work well together and focus on producing the best of all possible products.

Viewpoint of a New Media Designer

David Weisman
Design Consultant
Weisman Designs
New York, NY

What type of interactive projects do you produce?

Everything, from electronic interactive products to actual hands-on educational exhibitions.

How long have you been involved in designing these types of projects?

For about four years.

Why did you become involved in designing interactive projects?

I fell in love with it all. It's like graphic design grows up!

Were you a print designer before that?

Yes. Publishing and advertising mostly, for 15 years, which translates well into new media. Also, I am a musician and animator, the resources of which I can utilize in my own projects!

In print design it is customary to usually give three different design approaches. Do you do that with Web and other new media projects?

I'm a designer of conviction. I've been very successful with aiming at a singular approach. I do find that with Web projects, the design must be flexible to accommodate ongoing plug-in content which is what makes the Web so unique.

Do you ever do spec work for Web or new media projects?

No. My clients like to pay me. Besides, I think at this point everyone realizes the need for well-designed new media projects.

How do you find the interactive design process to be different from the print design process?

New media has absorbed many types of professionals from varied backgrounds and industries who are new to the design process compared with the print world, and often don't understand creativity, costs, and timeframe.

Do you think preliminary planning is important to the interactive design process?

It's really in the client's best interest to work with the designer to creatively and realistically clarify criteria within the time frame and budget, so the designer can create a stable foundation and frame work to build upon. The very nature of Web sites demand flexibility and are more easily re-adjusted, but of course just like a good magazine, must have a continuity of design structure.

What are the biggest design mistakes you see in interactive pieces?

Form without content. Lack of thought given to a harmonious balance of spatial relationships and design elements.

Why do you think these mistakes are made?

Everyone is drunk with enthusiasm.

Can these types of mistakes be avoided?

As far as design goes, hire trained graphic designers, not HTML experts.

How early in the development process are designers involved in a project?

It all depends on the mentality of the client, the need for design, and type of project. Sometimes with Web sites, designers are called in to create a second generation Web site—that's basically a graphic re-design of existing text only content. Other times designers are part of the "from the ground up" approach if the product is new or graphically driven.

Do you find it difficult to estimate design pricing for new media?

Yes, but I usually separate design and production—design is a flat fee, and production is billed hourly.

It really depends on the final medium, which also determines complexity and distribution. 3D animation, as well as 2D with sync'd sound is obviously very specialized and much more work-intensive than frozen image work.

What is the main piece of design advice you would give designers of Web and new media?

Train your clients to understand what good design is and address all areas of design issues, both aesthetically and technically.

What is the main piece of design advice you would give buyers of Web and new media?

Don't talk about money first, you are not buying a used car. Instead, create a framework of a design that works and then proceed from there. Look for a seasoned designer with whom you feel comfortable working. It is usually possible to work out an mutually agreeable fiduciary relationship.

A Lesson Learned

Kevin Kall
Kall Design
Scottsdale, AZ

What type of interactive projects have you produced?

CD-ROMs. The first one was last year. It was a database for libraries that helped children choose books via subject matter.

Why did you become involved in the project?

I had been doing print work for this client and we had an ongoing relationship, so they asked me to get involved in the project.

How was the interactive design process different from the print design process?

It was new to most of the people involved, and no one really knew how to plan and direct the project. The client changed direction several times. When we worked on print projects, everyone knew their jobs and things went relatively smoothly.

Things went wrong?

Well, yes. There was no focus, no storyline, no content developer, no writer. We had one internal person to oversee the job; one designer, me; a programmer, and an animator. We were trying to do too much with too few people on a very tight deadline. It was the first really interactive project the client had produced, and key internal people were left out of the loop until very late in development.

So preliminary planning is important?

Yes. The client really needs to be on top of the project and know what they are trying to communicate.

How early in the process should designers be involved?

As soon as the client solidifies the idea in their minds, they should build their team.

Did you underprice the job on your end?

Yes. I realized about half way through the job that I had put in too many hours and that the fee would not cover it. It was difficult to charge the client for changes because the job was never clear at the beginning. Since they were already a client, I wanted to keep the costs down, so we just kept working on it. I thought I'd be getting more work from it.

Did you get more work from it?

No.

Was the client happy with the job?

Somewhat, but because the client changed directions so much and nothing was written down in the beginning, it was difficult to say.

Would you ever work on another new media project?

Yes, but only if there is an appropriate team in place. I found the process fascinating. It really allowed me to stretch myself as a designer.

Do you ever do spec work?

No! You set a precedent and it pulls down the industry. I think it is a statement that says your time is not worth anything.

What is the main piece of advice you would give designers of new media?

Be sure you get all the facts—what are the expectations for the the project?

What is the main piece of advice you would give buyers of new media?

I would ask them to have done some planning. If there is no plan, they cannot expect to effectively direct the people working for them.

A Designer and Animator Speaks Out

Donald N. Heller
Interface designer and animator
Danbury, Connecticut

How long have you been creating new media projects?

Eight years, since Director was called Video Works. I was a MacroMind (now Macromedia) certified trainer for Director 1.0.

Why did you become involved in new media? What was your background before that?

Well, I have a background as a puppeteer and musician, and I worked in theater design long ago. I also did shadow theater, which is a sort of predecessor to screen animation.

What types of projects do you create?

I work on CD-ROMs, 2D and 3D animation, and I recently completed my first Web site.

How early do you get involved in projects?

Sometimes very early and those projects go well. If I am the whole process, that makes it even better. The projects that I am included in later in the process tend to go less smoothly.

Do you think it is important to be involved in the preliminary planning?

[He laughs at us in surprise.]

Sure. I always try to get my clients to include me in their brainstorming sessions with their producers and writers. That way, I not only become a more valuable team member, but I can help keep the project under control. That is not to say I want to control my clients, but this gives me the opportunity to raise flags in areas that might not be obtainable within the budget they have

planned—I give them a reality check. Also, it helps me a great deal in understanding what the client wants for the project. I would rather sit in on one or two of these meetings early on to get a better understanding of what they want than have to tell them they can't have something further down the road, when it may impact other elements of the piece. If you are going to ask to be included in these meetings, be sure you are ready to participate fully. You need to articulate your thoughts and contribute wherever you can. Don't just sit there. Participate!

It is always very important to take notes when you are speaking to your clients about a project. Once you think you understand what they need and are ready to estimate the job, give your client a list of assumptions and responsibilities based on your conversation. This will ensure that you both understand what is going on. It doesn't have to be too formal, but it does need to be clear. If your client is a reasonable person to deal with, he will appreciate you doing this. If he is an out-of-control client, it protects you.

In print design, it is customary to give three different design approaches to a project. Do you do that with new media projects as well?

If the client is very specific then, no. But if he does not know exactly what he wants then, yes. It all depends on the client and the project.

Do you ever do spec work?

Only if I feel the rewards to be gained are great enough. I do it by gut feel. If I think the client is for real, then yes. If I feel like he is just picking my brain, then no. If Voyager asked me to do something on spec, I would consider it an audition.

If it was just some person I didn't know, then I would be very leery. Also, if I had a really good client, I would certainly do a limited amount of spec work for them on occasion. But, I wouldn't work for free for a week for them.

How do you price your work?

First, I try to look at the macros and micros in a project. I also differentiate between concept work and well-defined work. With either, I start by outlining the overall needs of a project down to the smallest detail. Then, I attach hours to each item for how long I think they will take, add them all up and multiply by the rate I would like to get. For concept work, I further multiply that number by two or three depending, upon the complexity of the job. You may think that is crazy, but I find that it works well for me. Being an optimist, I always figure how long it should take if everything goes perfectly and forget that concepts always take much longer—there is always something for which you did not account. It's always a balance between time and money. Additionally, with concept work, I try to give my client a range for an estimate. This way, I have a little flexibility and they feel that I am not trying to gouge them. If your quote includes a higher number, you have working room. If not, you have no space to evolve a project.

What are the biggest mistakes you see in new media projects?

Two things: communication and low bids.

Being sure that the key players are in contact with each other is vitally important. If these people are not communicating directly with each other, things will fall through the cracks.

Quoting too low a price on a project just gets you stressed out and then your heart is not in the project. Always quote a price that will allow you to produce the piece in a professional manner.

Why do you think these mistakes are made?

As far as communication, I think that everyone thinks that the other team players are in their heads and that everyone is thinking the same thing. That is not always the case. Don't assume anything. A simple phone call can save a lot of trouble later on.

Artists are optimists and sometimes desperate for work. If a client pressures them to bid lower, they get nervous and often comply. They also want to believe that they won't run into any problems when they are creating the project. There is always some little detail you have not accounted for and the button that simply doesn't want to work properly. If you client balks at the price you have given them, explain that you will be glad to reduce the price if it takes you less time, but you don't want to promise a price and then have to come back later to raise it.

What is the main piece of advice you would give designers of new media projects?

- Listen to your client's needs.

- Check that both you and your client understand your respective responsibilities.

- Show projects to your client in stages for approval to proceed.

What is the main piece of advice you would give buyers of new media projects?

- Be ready to pay for quality work. In the long run, you will be better off. Cutting corners will lead to band-aids.

- Please pay your artists promptly. They will appreciate it more than you know and be ready to work all the harder for you.

Comments from a 3D Animator

David Teich
Owner
Mind of the Machine
Roosevelt, NJ
mindmach@aol.com

What type of 3D design and animation have you done for interactive projects?

Mostly I am building rather extensive environments—re-creating a real environment like the fairgrounds for the Horde Concert Tour or something completely metaphorical like the virtual village for the MCI kiosk that I just finished. It was like the E-world environment but in 3D. My CD-ROM–based work is usually managing the entire 3D part of the project. With Web-based work, you don't have the ability to move data around as much so it is more like smaller pieces of the site—like small animations, buttons, and illustrations.

How long have you been involved in 3D and animation?

Since about 1990.

How difficult was it to deal with 3D in 1990?

The speed of the CPUs was much slower and there were times that projects were compromised because we could not complete the kind of work we wanted in time. That is less true today. We can get a whole lot more accomplished now.

Why did you become involved in 3D design?

It was a personal decision. I saw some extruded letters in Step-by-Step Electronic Design and was amazed that you could do that—and with shadows, too! After that I was hooked.

What did you do before 3D?

I was doing type and logo design—two-dimensional illustration and graphic design.

Was the learning curve difficult for you?

Yes, at first, just trying to understand the 3D space. Getting the metaphor for 3D space was the hardest thing.

In print design it is customary to give three different design approaches to a client from which to choose. Do you do that with 3D and animation projects?

No, I learned not to do that a long time ago. I talk with a client and get a really good idea of what they want and go in that direction. I usually work with clients that know what they are after.

Do you ever do spec work for 3D projects?

Almost never. I would do it occasionally for a friend that is pitching a project and needs a 3D element, maybe a charitable organization. When I first started out I did some because I needed to create samples for my portfolio. But now, I don't feel that I should work for nothing.

I think that a lot of people are taken advantage of—especially young people just out of school. They are promised exposure and more work but usually never get it. That is unfair.

How do you find the 3D process to be different from the print design process?

It really isn't that much different. When I design a 3D piece for print, I work the same way as for other 2D design. For animation, the process is different from print, but more like for video and television—you create storyboards. Anything I design, I do in pencil first—whether it's a storyboard or for print. When you give someone a computer comp, it looks a bit too finished before it's really thought out.

Do you think preliminary planning is important?

Yes, very. It saves lots and lots of time in the long run. I'm usually involved at the initial planning stages. It works well that way because otherwise you are usually patching up someone else's holes.

What is the biggest mistake you see in 3D?

Relying on the technology and "cool tricks" without a good design in place.

Why do you think these mistakes are made?

The tools are getting easier to use, cheaper, and there is a prevailing attitude, reinforced by advertising, that owning the tool will make you a capable artist.

Can these types of mistakes be avoided?

On an individual basis, yes. Culturally I think the problem will get worse before it gets better.

Do you find it difficult to estimate 3D pricing for the Web and other new media?

Not really. I've been doing this for a pretty long time, and I now know how long it takes me to do things. I generally price it hourly and then give a project fee to the client for the overall piece.

So having an understanding of how long it takes to do things is important?

Yes.

Do you ever charge by usage?

Yes, particularly for advertising. If something is being used for a national magazine for many years, you would charge more than for something being done for a local magazine for a week.

So it's a combination of hourly, project, and usage?

Yes.

How do you balance that?

I take a guess [he laughs]. Actually, it's a combination of intuition, experience and negotiation. You have to know what the standards are in the industry, know your own worth, and know your client.

What is the main piece of advice you would give designers of 3D for Web or new media?

Learn the basics. The people that I know that are doing the best work came up through some type of classical training—like filmmaking, typography, and so on. I see a lot of people coming out of school who have never had that and it shows.

What is the main piece of advice you would give buyers of 3D for Web or new media?

I think buyers believe because it's computer-generated, that it is less work. That is not so. I would encourage them to learn more about the process. Don't expect miracles. It is a joint effort.

Chapter 3

In Summary

As with any type of design, designing for new media means more than dressing the page or screen with pretty type or art. You have to take many elements into consideration: the content, the audience, the navigation, the budget, and the timing allowed for the project. It is a balance of all of these and more that makes for an interesting and useful Web site or new media project.

Pricing for many parts of Web and new media design often boils down to figuring how much time the tasks take and how much to charge per hour. In the next chapter, we will look at rates and salaries for the different job functions.

"Confusion and clutter are failures of design, not attributes of information. And so the point is to find design strategies that reveal detail and complexity—rather than fault the data for an excess of complication. Or, worse, to fault viewers for a lack of understanding."

Edward Tufte

Rates and Pricing

It might be the "magic" of our industry that attracts us, but it is the pay-check—or at least the prospect of one—that keeps us coming back. Certainly, the issue of how much we are paid is one of the most difficult and sensitive aspects of the new media and Internet business. Despite the notion of *virtual* communities, offices, and workgroups, people demand *real* compensation for their work—and rightly so.

From the perspective of the business person, how much we pay our personnel, whether they are freelancers, contractors, or full-time employees, is one of the most significant aspects of determining the cost of the projects we produce. When you pay your designer $50,000 a year, and your programmer $125 per hour, those salaries are added to the other factors that determine how much you need to charge your client to break even on a given project. (Of course, there are other factors and we considered them in Chapter 1, "Business Basics").

AV Video and Multimedia Producer's Salary Survey Results

AV Video and Multimedia Producer's October 1996 Salary Survey shows that where you live does have an impact on what you make. Generally, people in the Los Angeles area command the highest salaries—about the mid 70s. New York, Boston, and San Francisco are in the average range—the low 60s. The Pacific Northwest and Midwest have the lowest salaries—about the low 50s. Additionally, women, although closer in salary than in the past, are still making slightly less on the average than men.

In this Chapter, We:

- Address the three basic types of new media employment options—freelance, contractor, full-time—and discuss the advantages and disadvantages of each.

- Present real-world hourly rates and annual salaries. A number of factors can determine hourly rates and annual salaries, such as the size of the company, the company's experience and expertise, where the company is located, the type of clients the company works with, the platform, and so on. We present a profile of each company so that you not only have a look at the actual numbers, but also a context for assessing the meaning of those numbers.

- Hear from consultants, experts, and recruitment firms as we try to paint a broad and informative picture of this sensitive subject.

- Sketch out basic teams and discuss how each team member contributes to a project.

- Present general hourly rates and annual salaries for each team member.

As we do all of the above, keep in mind that the new media and Internet industry is in a constant state of change. Some HTML pioneers, who at one point could command a hearty salary for their craft, might start to see their rates "pushed down" as more and more of the pack picks up one of the popular Web authoring tools, such as the Claris Corporation's Home Page or Adobe Systems' PageMill. Those same pioneers, however, might actually see their rates go up as they learn and apply newer and more complicated tricks and techniques.

In a bigger sense, in some areas of the country, Web development prices might rise or decline depending on the corporate community's mercurial attitude toward the Internet. CD-ROM developers might see their prices decline as more and more companies look to the Internet to communicate their messages and available work dries up. On the other hand, some CD-ROM developers might find that a slight downturn in the industry has put some of their competition out of business and that prices actually are rising. In short, an unimaginable number of factors affect our industry, making any attempt to define specific financial data difficult at best.

What's Hot in the New Media Industry?

**Judith Mayer
Scofield & Pixley
San Francisco, CA**

What is the focus of Scofield & Pixley?

We are employment recruiters specializing in technical writers, trainers, and programmers for the largest firms in Silicon Valley.

What is the range of hourly rates and salaries at which you place people?

Well, for contract work, we tend to be in the $50 to $70 per hour range. When it comes to full-time employment, we are looking at a minimum of $50,000 up to $100,000 plus, not including signing bonuses, stock options, and annual bonuses.

From the employment perspective, what's hot?

Java, Java, Java. Did I mention Java? Also C, C++.

Any and everything object-oriented. We are seeing tremendous need for programmers and developers in the area of networking development. That includes ATM, SMDS, and Frame Relay.

Database development is also one of the largest growing categories. In addition, Web development applications, such as video streaming, Internet-based phone technology, and more.

Essentially, the job market in San Francisco is not where the networks and the Web are today. The real market is where networks and the Web *will* be.

And that affects programmers, right?

Absolutely. What you also see on the West Coast is a broader range of employment opportunites at non-computer companies, even though this is Silicon Valley. There's a lot of need for applications developed for the financial industries and other sectors where businesses are using proprietary software to give them an edge.

That said, you make more if you are at a company that is selling a product based on your skills. A programmer's starting salary, for example, in a Silicon Valley company, is generally in the $50,000 to $60,000 range. For a non-computer industry position that starting salary might be $40,000 to $50,000.

What about technical writers? What is that job category looking like?

It is definitely growing. We are seeing salaries from $50,000 to $80,000 for people who can write manuals and instructions as they pertain to the Web and CD-ROM.

Interestingly, as manuals become more digitized, that is, they start to function more as an on-screen help mechanism, there is an even greater need for people who can create electronic tutorials.

Seems like an emerging job market for editorial talent.

Yes and no. Technical writers need to be able to connect with developers and programmers—they need to speak their language and turn it into English for the end user. This is a highly specialized skill. Although they don't need to be able to write code themselves, a good technical writer can look at code and understand it.

We get a number of people who come to technical writing from the creative side with the idea that they wrote poetry and short stories in college and have placed a few freelance clips in magazines, so they think they can make the jump to technical writing. It's not exactly the same thing.

So let's talk about the East Coast-West Coast rivalry...

You mean aside from the fact that we have better weather? Seriously, my experience has been that salaries are generally the same. That is not to say there aren't exceptions, but it is sort of amazing that despite the cultural differences and the distance, the numbers shake out in roughly the same way. You have to exclude Wall Street, which tends to skew the general survey data.

Any other differences...related to employment?

Actually, the difference is that the vendors, meaning the computer companies or the technology makers, tend to pay higher salaries.

It's also true that there's a slightly different employment culture here. There's that "start-up" folklore that people are always trying to tap into. When you get a job at a start-up out here you tend to get a signing bonus, a salary, and stock options. The security isn't the same as working for a non-computer company, such as a bank, or working at an established Silicon Valley giant, such as Adobe, but there is this lure of opportunity. Silicon Valley is full of opportunity and hope. The "potential" is greater out here and the culture sort of feeds that myth. It's also California. It's more relaxed. Programmers here can do what they want, because they are at the top of society out here.

All of the numbers presented in this chapter reflect the hourly rates and annual salaries being paid in the metropolitan areas of New York City and San Francisco. This is not to say that terrific new media and Web development is not taking place in Seattle, DC, Chicago, Boston, Austin, Miami, and other great areas to live and work. Whenever possible, we included profiles of and data from companies working in other areas of the country. In fact, the case studies in this book include outstanding examples of projects from DC, Boston, and Seattle.

We focused on New York City and San Francisco because there is no question that these are the epicenters of this industry and reflect the average salary ranges and freelance rates.

When we started putting this book together, we felt that we needed to include a chapter on hourly rates and annual salaries, and that we needed to have some of those rates and salaries presented with as much real-world information as possible. We reached out to many people. We collected a lot of data. And, we included as much information as we could without convoluting the message. These numbers, like anyone else's, are not a final word on the subject. Instead, we have given you a solid foundation from which you can arrive at what makes sense for you and your client.

In terms of determining rates and salaries, and using those numbers to develop your company's business proposals, there are three basic models that you can use to pay the people who contribute to your new media and Internet projects.

- Freelancers—typically paid by the hour

- Contractors—paid by a day rate, a project rate, or on retainer

- Employees—paid a salary

Our purpose here is to help companies assess strategies for determining the best options to establish fair rates and salaries and use those strategies in creating profitable business proposals and budgets. Let's take a look at the advantages and disadvantages of each type of relationship from the perspective of the employer as it relates to developing a sound business proposal and budget.

Paying a Freelancer by the Hour

Companies that pay people by the hour are typically are engaged in hiring freelancers. Many graphic design firms do this when they are in the middle of a busy period and their in-house design staff is "maxed out." The firm contacts freelancers and has them come in to work on a project. Those freelancers are typically paid an hourly rate.

The advantage? The company only pays the freelancer for what it needs. If the work load lightens, the freelancer is told the temporary need has ended. This affords the company maximum flexibility. You get what you pay for, and you only pay for what you need.

In freelance relationships there is little room for disappointment. For example, you need 10 pages of HTML. You hire someone. They agree to do the pages in 8 hours for $15 per hour. That's it.

Even though freelance relationships are probably the most common type of relationship in the new media and Internet industry, freelancing has its disadvantages. First, finding the right freelancers is not easy. Good people, the kind who can roll up their sleeves, jump right in, hit the ground running, and make an immediate contribution to the project the way you want and expect it to be done, are rare indeed. Second, everything takes longer than expected. It's the axiom that, "Every project expands to consume the time allotted to it." Here, costs can increase quickly and surprisingly.

Witness the words of one somewhat shocked new media developer who responded to an invoice from a freelancer by shouting, "Sixty-seven hours! Had I known that, I would have sent you home and done the job myself!" When it comes to paying people an hourly rate there is the fear that, "the meter is running." One CD-ROM producer said, "It's a lot like being in a cab that makes the wrong turn. You get this anxiety when you see the meter keep ticking away."

Finally, freelancers have hidden costs that might not appear on your project's balance sheet. Freelancers are unfamiliar with your company and the way it operates. If they are not in your office everyday, they might not know that the client doesn't want X, and amid the crisis you did not mention it to the freelancer who spent last night working on the project. Sure, greater communication could solve the problem. But greater communication takes time, and often, that is not a luxury you have.

There is also the reality that, in some cases, freelancers are naturally focused on their next job. Out of necessity, the job they are working on is *current* business, and some cannot help but focus on the *next* gig.

These comments are in no way intended to impugn the thousands of freelancers who work hard and offer their clients quality, work at fair prices, with a flexible schedule. In general, the system works everyday in offices across the country in nearly every type of industry. The point we want to stress is that paying people on a freelance basis has its benefits. It also has its drawbacks. It's something to consider when you figure out how to build your new media and Internet team. New media and the Internet create unique employment situations in which companies might need to evolve the freelance model to a more project-by-project employment arrangement.

Freelancer/Contractor or Employee?

Alan Rothstein, CPA
Rothstein and Company
Avon, Connecticut

Unfortunately, it is not up to the individual to pick and choose what's best for tax purposes. The specific set of circumstances that surround the contractual arrangement between the individual and the firm utilizing his or her services is what determines the status of the individual—employee or independent contractor. Depending on the individuals circumstances, there are advantages and disadvantages of each classification. The best action that you can take is to talk to your CPA or attorney.

In 1987, the U.S. Treasury Department issued revenue ruling 87-41, which identified 20 factors that the Internal Revenue Service uses to distinguish whether an individual is an employee or an independent contractor. The common theme of the 20 factors is the concept of control: Does the "employer" have control over the individual to such an extent that the individuals independent status can be questioned.

Recent tax legislation passed in 1996 established additional guidelines and a safe harbor to substantiate independent contractor status. If it can be shown that a significant person (more than 25%) of the industry utilizes freelancers/independent contractors to provide specific services, then independent contractor status could be justified.

What's the Difference?

The differences between an employee and an independent contractor are significant.

All of an employee's income is subject to withholding tax, both federal and state. Any unreimbursed business expenses incurred on behalf of the employer are limited to 2% of adjusted gross income and would be deductible if the individual is itemizing deductions as opposed to taking the standard deduction. On the plus side, the individual would be covered under workers compensation statutes in case of an injury while performing his job and would also qualify for state unemployment, should the position be eliminated or the individual laid off for lack of work.

Independent Contractor status could provide the individual with significant tax benefits. Unreimbursed business expenses can be used to reduce income before social security taxes are computed. Retirement plan contributions can be made based on the net income of the individual. Income from all sources where an independent contractor relationship exists can be combined for one "accounting," home office deductions are allowed and justified if certain criteria are met, and certain flexibility of timing income and expenses can be realized depending upon specific circumstances of the individual.

As stated above, the classification is not up to the individual. If the independent contractor status is preferred, there needs to be evidence to support this classification unless you can rely on the safe harbor provisions. If you desire independent contractor status and are unsure that industry guidelines will qualify for the safe harbor provisions the individual needs to establish him/herself as an independent business owner.

Strategies to Consider

There are several strategies to consider to keep your freelance/contractor staus: maintain several client relationships for whom you are providing similar services; have business cards and stationary prepared with your name and address; maintain a separate phone number (aside from personal). Register with the State Tax Department to collect sales and use tax as state law mandates. Finally, be able to justify/prove that you are self-employed and that you make your own business decisions, whether they be right or wrong. Your CPA should be able to provide the guidance you need in determining proper classification status; employee or independent contractor.

Paying a Contractor a Day Rate or Project Rate

Many companies recognize that the freelance model does present some risks. Freelancers themselves are starting to recognize the same. Paying team members on a day rate or a project rate is one way that both parties—employee and worker—are trying to establish a fixed rate relationship.

Suppose, for example, a CD-ROM developer needs a designer. The CD-ROM developer knows that his total budget for the project is $125,000 and that the project might take approximately 5 months. In the past, the developer has used a certain designer, on a freelance basis, at the rate of $75 per hour. The CD-ROM developer estimates that she will need the designer for approximately 10 weeks. Under the past terms, the designer would ask for $30,000 (10 weeks @40 hours per week = 400 hours × $75 = $30,000).

But on this project, the CD-ROM developer only has a design budget of $20,000. She talks to the designer and he agrees to do the whole project for $20,000—no matter how many hours it takes. Perhaps the designer is really excited about the opportunity to work on the project, or maybe it is a slow period for the designer. In this case, the CD-ROM developer has now capped her costs. She has turned a variable cost—one that varies dependent on how many hours it takes the designer—to a fixed one—one that does not fluctuate.

For the company, converting variable costs into fixed costs is an advantage. Although this approach seems to always favor the employer, it can have its disadvantages. The rate might be set too high. Suppose the designer efficiently creates a terrific interface in four weeks at a cost of $12,000. In this case, the CD-ROM developer overpaid by $8,000—a costly decision.

These types of relationships can be structured so that they are unfair to the worker and could have a negative impact on the project.

With every member of a team integral to the product's success, unhappy workers who feel that a deal has worked against them, will impede a company's ability to create its best work no matter how good the intention. Win-win relationships are the most important aspect of building a profitable company. Contractor relationships that are poorly conceived have the potential to reduce the quality of work produced. How do you put a price on that?

Another variation on this type of contractor relationship is the "split the pie method." In this approach, a designer, a producer, and a programmer, who each have their own small business, might pull together as a team and approach a client as a single unit, each offering his or her own unique skills to help produce the project. In these cases, one person takes the lead and writes the proposal, which includes the fees from each of the other team members. These situations, not uncommon in the new media and Internet industry, are potentially dangerous if one team member feels that the situation is not a fair one.

Here, too, the focus is on establishing fixed rates for the programmer, the designer, and the producer, respectively. An often overlooked aspect of the "fixed cost" approach concerns an important business principle: determining the true cost of producing a project. Take, for example, a Web developer who has three team members: a designer, a production artist, and a Webmaster. Each member agrees to work on the project, no matter how long it takes, for $10,000 each for a total of $30,000. The Web developer charges the client $60,000, pays his team members $10,000 each, and keeps the remaining $30,000. The Web developer oversees the project, everyone works 18 hours a day for six weeks, the project is done, and each team member takes their fee.

Six months later, the Web developer gets another contract to produce a Web site. The designer, the production artist, and the Webmaster are not available. How does the Web developer determine the actual cost of producing the project? It's not possible. The potential variable costs were converted into fixed costs. There is no way to tell whether at $60,000 he made money. Was the charge too little? He can't be sure. The Web developer is in the position of not knowing how much it costs to produce his product.

We posed this scenario to a studio manager at a small design firm. She didn't see the relevance until we took a look at a scenario that specifically applied to her studio.

The Westchester Design Studio (not the real name) had one senior designer and one junior designer on staff. The senior designer was paid $52,000 per year, the junior, right out of college, $28,000. Whenever the Westchester Design Studio went to pitch annual reports, the sales person would say, "We can do the book for $60,000." The client would balk and the firm would settle on $45,000.

Because the Westchester Design Studio had converted its variable costs—design—to $80,000 (the combined salary of the senior and junior designer), four annuals at the price of approximately $180,000 (not including printing) created what was perceived to be a profitable business. Adding in its other business, the company was "doing well."

The company, like many graphic design firms, never paid overtime. "We are all working to make this work," said the owner.

One annual report season, the Westchester Design Studio was also working on an interactive CD-ROM catalog for a children's clothing company and a Web site for one of the studio's newer clients. Both projects took the full attention of the junior and senior designer. The company had to hire two freelancers to keep up on the annual report work. The studio decided to pay the freelancers on an hourly basis. For the first time, the true cost of the design for the annual reports became apparent. If the studio had been paying the actual cost for the work it was getting from its senior and junior designer (overtime), it would have lost money on the annual reports. It did in one case.

The ultimate impact: what was once perceived as a "cash cow" for the company, was barely a break even if you totaled up the actual costs of the project.

Establishing a project rate works best when you want or need to hire your freelancer for a longer period of time and you cannot afford to pay your freelancer on an hourly basis. This type of freelance relationship can work for the freelancer because it gives her a guarantee of work for a specified period of time. In fact, many new media and Web shops are following this model and even "rent" space to freelancers, including computers, when not in use. This type of relationship has the potential to work for both parties if it is structured properly.

This model is likely to increase in the future given that, for better or for worse, our economy is heading in this general direction. Many larger firms are laying off their full-time employees only to hire them back as contractors on a project-by-project basis. Not only are full-time employees being downsized into this model, freelancers seeking more stable work are committing to it as well.

Some firms use a retainer model with certain key freelancers. For example, a company might find that terrific Java programmer and develop a relationship where it guarantees the programmer a certain fee every two weeks. In exchange, they reserve the programmer's time for a certain number of hours every two weeks. If the firm has work, the programmer commits to the number of hours agreed upon. If the firm doesn't have work, the firm pays the programmer anyway, generally at a rate up to half off the agreed upon guarantee.

Why would anyone establish a relationship in this manner? The firm wants to keep the programmer on retainer so that when it needs the programmer it can, on short notice, become the programmer's priority. The same type of relationship has been established for some designers. The designers agree that when the client they have a retainer relationship with calls, that client's needs move to the top of the list. Ultimately, any agreement structured this way boils down to an hourly agreement since the company is buying time at an hourly rate.

An Independent Designer Prices New Media Projects

**Heather Sommerfield
New York, NY
heather@lightbulb.com**

Heather Sommerfield's journey to the new media and Internet industry serves as an example of what can happen when a fine artist "goes digital." She began her career as a jewelry maker, working with wire and semi-precious stones, and painting works in oil, acrylic, and pastel. Then Sommerfield found the computer, where she admits for the first time in her life she found a tool that would enable her "to produce the creative vision she had in her head on a screen."

Sommerfield has provided design and production services for companies working on projects for *The New York Times*, IBM, Canon, Hewlett-Packard, The New School, the Parsons School of Design, Elecktra Records, Fruit of the Loom, Chase Bank, and Phillips.

Your clients ask you to work in print, new media, and on the Web. Do you have a favorite?

I like them all! They each represent a viable means of communicating messages, which is what I do.

I really enjoy the Web, but everyone is not wired and perhaps they never will be. I like to work on the Web to reach those who are there, but for those who are not, you have to reach them via print.

Besides, there is something about print. You can hold it. Walk around with it. You can be outside with it, instead of looking at it inside on a specialized device we call a computer. As a designer, you reach a point in which you realize that people react differently to color and images that are projected by the light of your computer monitor.

Images are about feeling. And in some cases, print is the only way you can get a certain feeling.

How do the percentages break down in your studio in terms of print versus new media versus the Web?

Right now half of my business is print work, about 40% is Web work. There's some other new media work, but it is relatively small.

Let's assume there are three basic ways, or models, in which you get paid—hourly, daily, or on a project basis. Which do you prefer and why?

There's no question that hourly is best. I know how many hours I put into every project that I work on and it is always way more than I ever imagined. If I am working on an hourly basis, I can really get into the work and do the absolute best that I can without saying to myself, "I can't spend any more time on this because the client is only paying me a lump sum of X." In that case, it is hard to know when to stop—your creative urges tell you to keep pushing the job, but your business sense says you have to stop.

What do your clients think of the hourly model?

While it works best for me, it has a tendency to be unrealistic.

For example?

Well, my hourly rate is generally about $50 per hour. Recently I worked on a project that took up all of my time. In fact, I ended up working on the project for approximately 500 hours in one month. If you do the math on that it amounts to $25,000 for one month of work. Granted, it was a rough month...but...

So what happened with your client?

They understood that was how many hours that I put into the project but there was no way they could afford that much to pay me. We worked it out and came to an adjusted hourly rate in the mid-$30 per hour range. It was a figure that we were mutually comfortable with. I have the kind of relationship with my clients where they rely on me and I rely on them...that way, what works for them ends up benefitting me in the long run.

So you found it in your best interest to adjust your hourly rate?

Of course. Keep in mind that I honestly believe that $50 per hour is not a lot of money for what I do and how hard I work, and I am sure there are a great many creative professionals who would agree with me. But what happens is that when your client hires you for such an extended period of time, in this case a month, you have to be prepared accept a lower hourly rate. You are sacrificing dollars paid per hour for the stability of longer term work—essentially a guarantee.

Didn't the client know up front that the job would be that involved?

Not really. In this case, they underbid the job with their client. In fact, they actually agreed to my $50 an hour rate up front. But they didn't really know what the full project entailed and I can't say that is entirely their fault. In this industry where everything that can go wrong does and everything takes three times longer than you ever imagined, it is very difficult to get a handle on this stuff. Proper planning and budgeting reduces the margin for error, but it is still a huge margin nonetheless.

But you had a contract?

Right. But my client was completely honest about the situation. They knew how hard I worked and they wanted to do the right thing, which made it easy to reach a compromise based on what was left in the budget. They basically said, here's what we have left in the budget. Can you live with this? The answer was simple: yes. We both did well on the job. It just wasn't what we thought it would be. That happens.

Ultimately the relationship is more important than the project. They did the best they could. I did what I could. We both were happy. Because I am viewed as a resource for my clients to better service their clients, all of my relationships are built on a win-win model.

If the hourly rate can present problems for your client's, what model do they favor?

Most clients want me to work on a project basis. They cap my costs no matter how much time I spend on the project.

How does that sit with you?

Working on a flat fee or project basis is dangerous. There is a tendency to take advantage of your time, even though it may be unintentional.

How so?

They make millions of changes! Remember we work for a client who has subcontracted us, which means they have a client to please. When that is the case, you have twice the number of people to please. As my production assistant Kate Harwood says "We are in the business of pleasing two clients."

Based on the fact that the hourly doesn't work for your clients, and a flat fee per project basis doesn't work for you, how does the day rate model work?

It's my favorite. My studio is in my home, so I tend to work odd hours. The day typically doesn't begin until 11 and it doesn't end until three in the morning. Working on a day rate, the client doesn't have the feeling that the meter is running all the time and I have the flexibility to be human—that is, run errands, actually go outside, stuff like that.

So what is your day rate?

Generally, $500 a day. Basically getting paid a day rate is better for the client, since you generally work more than an hourly, but it protects me from getting locked into a relationship where I am working on a project fee in which I work for long stretches of time and not get paid for it.

Are there any compromises in your day rate?

Sure. If someone hires me for an extended period of time it can drop as low as $300 to $350.

And how does the studio track its time?

We have pads of paper sitting next to every computer and we log our time on an hourly basis regardless of how we are being paid. We didn't used to do that, but since we have, we've been able to get a really good sense for how long a job is going to take and how much we need to accept—whether it is hourly, daily, or per project.

Paying Full-Time Employees a Salary

Much maligned as overhead that companies need to shed to be competitive, full-time employees have unquestionable advantages. Full-time employees are there...full-time. They are paid a salary, and they do what it takes to get the job done. They care about their work, they care about the company, and they pitch in when it is needed—at least in well-managed, win-win companies! They understand the company's mission and they are the real reason that a company succeeds.

As one CEO of a growing communications company declared, "Every business magazine I read tells me my employees are unnecessary. Downsize them. Get rid of them. Erase them from the balance sheet. Who writes this stuff? I look out my office and I see hard-working people who, each and every one, have made this company a success. I can't get enough good people to work here full time."

The obvious disadvantages to full-time employees: rising salaries and the cost of health care.

Then there's the issue of what you do when there's a slow quarter and you have people in what is referred to as "downtime." In addition, hiring full-time employees often means shooting for a jack-of-all-trades. When you are building a team from freelancers, you have the option of selecting the best designer, the best animator, the best videographer for the specific project. On the other hand, one entrepreneur declared, "There is nothing like having everyone in an office together, pulling in the same direction, producing its best work. It's why I do this."

The New Media and Internet Teams

Defining who's on the new media or Internet team is almost as difficult as finding out how to pay each team member. Vivid studios' *Careers in Multimedia* is one of the best and most comprehensive sources on the subject and a must read.

In some cases, larger entertainment companies, such as Disney, deploy 25 member teams—including executive producers, producers, 2D animators, 3D animators, programmers, videographers, voice over artists, beta testers, composers, editors, and sound professionals—to produce some of the products the venerable animation giant produces.

One aspiring animator looking at a major commercial CD-ROM commented, "I was depressed. I had been doing some work trying to put together an animated piece when I saw that CD-ROM. It was terrific, and at the same time, it made me want to quit. How could I ever pull something like that together. Then I saw the credits...it took no less than 32 people! If I had a team like that..."

Large staffs do not guarantee a successful product. Some of the best work in this industry has been done by pioneers orchestrating tightly knit units—witness Rodney Greenblat's *Dazzleloids*, any work done by the venerable artist/animator Jim Ludke, and the proficient staff at *Blender* (the CD-ROM magazine). Of course, then there's the legendary Miller brothers who created the blockbuster *Myst*.

Still, those of you running a business are unlikely to enjoy the luxury of 32 people working on your project. Let's face it, you are probably not going to have 10 people working on your project. In many cases, you might have only the services of a team of three. In any case, sketching out the types of roles that you are likely to need, and general salary guidelines for those roles, sheds some light on what you can expect to build into your new media or Internet project budget. Whether you can get one person in the office to perform more than one role, which is generally the case, is up to you.

Let's take a look at the roles and salaries for a new media and Internet teams.

New Media Project Roles and Salaries

How many people does it take to produce an interactive diskette or CD-ROM? One, if that person is a new media superstar and can do everything from project management and design to programming. Certainly there are many two-person CD-ROM shops that team design and production skills with programming skills to produce excellent work.

The basic team members we encountered when researching this book included a design person (creative director, interface designer, or graphic designer), a production person, a project management person, and a programmer/technical person.

The Voyager Company, a pioneer in the field of CD-ROM development, pairs its teams in groups of three including: a designer/production person, a programmer, and a project manager/editorial manager. From time to time, freelancers are called in to help with video or animation challenges and eager interns fill in the rest.

How good can your CD-ROMs get with a team of three? Check out Voyager's *Van Gogh: Starry Night: A History of Matter, A Matter of History.* The content is intelligent and Paul Schrynemakers' design sense engaging and elegant.

The actual team composition depends on your company, your staff, your project, and your budget. Here's a look at each possible team member.

Producer/Project Manager

The producer or project manager oversees the new media project from conception to completion and is often asked to serve as the team cheerleader and team psychologist. In larger firms, these duties can be hierarchically divided among an executive producer, senior producer, and producer. In traditional, non-new media firms, the role of the producer tends to fall under the title of project director or manager. More than any other member of the team, the producer/project manager is responsible for ensuring the product is produced on time and within budget.

Other Roles:

The producer/project manager is often called upon to serve as editorial director, writer, or editor.

Freelance Rate:

Producers tend not to be paid as freelancers although contracting producers to manage specific projects is common. Their rates vary widely and are based on time and the needs of the project.

Salary Range:

$55,000 to $95,000; $55,000 for producers and project managers. Senior producers start at approximately $75,000.

Editorial Director/Content Director/Editor/Writer

The editorial team member might be one of the most overlooked members of the team. Whether it be in the capacity of editorial director, editor, or writer, a professional editorial person is key to creating a product that is conceptually organized and makes intuitive sense. Good structure enables better design.

Other Roles:

This person sometimes does double duty as the project producer.

Freelance Rate/Salary:

Good copywriters and editors can command anywhere from $100 to $150 per hour.

Salary Range:

$40,000 to $60,000

Art Director/Creative Director

Many smaller teams do not have an art director/creative director. Overall, the art director/creative director is responsible for the identity of the project—the look and feel that the product maintains from the interface to the packaging and advertising. Good art directors can establish an identity that has the power to create a phenomenon—just look at the immediate impact *Wired* magazine, the bible of the digital age, made under the direction of the incredibly talented Barbara Kuhr and John Plunkett.

Other Roles:

This person is sometimes called upon to function as the designer working in tandem with a production assistant.

Freelance Rate/Salary:

The range is broad and can include anywhere from $60,000 to $80,000 or more depending on the size of your company.

Designer/Interface Designer/Graphic Designer

If the art director/creative director designs the garden, the designer/graphic designer is the one who plants the flowers. It is the designer that implements the vision of the art director/creative director. If no art director/creative director is present, the designer/graphic designer is responsible for shaping the look and feel of the project.

Other Roles:

The designer/graphic designer is often called upon to not only design the project, but handle all of the project's production as well. In many cases, the designer might also have illustration and photographic talent (namely using Adobe Photoshop) and be called upon to create the projects assets as well as lay them out into the project's design. This makes a good and versatile designer/graphic designer indispensable to the success of the project.

Freelance Rate:

$50 to $95 per hour

Salary Range:

$40,000 to $60,000

Production Artist

In most cases, the production artist is the project workhorse often called upon to implement all of the work on any given project. When text changes need to be implemented, it is the production person that is likely to have to do so. It is also often the production artist that is responsible for taking the rough designs and translating them into new media assets. Production artists tend to be jack-of-all-trades with the option of evolving their career into designers or art directors. Because they also tend to have technical skills, production artists also move into programming, mastering such programs as Macromedia Director as well as 3D, video, and animation. A solid production artist is often a producer's most valuable team asset.

Other Roles:

Often the most computer savvy (excluding the programmers), production artists are called upon to provide technical support to each member of the new media team. They are also asked to serve as beta testers, administrative assistants, and virtually every other aspect of the new media team.

Freelance Rate:

$35 to $55 per hour

Salary Range:

$30,000 to $50,000

Illustrator

The illustrator creates the assets that are used in the product's interface, including backgrounds, characters, navigational buttons, and so on. Because computer illustration files can be made very small, yet retain a powerful visual impact, good illustrators can be valuable contributors to a quality product.

Other Roles:

In many smaller new media firms, illustrators also serve as the designer for the project.

Freelance Rate:

$75 to $100 per hour; although negotiated project rates, in which the illustrator works for a project fee, not an hourly rate, are more frequent.

Salary Range:

$40,000 to $60,000

Photographers

Photographers provide product and people shots as well as images that can serve as the texture for an interface. With their understanding of visual presentation, photographers can serve as key project members by working with designers to provide assets—photographs—that can create stunning designs.

Other Roles:

In some cases, photographers with knowledge of Photoshop are helpful as production artists.

Freelance Rate:

Traditionally photographers work on a per assignment rate, referred to as piece work. In our industry, photographers are typically paid a day rate, ranging on the average from $1,000 to $1,500 per day. Although, there are a good many photographers that command a day rate over $2,500 and can be well worth the price.

Animator: 2D/3D

An animator creates 2D and 3D artwork for a project as well as composes animation for the new media project. Well-done animation has the power to create visually arresting works, such as Jim Ludke's work on the CD-ROMs *Freakshow* and *Bad Day on the Midway,* produced with the ultra-creative and talented music and new media ensemble *The Residents.*

Other Roles:

Generally high-end animators create nothing but animation in some very sophisticated programs. In smaller shops, the production artists, or the illustrator may get involved in creating 3D and animation in programs such as Specular's Infini-D.

Freelance Rate:

Good animators work exclusively as freelancers. Typically, a skilled animator can command as much as $100 to $150 per hour.

Videographer

When it comes to new media, many firms feel they can "get by" preparing their video themselves. The fact, however, is that a good videographer with an understanding of digital video and new media can add tremendous value to the quality of a new media product.

Other Roles:

On small projects, the production artist doubles as the videographer. On serious projects, there's no substitute for experience.

Freelance Rate:

$125 to $150 per hour or on a project basis

Sound/Composer/Musician

Unfortunately, the sound technician is in the same position as the videographer—most companies try to get by without one as they rely instead on music clips and desktop tools for their projects. The problem is that sound is more important than just an element you only notice when it isn't good. Good sound creates mood and environment—key elements in enhancing the experience for the user of your project.

Other Roles:

On small projects, the production artist doubles as the composer/musician. Again, there is no substitute for experience.

Freelance Rate:

$150 to $200 per hour

Programmer

The programmer is the magician who makes it all work by bringing all the elements together—adding function to the design, the animation, the video, and the sound. The programmer is also responsible for ensuring the program works on multiple platforms. Generally, the programmer has an assistant who helps and also does the product beta testing.

Freelance Rate:

$150 to $200 per hour

Salary Range:

$50,000 to 120,000; $50,000 to 60,000 for entry-level positions; $60,000 to $75,000 for intermediate positions; and $75,000 to $120,000 for advanced work

Internet Project Roles and Salaries

How many people does it take to produce a Web site? Excellent sites have been produced by a team of one. Larger Web sites can have as many as 10 to 15 members dedicated to them.

Small design shops are likely to have a team of three—a project manager, a designer, and an individual handling the HTML (the "HTMLer"). The design shop is likely to freelance programming work and maintain a relationship with an Internet Service Provider that works with the company to make sure that the Web site is uploaded to the server and adequately maintained.

The following classified ad was actually posted on a mailing list.

WANTED

A motivated and talented individual to build world-class Web sites for an Internet start-up firm. Individual must have one year experience designing and producing major Web sites...the perfect candidate will handle all Web site design and programming. Candidate must be proficient in Adobe Photoshop, HTML, CGI, Java, Macromedia Director/Shockwave, Real Audio, GIF Animation. Windows NT and Unix experience a plus. Copywriting skills a plus. Must be willing to relocate. Looking for team player with a good sense of humor. Send résumé and URLs to...

If you had to do all of the preceding as part of your job description, do you think you would have a good sense of humor on top of it? Get real!

There is a tendency in the Web developer community to have one individual responsible for too many varied tasks. We agree that there are some individuals who are enormously talented—individuals who are capable of managing design and programming requirements. Yet, overall, do you really think this is possible?

Why is it that many Web sites are criticized for their lack of content and artistic effect? The answer more than likely has to do with the fact that the majority of Web sites are not created by editors and artists, but rather programmers. This is not an assault on the creativity of programmers, which apply their own unique version of creativity to their craft. Yet, the fact remains: artists create, designers design, programmers program. Having one individual responsible for all of those aspects of building a Web site means that something is compromised along the way.

Here's a look at some of the members of an Internet team. Again, specific team members depend on the project.

Producer/Project Manager

The producer or project manager serves as the primary client contact on many new media projects is also very likely to be the one who writes the business proposal in addition to overseeing the conception of the site and its production.

Other Roles:

The producer/project manager might also be called upon to serve as the editor and even asked to pitch in and help with the HTML as well as help test the final site.

Freelance Rate/Salary:

Producers tend not to be paid as freelancers although contracting producers to manage specific projects is common.

Salary Range:

$65,000 to $85,000

Editor

The editor works with the client to determine what type of content is relevant to the site and also helps organize that content into a hierarchy that determines how the Web site is structured.

Other Roles:

The editor knows enough HTML to make changes and corrections to the copy and might also serve as the Web site's producer.

Freelance:

$50 to $100 per hour

Salary Range:

$45,000 to $55,000

Art Director/Creative Director

The art director/creative director works with the producer to create the design content for a Web site as well as oversees the design staff to ensure that the design concept is successfully executed.

Other Roles:

Might also serve as the Web site's designer.

Salary Range:

$60,000 to $90,000

Designer

In larger firms, the designer implements the vision of the art director/ creative director. In most firms, the designer creates the Web site design in a page layout program (such as QuarkXPress or Illustrator) and works with the production staff to convert that design to "Web-friendly pages" in Photoshop.

Other Roles:

The designer might be called upon to complete the production work for the Web site as well as handle the creation of the site's final pages using HTML.

Freelance Range:

$60 to $80 per hour

Salary Range:

$40,000 to $60,000

Graphic Production

The production staff works with the designer to translate designs into final Web pages. Good production team members enhance the development process by consulting with the designer on how to create designs that take into account the limitations that the Web places on the presentation of graphics.

Other Roles:

The graphic production person might be called upon to do HTML work and recently has also taken on the responsibility of managing a Web site's CGI scripts. Good production people also handle sound and video that is placed on the Web site for downloading.

Freelance Range:

$35 to $55

Salary Range:

$30,000 to $45,000

Illustrator

The illustrator creates assets in the form of designs, navigation buttons, and general interfaces that shape the look and feel of a Web site.

Other Roles:

Illustrators also serve as designers and production artists. Technologically savvy Illustrators also handle HTML. They are also moving into roles in which they create 2D, 3D, and basic animation.

Freelance Range:

$75 to $100

Salary Range:

$35,000 to $50,000

Photographer

Unfortunately, the majority of the Web developers we contacted for this book painted a sad picture for photographers: the majority of Web developers purchase stock photography or use digital cameras to provide images for their Web sites. Other companies pay their photographers to shoot images for the product shots in their catalog and use those images on their Web site. Because the Web presents images in low resolution, there is the perception that there is less incentive to hire professional photographers specifically for Web work. On the other hand, digital stock photography houses are gaining in popularity and offering photographers works for sale online.

Freelance Range:

The standard rate for photography: $1,000 to $1,500 per day

Production: HTML/CGI

The HTML / CGI production person is largely responsible for the creation of final pages in HTML as well as implementing necessary CGI scripts. This team member also tends to be proficient in tables and frames as well as implementing animated GIFs and "every other trick in the book" including Java.

Other Roles:

The HTML / CGI production person also doubles as the graphic production artist.

Freelance Salary:

$25 to $55, depending on the level of complexity

(We have also heard of a few shops in the New York area paying $15–20 per hour for HTML work, but we have to wonder what the expectation or quality of the work is like.)

Salary Range:

$25,000 to $45,000

Programmer

The programmer is one of the most important members of an Internet team and more and more programmers are coming to the Web as a medium to offer their talents. Programmers contribute by working with CGI, Java, and custom scripts but as the need for more complex Web sites grows, the need for programmers increases to providing the delivery of databases, on-line transactions, and Intranets.

Freelance Rates:

$100 to $125

Salary Range:

$90,000 to $125,000

Webmaster

The Webmaster is responsible for maintaining the server. The Webmaster also works with the designer to ensure that files are uploaded properly and also works closely with the programmer.

Other Roles:

Depending on his or her expertise, the Webmaster might double as programmer.

Salary Range:

$40,000 to $75,000

Rosanne Esposito and Todd Carter
Busy Box Productions
San Francisco, CA 94111
http://www.busybox.com
info@busybox.com

Busy Box has an impressive client list, including: Agence France Presse (AFP), Apple Computer, Associated Press, Digital Stock, Koyosha Graphics of America (KGA), Motorbaby/Rawkus Records, Photo Electronic Imaging (PEI), The National Basketball Association (NBA), Visual Communications Group, UK (VCG).

The company designs and delivers electronic business solutions for some of the world's largest media companies. The company's core competency lies in its unique approach to dynamic content programming.

Busy Box seems to have a specific focus on media companies. What is the company's background?

We were established in 1995 with the mission of conceptualizing and creating complex network architecture for the Internet and producing dynamic content programming that creates worldwide commercial opportunities for our clients. Our business focus is on self-organizing consumer/supplier communities, best demonstrated by the soon-to-be launched "Media Network" site we developed in conjunction with Apple Computer.

Why the emphasis on media companies?

It's where we came from and a logical extension of the industry we were trained in. Our core competency lies in our media-industry experience—the understanding and application of technologies, strategic marketing of online information services, and the development of interactive content.

By developing custom software, programming and information design informed by a fundamental understanding of interactivity and online environments, our company's products enable us to create effective synergistic marketing strategies that both exploit vertical markets and identify new markets to achieve greater market share and profitability for our clients [translation—we know our clients and their business so we can give them what they need].

In addition to you and Todd, who are Executive Producers? How is the Busy Box team structured?

We have a core team that includes the following members: Nick Black (Database Expert Extraordinaire), Jon Bloodworth (General Counsel), W. Michael Walton (Network Systems Doctor), Cloude Porteous (WebObjects Master), and Jon Grover (Applescript and Automation Applications Master Developer).

We also have a team of consultants including Donna Mann (Director, New Media Information and Publications, National Gallery of Art, Washington, DC), and Catherine Tierney (Chief Librarian Akron Beacon Journal).

In terms of Web hourly rates and salaries, what do you pay for a project manager?

Stock incentives and benefits not included, $40,000 a year for a full-time position, about $50 per hour for freelance rates.

For a designer?

$50,000 a year or approximately $75 an hour.

Illustrators?

$40 to $50 an hour.

Animators?

Basically, the same rate as illustrators.

How about programmers?

That varies. For programmers with C and Java experience, about $75 an hour or about $65,000 a year. For HTML and basic production work, $25 an hour. For CGI work, anywhere from $40 to $50 an hour.

And you pay copywriters...

About $35 an hour.

A Webmaster?

At an annual salary of $50,000 or about $60 an hour.

A Pricing Survey—Florida

José Lopez-Varela
CreatAbility.connected
Coral Gables, FL
http://www.creatability.com
info@creatability.com

CreatAbility.connected is not just an interactive house that "cranks out" Web sites. It's an integral part of the CreatAbility team, producers of award-winning general and Hispanic market advertising, marketing, and public relations. "We Build Smart Sites."

NEW MEDIA

	Freelance per Hour	Full-time per Year
Project Manager	$12 to $18	$22,000 to $35,000
Creative/Designer	$15 to $35	$28,000 to $45,000
Illustrator	$15 to $25	-
Photographer	$150 to $200	-
Animator	$15 to $18	$28,000 to $32,000
3D	$15 to $18	$28,000 to $32,000
Sound	$15 to $18	$28,000 to $32,000
Videographer	$150 to $200	-
Editorial Director/Copywriter	$15 to $25	$30,000 to $52,500
Production	$10 to $15	$18,000 to $22,000
Programmer	$15 to $20	$30,000 to $36,000
Lingo	$15 to $20	$30,000 to $36,000
C	$75 to $100	-

INTERNET

	Freelance per Hour	Full-time per Year
Project Manager	$12 to $18	$22,000 to $35,000
Creative/Designer	$15 to $35	$28,000 to $45,000
Illustrator	$15 to $25	-
Photographer	$150 to $200	-
Animator	$15 to $18	$28,000 to $32,000
3D	$15 to $18	$28,000 to $32,000
Sound	$15 to $18	$28,000 to $32,000

Videographer	$150 to $200	-
Editorial Director/Copywriter	$15 to $25	$30,000 to $52,500
Production: Art	$10 to $15	$18,000 to $22,000
Production: HTML	$10 to $15	$18,000 to $22,000
Programmer	$20 to $25	$30,000 to $36,000
CGI	$20 to $25	$30,000 to $36,000
Java	$20 to $25	$30,000 to $36,000
Webmaster	-	$50,000 to $75,000

A Pricing Survey—West Coast

Andrew Shakman
President
CyberSight
(aka Internet Marketing, Inc.)
Portland, OR and Santa Monica, CA
http://www.cybersight.com
info@cybersight.com

Key Internet projects the company has produced or contributed to include: Visa International, Molson Breweries, Stolichnaya Vodka, among others.

WEB

	Freelance per Hour	Full-time per Year
Project Manager	-	$20,000 to $40,000
Creative/Designer	-	$35,000 to $50,000
Illustrator	$15 to $35 for standard work; $35 to $55 for rush work	-
Editorial Director/Copy Writer	$10 to $65	-
Production: Art	$8 to $35	-
Production: HTML	$18 to $20	$15,000 to $25,000
Programmer (including CGI and Java)	-	$20,000 to $40,000
Webmaster	-	$25,000 to 40,000

A Pricing Survey—New York

Rich Shupe and Lynn Fischer
Fischer Multimedia Arts (FMA)
New York, NY
http://www.FMAonline.com
info@FMAonline.com

FMA is a full-service design and production house offering CD-ROM, enhanced CD, and online services. Specialties include Director/Shockwave, mTropolis, QTVR/RealVR, Apple Media Tool, JavaScript, and digital video and audio.

NEW MEDIA

	Freelance per Hour	Full-time per Year
Project Manager	$15 to $20	$30,000 to $35,000
Creative/Designer	$20 to $35	$35,000 to $45,000
Illustrator	$20 to $35	-
Photographer	$40 to $100	-
Animator	$50 to $100	-
3D	$20 to $50	-
Sound (desktop audio work, not including original audio composition)	$10 to $20	-
Videographer (professional cameraman)	$40 to $100	-
Editorial Director/Copy Writer	$10 to $20	$25,000 to $30,000
Production	$10 to $15	$25,000 to $30,000
Programmer, Lingo	$20 to $50	$40,000 to $50,000
Programmer, C	$50 to $100	$40,000 to $50,000

Most hourly rates and annual salaries for new media work are the same for Internet development work. With the exception of the following positions that are Internet job only:

INTERNET

	Freelance per hour	Full-time per year
Production, HTML	$15 to $35	$30,000 to $40,000
Programmer, CGI	$50 to $100	$35,000 to $45,000
Programmer, Java	$50 to $100	$40,000 to $50,000
Webmaster	$25 to $75	$35,000 to $45,000

A Pricing Survey—New York

Bill Nelson
Rare Medium
New Media and Web Developer
New York, NY
http://www.raremedium.com
info@raremedium.com

Rare Medium, Inc. is an award-winning, interactive design and multimedia creative house. The company has developed a specialty in creating engaging interactive content for international consumer brand marketers as well as for the arts and entertainment industry.

NEW MEDIA AND WEB

	Freelance per Hour (unless otherwise noted)	Full-time per Year
Project Manager	$20 to $30	$30,000 to $40,000
Creative/Designer	$30 to $50	$30,000 to $50,000
Illustrator	$35 to $50	$35,000 to $50,000
Photographer	$250 to $500 / picture	-
Animator	$25 to $50	$25,000 to $50,000
3D	$25 to $50	$25,000 to $50,000
Sound	$18 to $25 / per sound	-
Editorial Director/Copy Writer	$25 to $40	$25,000 to $40,000
Production	$15 to $30	$20,000 to $30,000
Production, HTML	$15 to $35	$20,000 to $30,000
Programmer, Lingo	$35 to $50	$35,000 to $50,000
Programmer, C	$35 to $75	$30,000 to $50,000
Programmer, CGI	$35 to $75	$30,000 to $50,000
Programmer, Java	$35 to $75	$30,000 to $50,000
Webmaster	$15 to $25	$20,000 to $30,000

A Pricing Survey—New York

Marc Infield
Geronimo Creative Service
San Francisco, CA
http://www.geronimo.com
design@geronimo.com

Geronimo provides full-service design and copywriting for clients in the sports/outdoor industry. Their mission is to provide quality writing and design to their clients, while trying to keep things enjoyable for everyone involved.

New Media and Web	Freelance per hour	Full-time per year
HTML	$10 to $16	$25,000 to $30,000
Project Manager	-	$30,000
Creative/Designer	-	$30,000
Illustrator	$200 to $600 per illustration	-

Photographer (For Web work, they pay less because color matching and the resolution is not as critical as in print media.)

	$1,000 per day (with studio).	-
Editorial Director/Copy Writer	$15 to $25	-
Production	$12 to $35	-
Programmer	$50 to $100	-
Webmaster	-	$25,000 to $45,000

A New York Recruitment Firm Tells All

Laura S. Hill
President
Able Associates, Inc.
New York, NY
http://www.ablesearch.com
laura@ablesearch.com

Able Associates is a management recruiting firm that specializes in searching for new media, advertising, and publishing professionals and executives. The firm's reputation for serving the staffing needs of New York area firms has been earned over 40 years and continues to evolve as the demands of today's employers change. We strive for the utmost level of professionalism and integrity as we assist our clients in finding and attracting the talent they seek to grow their businesses and stay abreast of the competition.

Able assists multinational entertainment giants, independent multimedia developers, and start-up new media firms with the following positions: Vice President, Applications Development; Vice President, Technical Services; Vice President, Human Resources; Director, Human Resources; Editor-in-Chief, Electronic Reference Products; Director, Media Programs; Director, Programming and Content Syndication; Director of Technology; Account Director; Director, Media Planning; Editorial Production Manager, Interactive Division; Product Manager, Business-to-Business Interactive; Webmaster; Online Marketing Communications Director; Producer; Senior Producer; Project Manager, Cable, Modem, and Television; Web Developer; Senior Web Developer; Program Manager, Online Financial Applications; Marketing Manager, CD-ROM; Public Relations Manager, Latin America.

As a recruitment firm specializing in new media and the Internet, you are on the front line of the job scene. What sort of trends are you seeing?

I am seeing a lot of job candidates who are skeptical of employment opportunities at start-up companies. While it's true that there is a serious need in the industry for technology skills, positions for junior-level talent are pretty much abundant. Job candidates right out of college—those in the trenches doing most of the work—find themselves in demand. In the early days of the industry, these types of candidates were impressed by things like stock options. Now they are more savvy. Start-ups trying to use a combination of stock options and salary to lure employees are having a difficult time, because they are competing against more established firms that can pay good salaries and offer good benefits. As a result, start-ups have had to offer higher salaries than more established firms.

Anything else?

The cable modem industry is hot, hot, hot. There's also a growing need for high-end sales representatives. Top management and executives are also hard to find.

The commercial CD-ROM business is dead. Business-to-business use of CD-ROM, though, is doing well.

Any surprises?

The wireless industry is becoming increasingly active as of late.

How about in terms of programming?

Simple: C++, Java, Microsoft Tools, and Windows NT. There aren't enough programmers.

Let's talk about project managers, or producers. What kinds of salaries are you seeing for this position?

Overall, I would say that the type of salary being offered varies greatly based on two factors: the candidate's experience and the specific needs and demand of the employer, which are unique to each situation.

In general, a project manager or producer position varies from approximately $55,000 to $75,000. Senior producers can command anywhere from $80,000 to $100,000.

It's important to note, however, that every position is unique.

For example?

In some cases, the producer has no technical skills. In others, the producer is a C++ programmer with production experience. Some producers come from a design background, some from an administrative background. Depending on the circumstances, the producer might roll up his or

117

her sleeves and do much of the work on a project or they might simply oversee and manage a project or product. Then there are producers with an editorial background—content producers.

It is also worthy of note that sometimes the "better" jobs do not pay as much.

Can you elaborate on that?

Sure. A firm that has an excellent reputation, offers a solid career path...often to mid- and upper-management...and stability is particularly attractive to the best job candidates. They have the luxury of having good people that want to work for them. They are in a position where they can actually offer lower salaries and still attract the best talent. This is the case for almost all of the positions in our industry.

What kind of salaries are you seeing with the difficult to define title of "Webmaster"?

This is one of the most confusing job titles to fill in the marketplace. Some Webmasters have a technical background, some an administrative background. We have also seen Webmasters with content or marketing experience command excellent salaries.

For job candidates without a college degree—they may still be in school—I have seen annual salaries range in the mid $25,000 range. With a degree and six months out of college, approximately $30,000 to $40,000. If, however, you are a Webmaster with programming experience, you can command $70,000 to $75,000.

How about creative positions? What titles are you seeing being used to describe the creative talent in the industry?

There tends to be title inflation in this area, so you see anywhere from creative director,

designer, art director, senior art director, graphic designer. Interestingly, my experience has been that titles are less important to the actual job candidates. They are more concerned about what creative challenge a position offers as well as what medium is involved, such as the Web, interactive television, and so forth.

Designers make in the range of $35,000 to $55,000. Senior designers or art directors can make anywhere from $55,000 to $75,000. If the designer has solid project management experience and supervisory responsibility, the salary can be $75,000 plus. The drawback for the creative talent can be that at that level they are doing less hands-on work, which might be their true love, and doing mostly mangement work.

How about salaries for Illustrators?

Our experience has been that illustrators tend to be freelancers who have established their own network for employment.

And photographers?

The same situation as for illustrators.

How about animators?

We have seen that animators, as well as sound and video skills, tend to fall under the jurisdiction of the technical staff or handled by the designers or production people.

Speaking of production, how do you draw the line between the creative and production side of the industry?

The distinction between the artistic side and the production side tends to be determined by whether or not the candidate has an art degree, usually a Bachelor of Fine Arts.

Designers tend to move up the creative ladder into director and manager positions. My experience has been that production people tend to progress into producer roles.

How about production salaries?

I would say they range from $25,000 to $50,000.

How about the content side—editorial?

There seems to be a good supply of people relative to demand in this area. Whenever there are more people looking for jobs, than jobs looking for people, you tend to see salaries decline. A good editorial person can expect a salary in the $45,000 range.

That said, there are cases in which an editorial person will have a specific expertise—an exact match for a company's content, such as the travel industry or the food industry. In those cases, the "expert" is in a strong position to comand a salary as high as $100,000. Sometimes more.

And then there are the programmers. They can name their price! In general, programmers tend to choose the positions they accept based on the challenge. Programmers right out of school can start at $50,000 to $55,000.

And how about those with more experience?

Let's put it this way...we have heard of some programmers getting $500 an hour for Java. Salaries as high as $150,000 to $180,000, on a contract basis, are not unheard of.

One of the biggest factors affecting programmer salaries in Manhattan, for example, is that new media and Internet companies have to compete with Wall Street. Wall Street can afford to pay more salaries and greater benefits, as well as offer tremendous challenges and excellent career paths. The job market for programmers is totally affected by that.

What about other positions in the areas of marketing and business development, for example?

There are a lot of highly talented people looking for marketing and business devleopment jobs, which range in salary from $70,000 to $100,000. While we have placed people in these types of jobs, it's not a frequent occurrence.

Why is that?

First, by definition marketing people tend to be social animals. Their career is often based on their contacts. They know the players in the industry and when a position opens they tend to know about it. Many of these jobs are filled through "networking."

Second, you have a lot of people competing for higher salary jobs. There are simply fewer of these types of jobs available.

Any final thoughts?

This industry is so new that clear patterns have yet to emerge. Many of the job titles and requirements overlap. Job functions are blurred and many candidates have so many skills that they can oftentimes fulfill one, two, or three positions at a company. That, and the fact that many companies' needs are constantly evolving, means how much you get paid, or pay, all comes down to the negotiation between the employee and employer.

NewMedia Magazine Salary Survey 1995

NewMedia magazine specializes in comprehensive comparitive product reviews, industry news, and feature articles for professionals who buy and use digital media products and services. Their 1995 salary survey shows that the average multimedia professional made $61,180 per year. Across the markets of commercial, corporate, and educational media, the salaries were about the same.

Some specific job titles and their salaries are:

Producer	$55,640
Design Director	$55,310
Software Engineer	$47,500

Source: *NewMedia* magazine, July, 1995.

HOW Magazine Salary Survey 1996

HOW magazine, a well-respected design resource, conducts yearly salary surveys for the design industry. Their last survey, in June of 1996, showed the following results for designers across the United States:

Average Salaries for Designers by Region

Northeast	$46,822
West	$43,328
North Central	$42,762
South	$42,559

Freelance designers averaged $52 per hour.

Average Salaries by Job Title

Principal/Partner	$53,686
Creative Director	$55,040
Art Director	$46,718
Senior Designer	$45,371
Designer	$37,479

Men still made, on the average, more than women, and designers in metro areas made more than non-metro areas. For a complete report, contact *HOW* at (513) 531-2690, ext.328.

In Summary

The information in this chapter has given you a place to start in pricing your new media or Web project. It is important that you do not try to get one person to do too many things, although, that is not to say you should never overlap expertise. Each project is unique and requires a unique set of talents. Break down your needs and budget your hours and rates carefully. Try to take every detail into account and do not try to get the cheapest talent you can find. Hire people who have experience in their area, are interested in the project, and are willing to work as part of a team.

Building a Budget

A good budget defines a project on a line-by-line basis. It's often said that when you build your budget what you are really doing is drawing a line where aspiration meets reality.

In This Chapter, We:

- Look at how businesses can use budgets as a project management tool.

- Build a budget for the Joe Breeze Cycles business proposal we presented as an example in Chapter 2, "The Business Proposal."

Every aspect of your project has a cost attached to it. When you talk on the phone with a prospective client, that phone call takes time and represents the cost of sales. The cost of the CD-ROM package represents a cost of production. When you spend two days writing a press release announcing the release of your final product, that represents a marketing and public relations cost, whether you do it yourself or hire a firm to do it for you. In short, everything you do in your business costs something—from the space you rent for your company to conduct its business, to the office supplies and computers your company uses, to the Web site you are building for your largest client.

Every action and expense pertaining to a project should have a corresponding line item in that project's budget. As Matthew Winston, one business savvy new media developer, declared: "The budget is a project's definition." The budget is also the driving force in the project. In a successful company everyone knows where the actual budget stands. They know what the budget contains. And more important, they know what it does not contain. In a successful company, everyone also knows and understands the process by which the budget was created. Successful companies use the budget to guide the company's operations. You may think that this type of employee involvement challenges traditional business practice. Well, it does, and it seems to be working! In John Sculley's *Odyssey* you can read about how Apple utilized this approach and SCP/Medscape (one of our case studies) has done this successfully as well.

For example, a designer knows he has up to 30 hours to design the client's interface and subsequent screens. A producer knows that his CD-ROM goes into a four-color box and can cost no more than $2 per unit to print, score, fold, and collate. The person on the team responsible for creating the CGI scripts knows he or she has two days to write a script and one day to implement that interactive form on the client's Web site—testing not withstanding.

A good budget also enables effective project management. For example, in one company, every Monday morning, team leaders get together for breakfast. Revised budgets for all projects are passed out for review. Team leaders review the budget comparing the company's initial estimates with actual, up-to-date budget numbers on the project. Team leaders also discuss projections for the future, making sure to note upcoming project milestones while also paying careful attention to remaining budget resources. Of course, in this case, up-to-date and accurate time sheets are critical.

Building a Budget

Building a budget is a straightforward and simple exercise. It is important to recognize that you will inevitably make mistakes. Making CD-ROMs and building Web sites is not an exact science—it's an art form. The trick to developing a solid budget is not unlike trying to put your arms around a pile of leaves—no matter how careful you are, some of the leaves will fall to the ground. You will omit line items in your budget. You are also likely to underestimate the amount of time it takes to design an interface, program an interactive database, and manage your client. One of the golden rules of life seems to be that everything takes far longer than you expect, and almost always twice what you planned for. Relax! Even the most experienced producers admit that their budgets are "best guess" assumptions.

Chances are good that if you work efficiently and communicate with your client and other members of your team, you can more than offset your errors by coming in under budget in regard to other aspects of the project. By using your budget to manage your project, you can make mid-project adjustments that will enable you to minimize your costs to the greatest extent possible if not recoup your costs entirely. Certainly, this approach—open communication and careful review— is more likely to yield positive and profitable results than signing a contract, completing the project, and settling the score at the end.

With each project, your budgets will become more and more accurate. As you use your budget to improve the management of your projects, it will develop into a comprehensive document that takes on greater definition—in short, a document that paints a more realistic picture of the products you develop, creatively and financially.

Let's take a look at preparing a budget for the business proposal that we presented in Chapter 2, "The Business Proposal."

Budget Categories

When you prepare your budget, you want to go back to the items that you presented in the step-by-step development process that you communicated to your clients in your business proposal. Here are the steps that were outlined in the program development for the Joe Breeze Cycles Web site:

- **Editorial Development.** Review all of the editorial material available regarding Joe Breeze Cycles (including history and background, catalogs, product reviews, information on Team Breezer, and so on) and work with Joe Breeze to determine what material will be included on the site. This proposal assumes all content is provided on disk by Joe Breeze Cycles.

- **Site Architecture.** Categorize all of the available content into sections for the Web site, create hierarchies of information, and structure each section on the site. In addition to defining the site's structure, this step includes creating a site blueprint, presenting the diagram to Joe Breeze Cycles for approval, and incorporating client changes.

- **Design.** Create initial site sketches based on one design concept, incorporate client approval and receive final sign off on initial sketches, create final page designs and all site assets (including photographs, illustration, navigation buttons, icons, and so on), and manage revisions and final approval with Joe Breeze.

- **Production: Graphics.** Optimize all design elements and site assets for the Web, including conversion of artwork from Illustrator to Photoshop, indexing, reviewing graphics in multiple browsers, and making final adjustments of graphics after indexing.

- **Production: HTML.** Create page templates and combine all design elements and site assets into final Web page creation.

- **Site Review and Testing.** Proof and review final HTML files for content accuracy, check design consistency, and verify all links and navigation. This also includes final client approval.

- **Uploading to Server.** Place files on the server, test all links, as well as incorporate any last-minute changes and additions from the client.

- **Marketing.** Register the site with various search engines as well as surf the Web for online bicycle magazines and mountain biking related Web sites, and notify them that Joe Breeze Cycles is on the Web! This step is important in that the bicycling community has a strong presence on the Internet, including bike manufacturers, riding clubs, retailers, catalogs, and more.

These descriptive terms, from editorial development to marketing, were presented to the client in the business proposal. These terms serve as the general categories for your budget. Every company describes what it does and how it works for its clients using the terms and descriptions with which it is most comfortable. These categories define the language used between the company and the client to describe the process of producing the client's product.

After you have created a business proposal and defined this process using terms that are clear and understandable for you and your client (and you and every member of your team), keep a general list of your budget categories. Periodically review the list. Ask team members if there is better language that can substitute for each of these budget categories. Everyone on the team should know what the budget categories are, what they mean, and how they are used to describe the production process. This communication enables team members to talk to the client in a clear and consistent manner. It also enables each of the team members to communicate among themselves with the same success.

We know of successful companies where the sales team not only understands the terms, but also plays an important role in their creation. That way, when they speak to the client, they are effectively communicating about the project.

One company we know of actually spends time making sure everyone at the company understands the language presented in both the business proposal and the budget. Why? Says the CEO of the company, "so that every person who answers the phone, and takes a message from a client, understands what the client is asking and can relay that message clearly to anyone else in the company."

In many cases, clients have their own terminology to describe the production process. For example, some, correctly or not, view HTML as programming. For that client, your budget categories should be restructured to match the way the client defines the production process. To do so will make communication easier in the long run.

When you create your first budget, begin with each project development category and create a step-by-step list describing everything necessary to fulfill that category. Let's take a look at the step-by-step items necessary for each of the categories presented in the business proposal to Joe Breeze Cycles.

Costs of Budget Development

The first element presented in the business proposal to Joe Breeze Cycles concerned editorial development. Some editorial development was necessary to create the initial business proposal. Some developers and design shops are in the position where they are hired to produce that editorial development—a business profile, research a market, create a content analysis, concept, and treatment—for a certain stipend ranging from $5,000 to $25,000. This situation is optimal. In many cases, however, the client does not understand or value the process and is reluctant to pay for the development of a concept, a business proposal, and budget in addition to the actual product itself. Part of this is because many clients have projects in which the budgets do not make it possible. Others feel that given the competition in the industry they can get it free, but that's another story.

In comparison to the rest of the manufacturers in the mountain bike industry, Joe Breeze Cycles is small. In fact, when we called the company, Joe himself answered the phone. Proposing that Joe hire us to do a concept and treatment would have been inappropriate. We made the calculated risk that we could recoup the cost of developing the business proposal and budget by selling Joe on the Web site. It was a gamble and fortunately we were right. Still, creating a client profile and needs analysis for Joe Breeze Cycles took time to research and develop. Fortunately for us, mountain biking is a hobby, so it was fun. Our research yielded enough information to present to Joe in our business proposal.

Many companies handle this initial project investment differently. Some do not track the time they spend developing business proposals. Others identify the number of hours they spend soliciting new business development. They track this for each specific project that they pitch. If they win the job, that time spent is folded back into some line item in the budget where it gets inevitably charged to the client. Or at the very least, the cost is reflected in the project's overhead as the "cost of sales."

If a contract for the job is not won, the total amount of time spent, and its associated cost, is earmarked "sales" or "business development" and written off as a loss. Good accounting practices include these costs in the company's general overhead. (There will be more on overhead later in this chapter.)

Unfortunately, for most companies, business is generally pitched on "spec," which means that the company pitching the business creates an editorial concept, develops a design, and presents a business proposal to a prospective client at no charge. As you read in Chapter 3, "Designing for New Media," freelancers and small companies are leery of spec work and some will not do it at all. There's no guarantee that any of their work will ever yield a return on investment. Clients who are not willing to pay even a small fee for this development are doing themselves and their suppliers a great disservice by devaluing the work—it is not worth paying for in their eyes. In the long run, this increases development costs overall and clients can miss out on great talent because of this practice. How your company addresses this issue depends on your business. At some point, the cost of sales can amount to a significant investment of time and money. We have heard some companies, frustrated at the ratio of business proposals they need to write to make a sale, claim "you wonder if we develop Web projects or just write proposals."

If your company spends an inordinate amount of time and money "chasing" clients and never winning their business, that is one sign that something might be wrong. Perhaps you are not being realistic about the type of business that your company is targeting, you are targeting the wrong clients, you are approaching your clients the wrong way, or your prices are too high. In any case, while the answers to these questions might necessitate a long and realistic assessment of the company's focus and capabilities, they are issues that sooner or later must be addressed. A company without sales is like a car running out of fuel.

The more efficiently your company can produce business proposals and budgets, the lower the cost of your sales will be. Again, open communication and teamwork can enable a company to go after *more* business with *less* resources.

The approach we took in developing the Joe Breeze Cycles Web site was to include the cost for much of the initial conceptual work in the proposal in the editorial development component of the budget. Certainly the site required more editorial development than initially was proposed in the business proposal, so the initial work was leveraged with future editorial investment.

We have seen some examples where, in certain industries, charging the client for the proposal was actually a line item in the budget or folded into overhead costs. Regrettably, we haven't seen this form of recouping costs as a standard operating procedure in our industry.

Breakdown of Budget Categories

Back to the budget categories for our example, the Joe Breeze Cycles Web site. Based on our business proposal, here are our budget categories:

- Editorial Development
- Site Architecture
- Design
- Production: Graphics
- Production: HTML
- Site Review and Testing
- Uploading to the Server
- Marketing

The next step is to create the line items for the budget.

Editorial Development

Editorial development for the Joe Breeze Cycles Web site required the following basic steps:

1. Create the client profile.
2. Create the client needs analysis.

127

3. Review the client's editorial material.

4. Talk to the client about the profile and needs analysis that was created. Also, work with the client to finalize the editorial material.

Site Architecture and Navigational Maps

Developing the site architecture (or navigation) is one of the most important aspects of developing a CD-ROM or Web site. This is a lot like working with an architect to design your house. The more planning that goes into the initial phase of the house, the more efficiently the rest of the house can be built. The same is true for Web sites and CD-ROMs. Check out CNN's Web site. Despite the enormous amount of content you know where you are and how to get where you want to go. Now that's site architecture!

Site architecture for the Joe Breeze Cycles Web site required the following basic steps:

1. Reviewing the company information and grouping it into sections.

2. Drawing a diagram for the site architecture reflecting those sections. The diagram included the hierarchy of the sections as well as the navigational paths among each section.

3. Creating a blueprint.

4. Working with the client to revise and finalize the site architecture.

Design

When it comes to design, every company has its own time-tested development technique. Telling someone how to structure their design process is a lot like telling Bill Gates how to run Microsoft. You could try, but could you really make the company *more* profitable?

The design for the Joe Breeze Cycles Web site required the following basic steps:

1. Creating an initial design concept which included rough sketches and storyboards.

2. Translating those concepts into the computer (design development).

3. Creating design assets: for example, icons, navigation buttons, background patterns, and so on.

4. Working with the client to revise and finalize the designs.

5. Applying those designs to final pages.

Production

After the final designs are approved, the assets have to be translated into files that are appropriate for Web viewing—that is, GIFs, animated GIFs, JPEG, HTML pages, and so on. This process can seem to take too much time to a client because she has already approved the designs. Be sure that she understands that there is still a fair amount to work to be done—educate her.

Production for the Joe Breeze Cycles Web site required the following basic steps:

1. Converting the design and design assets to appropriate Web formats.

2. Creating HTML page templates.

3. Completing the HTML for all of the pages.

Site Review and Testing

Once everything has been completed, many people think that the job is done, and little if any time is spent on testing the site. Believe us when we say you will find things wrong with the site during a review and testing process. Don't let your client push you into skimping on this final stage—it is vitally important. There is nothing worse than a beautifully designed site that doesn't work properly. Although this is true for all new media projects, it is especially true for CD-ROMs. There is so much content that until you sit down and start to use the work, you usually don't see the problems.

Site review and testing for the Joe Breeze Cycles Web site required the following basic steps:

1. Reviewing and proofreading the content.

2. Reviewing the design.

3. Testing all the links, and so on.

4. Working with the client to review, revise, and approve the final site.

Uploading Content

Uploading content to a server is a simple process. Once your pages are completed, you simply dial into the server with your password and send the files to the appropriate location via a program such as Fetch™. Then someone at the server site will check the content and have it active shortly thereafter.

The amount of time that it takes to activate depends on the size of the site and the content.

To upload the Joe Breeze Cycles Web site to our server, we needed to do the following:

1. Create a file structure.

2. Upload the files to the server.

3. Test the entire site online "live."

4. Make time for any final client changes or additions.

Marketing the Site

Once the site is active, you need to tell people about it. Sometimes, this can be quite an extensive marketing campaign tied in with the client's other company activities or as simple as listing with a few search engines.

As far as marketing the Joe Breeze Cycles Web site, we needed to do the following:

1. Register the Web site with the various search engines.

2. Establish links to other relevant and interested sites.

3. Create a press release.

4. Work with our client to send the press release to relevant magazines.

In defining a step-by-step process for our budget categories, what we have done is define the line items in our budget! If you have never created a budget before, or if you've been afraid of the budgeting process, you now know it's really that simple and straightforward.

That's it. Those are the line items in our budget for the Joe Breeze Cycles Web site. Of course, we are still missing the numbers attached to those line items, but that's next.

Administrative and Maintenance Costs

There are elements that are not in this budget that some Web developers will have to include, such as a monthly hosting fee, registering a domain name, DNS, and so on. Other developers might also have their own terms and descriptions to define the process. They might even have plenty of other steps that they need to produce a site (programming, for example). But remember from our proposal that this is a simple site that will be hosted in the mall section of an already established Web site, so these charges are not relevant in our case.

In the case of CD-ROMs or other new media, you would need to determine packaging, mastering, and replication costs as well. Mastering is generally in the $1,000 to 1,500 range and replication can range widely depending on the amount of duplicates you are looking for. Compare prices and get references from those who you are considering for this important process. Packaging is another broad variable. Use your good common sense and package your product as the products needs demand.

We encourage you to develop your own line items, based on the type of projects that you work with, according to the way you work. What we present here is simply an insight into the process.

Again, after you have created your budget categories and your final budget line items list, it is a good idea to circulate it to every person at your company—from the receptionist to the CEO. You will be surprised at all of the excellent suggestions you will get. Most of the time the best suggestions come from the administrative assistants. The so-called "people in the trenches." After all, who is in the best position to know all of the details about what it takes to produce a project than the people who actually do the work?

Have everyone in the company approve the list. Have them approve the language. Create a definition for each step and term and keep a glossary handy for people to look at and update along the way. Communication and participation in this regard is key. People need to understand that if they are working on a project, what they are doing corresponds to a line item in the project's budget. They also need to know that if they are working on something that is not in the budget they can come to someone who will add it. That's how budgets are revised. That's how budgets and companies grow productively.

We know of one situation at a company where there were a few people who disliked the project manager. Those people took great joy in pointing out that "the budget didn't include a line for this... the budget doesn't have that." Little did those people know, that despite their behavior, they were making significant contributions to the company's development. "At first, I took it personally and got defensive," the project manager later noted. "Then I realized how lucky I was. Here were people who, whatever their motivation, were giving me unbelievable feedback!"

Now that the budget categories are created, your next step is to build the actual spread sheet.

Creating the Spreadsheet

We will create the spreadsheet for our Web site in Microsoft's Excel. Despite the fact that attacking Microsoft seems to have surpassed baseball as our national pastime, Excel is the standard spreadsheet program for the Macintosh and Windows. In fact, during our research for this book, we can say that not one of the people we talked to used anything other than Excel.

That said, this is not a book on Excel. There are plenty of excellent books on the market that offer a step-by-step look at Excel. In addition, the manuals that come with the program are very comprehensive and helpful.

In setting up your budget, let's take a look at what you want to include in your budget's spreadsheet:

Budget Category. The general section of your budget, such as editorial development, design, marketing, and so on.

Budget Line Items. The descriptive steps that define each item within your budget category. For example, "create assets," and "HTML for all pages."

Explanation. A space in the budget where you insert any necessary descriptions and explanations for specific line items. Qualifiers and notes you place in the budget to serve as reminders and help notes.

Type of Unit. One word that describes the nature of your budget line item. For example, a one-time fee, an hourly charge, and so on.

Number of Units. Defines the estimated number of units in your budget line items.

Unit Cost. Includes the cost to your company (not including overhead) regarding a specific line item.

Total Cost. The number of line item units multiplied by the cost for each unit. This is the total cost of the line item with your company.

Client Unit Cost. The per unit cost that you charge your client.

Total Client Cost. The number of units multiplied by the client cost.

Contribution (to profit). The amount remaining when you take your total cost and subtract it from the amount you are charging your client.

Here's what the complete budget would look like:

Editorial Development

Line Items	Explanation	Type of Unit	Number of Units	Unit Cost	Total Cost	Client Unit Cost	Total Client Cost	Contribution
Create client profile	For proposal	Hour	8	40	320	100	800	480
Create needs analysis	For proposal	Hour	8	40	320	100	800	480
Review editorial	Not Apply	Hour	16	40	640	100	1600	960
Client revisions	Not Apply	Hour	8	50	400	100	800	400
Sub Total					1,680		4,000	2,320

Site Architecture

Line Items	Explanation	Type of Unit	Number of Units	Unit Cost	Total Cost	Client Unit Cost	Total Client Cost	Contribution
Group into sections	For proposal	Hour	8	40	320	100	800	480
Create diagram	For proposal	Hour	4	40	160	100	400	240
Blueprint	Not apply	Hour	4	25	100	50	200	100
Client revisions	Not Apply	Hour	8	50	400	100	800	400
Sub Total					980		2,200	1,220

Design

Line Items	Explanation	Type of Unit	Number of Units	Unit Cost	Total Cost	Client Unit Cost	Total Client Cost	Contribution
Create design concept	For proposal	Hour	12	75	900	150	1800	900
Input into computer	For proposal	Hour	4	75	300	150	600	300
Create assets	Not apply	Hour	20	75	1500	150	3000	1500
Client revisions	Not apply	Hour	8	50	400	100	800	400
Create final pages	Not apply	Hour	16	75	1200	150	2400	1200
Sub Total					4,300		8,600	4,300

Production

Line Items	Explanation	Type of Unit	Number of Units	Unit Cost	Total Cost	Client Unit Cost	Total Client Cost	Contribution
Convert design/assets	Not Apply	Hour	12	25	300	80	960	660
HTML templates	Not Apply	Hour	4	30	120	80	320	200
Create all site pages	Not Apply	Hour	16	30	480	80	1280	800
							0	0
Sub Total					900		2,560	1,660

Site Review

Line Items	Explanation	Type of Unit	Number of Units	Unit Cost	Total Cost	Client Unit Cost	Total Client Cost	Contribution
Proof/review content	Not Apply	Hour	8	40	320	100	800	480
Review design	Not Apply	Hour	4	50	200	125	500	300
Test links	Not Apply	Hour	8	20	160	50	400	240
Client approval	Not Apply	Hour	8	50	400	100	800	400
Sub Total					1,080		2,500	1,420

Server Upload

Line Items	Explanation	Type of Unit	Number of Units	Unit Cost	Total Cost	Client Unit Cost	Total Client Cost	Contribution
Create file structure	No charge	Hour	0	75	0	145	0	0
Upload files	Not Apply	Hour	4	20	80	50	200	120
Test Online	Not Apply	Hour	4	20	80	50	200	120
Client approval	Not Apply	Hour	0	50	0	100	0	0
Sub Total					160		400	240

Marketing

Line Items	Explanation	Type of Unit	Number of Units	Unit Cost	Total Cost	Client Unit Cost	Total Client Cost	Contribution
Reg. w/Search Engines	Not Apply	Hour	4	20	80	60	240	160
Establish links	Not Apply	Hour	10	20	200	60	600	400
Create press release	Not Apply	Hour	8	75	600	200	1600	1000
PR with Mags	Not Apply	Hour	0	50	0	100	0	0
Sub Total					880		2,440	1,560

									Contribution Margin Ratio
Gross Totals					9,980		22,700	12,720	56%
Less overhead (30%)								3,816	
Net Totals								8,904	39%

Figure 5.1
An Example of a Complete Budget

Looking at the complete budget, we can see that the gross totals for the project are as follows:

Cost to develop the site:	$9,980
Cost to the client:	$22,700
Gross contribution:	$12,720

Before we go on, let's evaluate the margins of these numbers.

Margins

Margins are perhaps one of the most confusing terms to deal with in our industry. We have had lots of discussion on margins with lots of companies and we all agreed—it is surprising how many of us really don't understand the concept of margins. We turned to *Accounting: The Basis for Business Decisions* by Robert F. Meigs and Walter B. Meigs. Meigs and Meigs define the contribution margin *as the amount of revenue in excess of cost.*

So in our example, the contribution margin is:

$22,700 (cost to client)

− 9,980 (cost to produce project)
_____

$12,720 (contribution margin)

Actually, Meigs and Meigs suggest that the contribution margin is the portion of the revenue available to cover fixed costs after the variable costs have been covered.

For the budget we presented here, we convert everything to fixed costs. For example, if the design on the project takes longer than we expected, we are not going to bill our client for that time. Therefore, the budget presents a fixed cost. In addition, if working with the client takes longer than 8 hours (the time we budgeted), we will bill the client separately for that excess time. Since that additional billing opportunity will occur later in the project, and is impossible to determine up front, it would be evaluated in the budget versus actual analysis of the project.

So, what we now have is a gross contribution margin of $12,720 for our project. Let's look at the contribution margin ratio.

Margins in the Graphic Design Industry

Carol Layton

A 14-year veteran of graphic design firms, Carol Layton has worked at some of the biggest names in the business—Milton Glaser, Walter Bernard, and Pentagram Design. Her roster of clients has included *Worth* magazine, Time Warner, the *Washington Post*, and more. She is currently the art director of a new magazine, *Bloomberg Personal*, for the venerable Bloomberg Financial Markets located in Princeton, New Jersey.

You've worked in quite a few design firms. What is the acceptable range of margins that most graphic studios are operating with?

I would say that margins of 20% represent the lowest acceptable, 30% is about the average, and 40% is on the high side.

What sort of things does that include?

In the traditional studio sense, labor, printing, and production costs.

Does that include general overhead? Such as rent, utilities, phones, and so on?

Excluding overhead. Not many companies include an overhead in their mark-up or margin. It's also very important to note that in the budget it needs to be clear that any changes—involving labor or other expenses—are outside the budget and will be billed accordingly. Almost as important as what is in the budget, it what is not in the budget. Those assumptions must be stated up front.

In terms of new media and the Internet, do you think traditional graphic design studios will see those 20 to 40% margins rise or fall?

It's hard to say right now how new media technologies will affect traditional margins. I think it is hard to tell because it is still early.

Any suspicions?

My guess is that margins will rise. For one thing, there's more technology involved in the creation and delivery process, so there is more billing opportunity. Also, the scope of this technology makes it possible to reach far larger audiences than traditional print media. That being the case, there's certainly a rationale for charging more.

Contribution Margin Ratios

Turning to Meigs and Meigs again, we find that the contribution margin ratio is expressed as a *percentage of revenue*. Meigs and Meigs offers the following formula:

Total Contribution Margin ÷ Total Revenue = Contribution Margin Ratio

In terms of the previously mentioned budget, we have a gross contribution margin ratio of:

$12,720 ÷ $22,700 = 56%

Now that we have our gross contribution and gross margin ratio, let's factor in our overhead to paint a final financial picture.

Although Meigs and Meigs are talking about traditional manufacturing, their insight is helpful for our purpose. Meigs and Meigs define three types of cost:

- **Direct materials.** The cost of materials used for a specific job.

- **Direct labor costs.** The cost of labor for a specific job.

- **Manufacturing overhead.** A "catch all" classification, including all manufacturing costs other than the costs of direct materials or direct labor. Examples include depreciation on machinery, supervisors' salaries, factory utilities, and equipment repairs.

Overhead

In terms of new media and the Web, overhead refers to anything not related to the specific project. For example, when you purchase Adobe Photoshop, that software is used for more than one project.

The same for a CD-Recorder, the Internet connection, a Web server, fees to attend conferences, the company phone system, office supplies, magazine subscriptions, employee health benefits, office pizza parties, and so on.

The general standard when determining what is overhead is to define overhead as anything that is used for more than one project. Of course, in this industry, nothing is really black and white. It's more likely 256 shades of gray! For example, all the time you spent learning how to index graphics for one client's Web site benefits other clients.

There are many ways to determine a general company margin, and there is no one way. It's best to work on the margin with your company's accountant.

Some companies put aside a total number at the end of the year—for example, $100,000—and then divide that number across all the projects the company has produced.

If the company produced four projects and Project 1 was 25% of the company's total revenue, Project 2 was 50% of the company's total revenue, Project 3, 12.5%, and Project 4, $12.5%. The $100,000 of overhead is then allocated to each project as:

Project 1: Pays for $25,000 of the overhead

Project 2: Pays for $50,000 of the overhead

Project 3: Pays for $12,500 of the overhead

Project 4: Pays for $12,500 of the overhead

This is only one of many ways to determine margins. There is also a percentage basis for overhead in which the company figures a general percentage based on every dollar earned. For example, the company determines that for every dollar it makes, the company overhead requires .30 or 30% of net revenues. Looking at the net margin contribution and net margin contribution ratio for our budget, we see:

(Remember that $12,720 is our gross margin contribution.)

Our company has determined its overhead at 30%. So, what we see then is that $12,720 multiplied by 30% is $3,816.

Therefore, our final project numbers are as follows:

Gross billing to client: $22,700

Our cost to produce the project: $9,980

Our gross margin contribution: $12,720

Our gross margin contribution ratio: 56%

Overhead: $3,816

Net margin contribution: $8,904

Net margin contribution ratio: 39%

Determining a target margin, both gross and net, is a very difficult task that depends on a wide range of factors.

In the case of Joe Breeze Cycles, we determined that our gross margins on all projects needs to be in the 60% range and our net margins should be in the 30 to 35% range.

Every company has to determine what it considers an acceptable range of margins for its projects. Some companies with larger overheads might shoot for higher margins. Smaller companies might also target higher margins, or they might define a range that is more realistic given the types of clients they work with and the types of overhead in which the company is willing to invest.

For example, a small design studio might determine that it doesn't want to host Web sites in its office, but instead may want to partner with a local Internet Service Provider (ISP). This lowers the company's potential overhead—it doesn't need a server and a high-speed Internet connection—and with its lower overhead, the company might feel that it can lower its prices, thus making it more competitive in the marketplace.

In any case, new media and Web business is a relatively new industry. Patterns of high, low, and medium prices haven't yet begun to emerge. This is why the same Web site might vary in price from $10,000 to $100,000—or margins from 10% to 1,000%.

This can be expected in any new industry. As patterns develop, more general benchmarks are likely to emerge as they have in the graphic design business.

For example, if you ask most designers how much it costs to produce an annual report they pretty much know—about $50,000 to $70,000—depending on the size of the book. Standards for new media and the Web will develop the same types of guidelines eventually.

One factor that might not make that possible in the very near future is that the technology is in a constant state of flux and new tools are constantly emerging. Today's HTML gives way to tomorrow's CGI, which then in turn gives way to Java, and so on and so forth.

Although only time will truly tell, one potential factor pointing in the direction of general new media and Web benchmarks might come from the client. As one marketing representative of a very large telecommunications company observed, "Developers need to remember that what will determine prices in this industry is not what the developer needs to make on the project to stay in business, but rather what clients are willing to pay."

Presenting the Budget to the Client

After you complete your budget, you need to create the page that you present to the client in your business proposal.

Again, there's no one right way to present the budget. Much of how you present the budget to the client has to do with your relationship.

For example, one simple approach would be:

> Cost to produce the Web site: $22,700

No matter how good your relationship, your client will like to see more words than that before they hand over a large check.

Another approach might be:

> Cost to produce the Web Site: $22,700
>
> Which includes the following:
>> Editorial Development
>>
>> Site Architecture
>>
>> Design
>>
>> Production
>>
>> Site Review
>>
>> Upload to Server
>>
>> Marketing

The approach we tend to favor is providing the client with all the information he needs to understand each phase in the project. In doing so, we don't advocate telling the client how much each line item will cost, because he then is in the position of "cherry-picking" away at each line and what you are left with is the low margin grunt work that makes the project unprofitable. Here's how we presented the proposal page to Joe Breeze Cycles.

Web Site Budget for Joe Breeze Cycles

Editorial Development

- Develop client profile
- Develop needs analysis
- Review editorial material
- Client revisions

Site Architecture

- Group editorial into sections

- Develop site diagram
- Create site blueprint
- Client revisions

Design

- Create design concept
- Develop design
- Create design assets
- Client revisions
- Create final pages

Production

- Convert design assets
- Create HTML templates
- Create all Web site pages

Site Review

- Proof/Review content
- Review design
- Test links
- Client revisions

Upload Site to Server

- Create file structure
- Upload files
- Test live
- Client revisions

Marketing

- Register with search engines
- Establish links

- Create press releases
- Public relations

Total $22,700

Joe Breeze appreciated this itemized breakdown of costs just as you see it here. If a client wants more detail about costs, then simply ask her what about the price is bothering her and try to get some insight into whether she agrees with the assumptions. Your costs should be based on an entire package of service and if she wants to revisit the assumptions, you should present her with a new number. Taking apart your numbers leaves you open to allow cherry-picking of each item and that ultimately leads to a nightmare in terms of designing and producing the job.

Finally, budgets are simply sets of assumptions about the definition of a project. For example, the budget says, "Assuming we do this amount of work, we will be paid this amount of money." The budget, and then the Letter of Agreement, carefully define what the amount of work is, and what the amount of money for that work will be. It is important that all assumptions about the project are stated as an addendum to the budget.

Budget Assumptions

Here's how we presented the set of assumptions for the business proposal for the Joe Breeze Cycles Web site.

Editorial Development

- All material provided by client on disk
- Includes 8 hours of client management and revisions (additional time will be billed under separate agreement)

Site Architecture

- Includes 8 hours of client management and revisions (additional time will be billed under separate agreement)

Design

- Includes the presentation of one design concept
- Includes 8 hours of client management and revisions (additional time will be billed under separate agreement)

Site Review

- Includes 8 hours of client management and revisions (additional time will be billed under separate agreement)

Marketing

- Assumes client mails the press release to national bicycling and health and fitness magazines

All of the budget items, and subsequent budget assumptions, form the basis for the final Letter of Agreement of contract with your client.

In fact, some companies actually attach the budget and the budget's assumptions as an addendum to the contract. In these cases, the up front part of the contract deals with the legal relationship between the developer and the client (who owns the material, payment terms, and so forth) and the budget and proposals defines the specific relationship with the client.

The Web Pricing Index (WPI)

**Matt Carmichael
Associate Editor,
*Interactive Media and Marketing
Advertising Age*, a publication of
Crain Communications Inc.
http://www.adage.com
mattc@netb2b.com**

Matt Carmichael graduated from Northwestern University's Medill School of Journalism in 1996 with a BSJ. He is a freelance writer and photographer with an emphasis on music and technology. He managed the development of several Web sites and developed one from scratch www.rocknroll.net—from running the server to creating the design and content.

What exactly is the Web Pricing Index?

The Web Pricing Index, or WPI, is a survey/study of pricing for Web development services around the country.

How is the WPI put together?

Working with several area developers, we created three corporate scenarios for three mythical companies. We then decided what sorts of Web services they would be looking for. We took those descriptions around to 20 developers, four in each of five cities, who returned a projected bid for the projects.

The participants are a cross-section of the Web development community—large and small, traditional agencies, and developers. Each month, we add a new feature to the descriptions and price that out independently. For example, in one particular month we added chat services to the prospective bid.

What was the motivation for the WPI?

Currently, there really isn't any real data about pricing on the Web. With costs being as widely varied as they are, it's a major issue for everyone involved—from both developers and their clients.

Should companies go with higher-charging developers because they seem to be more professional or is a moderately priced developer going to give the same value in the site?

On the other side of the coin, should developers charge more so that they're taken seriously by the larger accounts, or charge less and risk looking like they offer less perceived value?

With the WPI, we saw a chance to put together an ongoing survey to try and quantify some of these issues, or at least bring them out in the open with some real data behind them.

And how have people responded to it?

Response has been mixed somewhat.

Almost everyone agrees that it needed to be done. Some of the developers felt it was right on, and some got a little defensive. Of course, the developers who charge higher rates have reasons for doing so, and those who charge less do as well.

Some of the developers voiced their concerns that some of the other participants didn't have as much experience putting together sites, and that they didn't know what they were getting into when they bid so low.

But overall I would say that response to the WPI has been tremendous. We've gotten lots of interest from developers who want to participate and from people who want reprints and so on. There's no question that the WPI has sparked everyone's interest. From all sides of the Web development process, people are watching this project and are quite curious to see just where it goes and how it develops.

M-14 OCTOBER 1996

NETMARKETING

Adding customer chat can be inexpensive

By Debra Aho Williamson and Matt Carmichael

For many marketers, making a Web site more interactive is as easy as adding a little conversation.

Already, a variety of tools exist to create formatted discussion boards. And real-time chat, a hallmark of the commercial online services, is about to explode on the Web as new software becomes more widely available.

NetMarketing asked developers and ad agencies what they would charge to add chat and discussion features to a site. Each developer received the same marketing scenario.

Median prices range from $2,150 to install shareware software on a small site to $5,000 for a password-protected board on a midsize site to $38,750 for Java-based real-time chat. *(See chart below for details.)*

NOT FOR EVERYONE

But chat and discussion boards aren't a good fit for everyone. Marketers must devote staff to monitor discussions, and must be prepared to respond if users are saying negative things about the company.

"That's definitely a two-edged sword and a danger," said Brock Stanton, interactive marketing executive with WestWayne, Atlanta.

What can a marketer accomplish by adding discussion boards or chat? Developers say communications can extend the product message. But they caution against making the brand the sole reason for the discussion.

DEBATING PLASTIC WRAP

Few Web users would be interested in debating the strengths of plastic wrap, for example, but they might be interested in chatting with a chef.

As with last month's Web Price Index. *(See chart at right)*, this survey showed wide variation in pricing. Developers bid anywhere from $8,000 to $500,000 to construct the Java chat.

"We are all still on a quest to define the value equation for new media," Mr. Stanton said. □

Next month

Following up on this topic, we'll compare the costs of adding chat and discussion to a site. Web developers will be asked to bid on creating a site that lets users participate in a monthly formatted chat. Watch the *Net Marketing* Web site—www.netb2b.com—for Web Price Index updates in the coming months.

NETMARKETING

Web Price Index

We asked Web developers and ad agencies in five key cities to tell us what they'd charge to build sites for three hypothetical marketers. Here's what they said.

The results (by median price):

	New York	Chicago	San Francisco	Dallas	Atlanta
Small site	$35,000	$77,375	$92,500	$10,325	$15,925
Medium site	$98,150	$216,125	$258,750	$81,750	$73,063
Large site	$302,550	$736,500	$1,037,500	$312,500	$596,073

The "marketers":

Small: ACME Sprockets

A marketer of widgets, sprockets, etc., for distribution to construction contractors. The company wants to be "on the Web" but still isn't really sure what that entails. It will need basic services like hosting, a virtual domain and some form of getting e-mail.

The site will feature tables of parts specs and corporate information. On the back end, ACME will need an easy way for its people to update documents without having to learn HTML and FTP. This company is not very wired in its own offices and is getting online largely to provide easy access to information for its customers and distributors.

ACME has logos of its own already, which it would like to incorporate into the site, and the company really likes those "animated picture thingies." Executives will need a lot of tutoring and hand-holding.

Services:
- Look and feel (design/site mapping) for about 20 pages
- Virtual server
- Publishing tools
- E-mail/fax software
- Training/tutoring
- Internet service (dial-up) provided by developer or contracted out

Medium: Investments-R-Us

A n investment brokerage firm with its own intranet. The company needs a server and domain, something small to inter-

clients. Investments-R-Us handles customers ranging from individuals to large corporations, so executives...

Services:
- Look and feel (design/site mapping) for about...
- Virtual s...
- Pub...

Web Price Index: Cha...

Web Price Index: Chat

What it costs to add discussion boards or real-time chat to a Web site.

The results (by median price)

	Median price	Low	High
Small site	$2,500	$200	$50,000
Medium site	$5,000	$500	$100,000
Large site	$45,000	$8,000	$500,000

The marketers' requirements:

Small: ACME Sprockets

ACME realizes there isn't a whole lot of reason to have chat or a discussion board on its site, but the company thinks it would be cool to give manufacturers a place to talk about widgets. In fact, ACME wants to be the place on the Web for the active discussion of widgets. The CEO's son found a site that has free scripts (http://www.worldwidemart.com/scripts). ACME wants its developer to download this Perl script, configure it and get it running.

Medium: Investments-R-Us

This company wants to use chat to allow its sales reps to communicate with each other. The idea of a public chat forum worries the company, so it needs to have this feature password protected. One threaded discussion at a time is enough.

Large: Blockmonster Entertainment

Blockmonster wants to keep pushing the envelope. The company wants to develop a Java-based chat system where people can start their own areas, have private areas, link to pictures with their posts—the works. Executives want a nice front end, to make it simple. They are willing to buy another server to host the chat.

Medium: Investments-R-Us

An investment brokerage firm with its own intranet. The company needs a server and domain and outside e-mail to interface with its internal mail.

The company has a lot of proprietary investment data it wants its clients to be able to access, but no one else. The data must be searchable and sortable.

The company also needs an "about us" section with information for its clients and prospective clients: Investments-R-Us handles customers ranging from individuals to large corporations, so executives want to use this site in sales pitches as an example of the excellent customer service that they provide.

It must look nice, be a tad flashy, but mostly be very, very functional and get users quickly and easily to the data they need. Those Java "stock ticker-tapes" make their eyes pop out.

Services:
- Look and feel (design/site mapping) for about 100 pages
- Virtual server
- Publishing tools
- Training/tutoring
- Internet service (dial-up) provided by developer or contracted out
- Custom programming of the stock ticker
- Search engine
- Password-protected directories
- Database services (minimal)

Large: Blockmonster Entertainment Corp.

A chain of record/video/software superstores. This company wants the works. Content tests and promotions. Shockwave games. A database of reviews (both professional and generated by visitors) that is searchable and can be used to create on-the-fly pages based on a user profile that site visitors fill out and that gets databased.

The audience consists of young music/entertainment fans who want to talk about the music they listen to, so they need a chat feature as well. Full-out ad campaign with a media buy on several major sites and engines.

The company wants to use frames for easier navigation. It's not sure whether it wants to sell products over the Internet, but it's willing to test the waters with some special orders, so the company needs secure transaction capability.

For other orders, the company wants a locator guide so people can enter a ZIP code and come up with a detailed map showing where they'll find the nearest branch.

Blockmonster is going to want all the stops pulled out, and as new technologies come out, it wants a fast response of well-thought-out applications. Developer will also host the servers necessary to run this type of operation.

Services:
- Server hosting and maintenance
- Publishing tools
- Training/tutoring
- Internet service (dial-up) provided by developer or contracted out
- Custom programming/development of Java applets, locator and Shockwave files
- Search engine
- Password-protected directories
- Database services (extensive)
- On-the-fly page generation
- Digitization and integration of sound/video
- Secure transaction capability
- Working with the company's agency to provide:
  - Look and feel (design/site mapping)
  - Plans for the media buy/ad banner design
  - Content for promotions
  - Integration of existing materials into the site

The agencies participating in this study:
New York: Agency.com, Poppe Tyson, Kirshenbaum Bond & Partners, i33 Communications Corp. **Chicago:** Streams Interactive, The Leap Partnership, Neoglyphics, McConaughy, Stein, Schmidt & Brown. **San Francisco:** Vivid Studios, Red Dot Interactive, U.S. WEB, J. Walter Thompson USA. **Dallas:** IBDG Interactive, Generation Z, Hays Internet Marketing, McMann & Tate. **Atlanta:** The Kilgannon Group, Action Net Communications, Pollak Levitt Chaiet, WestWayne.

Figure 5.2
The Web Price Index is a Monthly Survey of Web Development Pricing

In Summary

Building your budget is a detailed, step-by-step process. It is not difficult, but it is time-consuming, and you need to know your business and how much time it takes to accomplish certain tasks. Once you know the answers to these items, it's easy.

Legal Landmines

This chapter was written under the guidance and advice of Jerry Spiegel.

The desktop digital revolution is barely 20 years old, but the explosive growth of digital media, and especially the World Wide Web (WWW), has already created business opportunities, the variety and potential of which have rarely been seen before.

The seemingly endless chain of youthful millionaires, made rich by public stock offerings in businesses often just a few years old, has created a gold rush mentality among digital entrepreneurs. This time, however, the gold is not a tangible yellow metal dug from the earth. It is the intangible bits and bytes of digital media, containing the multimedia elements of text, images, and sound. These elements make up the multimedia programs stored on CD-ROM (or other physical storage medium) or accessible by pointing your browser to a site on the Web.

These intangible assets exist as the direct result of our legal system. They are known as *intellectual property rights*, property that is the product of minds and imaginations. These are the legal concepts of copyright, trademark, and patent, as well as their lesser-known siblings, trade secrets, rights of privacy and publicity, and moral rights (or *droit moral*).

In our digital world, atoms turn into bits, the tangible becomes intangible, and the real becomes virtual. The only way to evidence and control the products of digital machinery is through governmental regulation (such as copyright law) and consensual arrangements (such as written agreements between participants). This is not only applicable to the products themselves, but also to the means of distribution. Thus, the ability to control a market by controlling a key physical aspect of distribution (such as the street corner or the shelves in the local software outlet) is eroding. As more and more business moves into cyberspace, the ability to protect and manage intellectual property rights becomes increasingly important.

Perhaps one of the most intimidating aspects of establishing and running a new media development business is finding and working with competent legal counsel. The purpose of this chapter is to help you know what you need from your lawyer—in short, how to help you help your lawyer help you.

This chapter is not filled with legal citations and references. It has been written from a conceptual viewpoint to help you understand why you need a lawyer, how to select one, which issues your lawyer must help you with, and how you can get the most out of your lawyer. This chapter will also help you to understand some of the legal terminology associated with the creation, protection, exploitation, and management of intellectual property rights. These are serious matters. Your failure to consult with counsel on any of these issues can result in substantial costs or liability to you and your business. So, please use this material only in conjunction with your lawyer and not as a substitute for proper legal counsel.

Your First Contact with a Lawyer

If you're an entrepreneur, your first contact with your lawyer will be during the planning stages of your business.

- You should have a *business plan* before you start your business. Although a business plan is supposed to be a formal written document with detailed revenue and expense projections, a business plan can also be nothing more than a clear understanding of what you are trying to accomplish, what it will take to accomplish it, what the risks are, and last, but certainly not the least important, how you plan to exit your business when needed. Your lawyer can help you to understand many of the issues and risks of opening your business.

- Your lawyer should play a significant role in helping you to formulate your business plan. In conjunction with your accountant, your lawyer should advise you on:

    - The legal form for your business

    - Where the business should be established

    - Applicable regulation compliance

In addition, your lawyer should be responsible for creating the essential organizational agreements, such as a shareholders' agreement and appropriate form agreements you should implement in your business.

A lawyer who has experience representing clients in the business, or in related businesses, will have an advantage in knowing what is necessary and appropriate (and what is not). A good business lawyer knows that legal knowledge must be tempered with practical, on-the-job experience. An experienced lawyer knows how to avoid over-lawyering a deal, as well as how to manage legal issues efficiently, without unnecessarily long or overbearing agreements. Knowing what concerns each party to the deal will have can help you and you lawyer close deals quickly, with a minimum of hassle. A lawyer with experience in your business can also help you to avoid potential problems before they develop.

What Your Lawyer Should Do for You

Jerry Spiegel
Attorney at Law
Partner, Head of the New Media Group
Frankfurt, Garbus, Klein & Selz, P.C.
New York, NY
jbspiegel@aol.com

Jerry Spiegel graduated from the New York University School of Law in 1973. He practiced corporate law for a number of years in Manhattan where he developed a general practice structuring leasing agreements for large computer systems such as IBM. In 1985, long before the onslaught of the Web, he landed his first on-line client, Baseline, an electronic publisher that built large databases comprised of credit information on film and television.

"Say you are making a movie and you need a lighting technician," Spiegel explains, "And someone says, '"Who's the guy who did the lighting on *Bladerunner*? That was fantastic.' They check Baseline." He notes that, after 10 years, Baseline has become a verb (to "Baseline" someone) and remains a key Hollywood resource.

At first, Baseline's delivery mechanism was based on the French Minitel service, which had become very popular in France in the mid-1980s.

"The system hosted information that providers wanted to make available to Minitel subscribers, so they came to the U.S. and set up offices," he explains. As a result of his experience with Baseline, Spiegel was retained to represent some of these firms in setting up their business. One customer was a computer service to *Penthouse* magazine called Pet-Line, which offered users the capability to chat and download pictures on a BBS.

"We found out early that sex chat was the killer interactive application," he jokes. "The product was a huge success."

In 1991, Spiegel negotiated license agreements for the Microsoft movie guide, which later became the very popular product *Cinemania*. After that negotiation, he was beginning to sense that a new media business was emerging. He convinced Frankfurt, Garbus, Klein & Selz that the business was real. After some investigation with clients, the New Media Group was launched in 1981.

"It was interesting," he says. "I literally had people coming by my office and laughing at me that there was no business in the on-line world. They were convinced I was weird. But I couldn't help it. This stuff was so fascinating"—and profitable.

Spiegel's firm, which has always had a media industry focus, started analyzing ways it could help its clients understand the convergence of various media properties—print, film, television, music, new media, and the Internet. What followed were CD-ROM licensing deals for the NBA, the NHL, Scholastic, and others. The firm also moved into the interactive television arena, representing Time-Warner on its full-service, interactive television network in Orlando, Florida.

As the on-line business started to take off, the firm represented its clients interests on America Online, CompuServe, Prodigy, the Microsoft Network, and the Web.

As a business attorney, Spiegel believes his most important role is in helping his clients avoid problems, having clear contracts, and helping his clients anticipate potential problems before they happen.

So what are the potential legal landmines?

I would say they are the basics: setting up your business, establishing thorough contracts, the exact terms of the relationships in the business, creating the proper incentive agreements, and raising capital.

What do you find are the biggest potential mistakes a new company is likely to make?

The most flagrant mistake is not putting in writing the terms and agreements with respect to work being done at a company. The first thing that I ask new clients is, "Do you have proper contracts with your staff members and employees?" That needs to be addressed first.

I also find that people fail to check the name of their business before they start doing business under that name. Invariably they run into trademark problems and, in terms of the Internet, problems in registering domain names.

There are also special cases in which I have software clients performing custom software development that don't have the proper agreements with their customers.

As an attorney, then, you function as both a business and legal advisor?

Right. My job is to be an effective advocate for my clients and properly represent them in their business negotiations. Therefore, I need to understand their business.

In what way?

First, the industry they are in. Understanding the industry my clients are in is incredibly important. It's key to understanding where the problems are likely to be, what the solutions are, and where the legal landmines might be.

It's also important to understand a client's own interest in the business. Who are they? What are their strengths? What do they want to accomplish? What is important to them? In order to function as a business and legal advisor, I need to know these things on a personal level as well as a business level. It's part of helping clients accomplish their goals.

How do you ensure that happens?

I encourage my clients to keep in touch with me, to keep me advised on what they are doing, and to keep me in the loop.

At what point does cost enter into the relationship?

Most lawyers bill on an hourly basis. In almost all

cases I prepare an estimate regarding my fees and how much I anticipate it will cost the client. Sometimes I agree to put a cap on my fees so that the client can manage that expense as a fixed cost. It all depends. Over the years, I have developed a way of working with my clients that they are comfortable with—a routine. I try to call every one of my clients at least once a month just to check in and see how they are doing. There is no charge for that sort of relationship building.

This brings up the point of the lawyer's bill. A client should never regard a lawyer's bill as unquestionable. The bill should be clear and detailed in documenting what work was done, by whom for how long, and how much. I encourage my clients to question what's on their bill. If the communication process is clear and open, everything should be straightforward.

Any final advice?

Above all else, you have to be comfortable with your attorney. In the course of doing business, you might have to tell your attorney awkward and confidential information. You want to talk about those things with someone you are comfortable with.

In the case of my smaller, start-up clients, they might not have a partner. An attorney with a keen business sense can offer valuable advice that, for the price of a $150 phone call, can save or make them thousands of dollars.

Aww—It's More Paperwork!

Perhaps you're one of those who think that "paper work" is just "make work." "Why should I worry about the details when I'm struggling just to manage my business to make a profit?" Well, the truth is, as you will learn later in this chapter, any business built on intellectual property rights is only as strong and as valuable as its written agreements. And without the right agreements in place, all the hard work of building your business can be for naught.

You don't need to spend a lot of money on legal assistance. A competent, experienced lawyer should be able to quickly generate the necessary agreements based on forms developed and used in representing other similar businesses. In no other business endeavor is it more true that an ounce of prevention is worth a pound of cure. It is always cheaper to have the right agreements done at the start (and you sleep a lot better, too). Experienced legal counsel can provide a solid foundation of form agreements. These agreements should be reasonable in their terms to minimize the necessity of negotiating each transaction but should reflect the company's desired strategic approach to the management and control of intellectual property rights. To be effective, counsel must be thoroughly familiar with the client's business and the issues that confront and challenge that business, both on a daily basis and over the long term.

Counsel also should be responsible for maintaining the completeness and accuracy of your executed contract files. The importance of this function may not become obvious until you seek financing or engage in a sale or business reorganization, but when you do, you'll be glad you followed this advice. The thoroughness and accuracy of these files will enhance the credibility (and value) of your company in the eyes of third parties contemplating any such transactions with you.

Likewise, the terms of your company's agreements will have a significant effect on the future success and value of your company. You should establish, at the outset, guidelines for the operation of your business. In addition to identifying the type of content in which you want to specialize or concentrate, these guidelines should reflect the terms on which you desire to publish products. The terms should be flexible enough to accommodate the various circumstances you might not expect to encounter.

Legal counsel can play an essential role in the running and building of a successful new media business. But, remember, your lawyer can't—and shouldn't—manage your business. That's your job.

Setting Up Your Business from the Start

Having decided to start your business, you will be confronted with many decisions. One of the first is the form your business should take, which forms are dictated by state and local regulation and by federal tax law. You should consult with your lawyer as to the most appropriate form for you. Each type of business organization has its own distinct advantages and disadvantages. There are four basic types of business organization: sole proprietorships, partnerships, corporations, and limited liability companies.

Sole Proprietorship

Sole proprietorship is the simplest form of legal entity recognized under common law. Common law is based on precedent going back to the English judicial system. It is distinguished from laws enacted by legislative bodies, such as Congress or state legislatures. Common law is the alter ego of the individual who elects to do business under an assumed (or fictitious) name (thus, the *d/b/a* notation which you frequently see). The individual assumes all liabilities of the business, and all business income is reported on the individual's personal income tax return. Because a sole proprietorship consists of an individual, no organizational agreement is necessary—just a *Fictitious Name Certificate*, which is usually filed in the county clerk's office.

Partnerships and Limited Partnerships

A *partnership* is the multiparty counterpart of a sole proprietorship, established under common law and recognized and governed by state partnership law. Sometimes referred to as a *general partnership,* it exists when two or more individuals (or corporations or other legal entities) decide to do business together as partners under an assumed name. Each partner is fully liable for the unpaid obligations of the partnership. Partnership income is included on each partner's personal income tax return. A written agreement is essential to address issues of relative ownership, financial obligations, responsibilities and duties, disagreement, disability and death, in addition to a certificate of partners usually filed with the county clerk's office.

Limited partnerships are creatures of state statute. Currently, 49 states and the District of Columbia have adopted the Uniform Limited Partnership Act (ULPA) in some form or another. A limited partnership consists of one or more general partners together with one or more limited partners. The general partners are liable for all unpaid obligations of the limited partnership. The limited partners usually agree to contribute a specified amount of capital to the limited partnership and have no further liability. Income or loss from the limited partnership is reported to each of the partners and included on their respective personal income tax returns, just like a general partnership. This makes limited partnerships a popular form for raising investment capital.

The ULPA sets forth very specific requirements for the creation of a limited partnership, and the failure to comply with those requirements will result in the entity being deemed a general partnership, subjecting the limited partners to liability for the partnership's unpaid obligations. An agreement of limited partnership spelling out the relative rights and obligations of the parties is necessary. A certificate of limited partnership also must be filed. In New York, an advertisement also must run for a minimum number of weeks in a specified periodical, resulting in substantial additional costs.

Corporations

Corporations are the basic building blocks of our capitalist, free market economic system, and they are the primary vehicle for the raising of investment capital. As creatures of state law, they are formed upon the filing of a certificate of incorporation with the appropriate state office (typically the state's secretary of state). Corporations are legal entities existing independently of their constituent owners, the shareholders, who have no liability for the unpaid obligations of the corporation. Corporations have a centralized management structure under which the shareholders elect a board of directors charged with the overall responsibility of running the business. The board of directors, in turn, elects officers who run the day-to-day operations of the corporation. Because of the formal management and financial structure, as well as the insulation from liability afforded to shareholders, corporations are an ideal vehicle for raising investment capital.

Federal income tax law recognizes two types of corporations: *C corporations*, which pay tax at corporate rates and are otherwise treated as independent tax entities; and *S corporations*, which are treated as partnerships for federal income tax purposes.

S corporation status must be elected by the corporation within 75 days of incorporation or at the beginning of any tax year. S corporations are popular because they combine corporate insulation from liability with the avoidance of double taxation and simplicity of organization. Historically, federal tax law has limited the number of shareholders to 35 individuals, none of whom may be a non-resident alien, and otherwise restricted the way that S corporations can operate. Commencing on January 1, 1997, however, IRS regulations will be eased, increasing the number of permitted shareholders to 75, easing the restrictions on who can be a shareholder, and permitting S corporations to own subsidiaries.

Limited Liability Companies

Limited liability companies are a modern development, invented to bridge the gap between partnerships and corporations in a more flexible way than limited partnerships. They were first recognized by Wyoming in 1977, but have since been adopted by the District of Columbia and all but two states, Hawaii and Vermont.

A limited liability company is defined as an unincorporated association of two or more persons formed under a limited liability law as adopted in one of the foregoing jurisdictions. (There are a few states, such as Texas, that permit a limited liability company to be formed with just a single person, but such an organization would not be treated as a partnership for federal income tax purposes.) The growth of limited liability companies was a result of the IRS approving a of partnership classification in 1988 for a Wyoming limited liability company for federal income tax purposes.

Instead of shareholders, a limited liability company has members who agree to contribute investment capital in exchange for membership interests. The members sign an operating agreement that spells out the manner in which the limited liability company will be operated and the relative rights and preferences of the members. Typically, the members elect a board of managers who are responsible for the management of the business like the directors of a corporation. The managers then elect officers who operate the business. But the management structure also can be altered to resemble a partnership. The flexibility afforded by the limited liability company is unique, but that flexibility comes at a cost. There is not only the expense of drafting an operating agreement, but the cost of publishing a legal notice, which in the New York City area can cost upwards of $2,000.

Where you do business will be the most important factor in determining under which laws you organize your business. But it's not the only or last factor, which can include having employees, assets, or in our digital world, perhaps a Web site on a remote server.

Thus, if you maintain just one place of business in New York City, the laws of the state of New York will apply. And, because your business will have to comply with those laws, including the tax laws, organizing as a New York corporation or limited liability company would be most efficient. In any event, to do business you must qualify in each state in which you establish an office or are otherwise deemed to be doing business. Of course, you should discuss these options with your lawyer before deciding how to proceed.

Your primary concerns should be limiting your liability for unpaid obligations of the business and controlling the cost of organizing the business. But, believe it or not, this is also the moment at which you need to think about how you're going to exit the business if it is unsuccessful. It may seem cheapest and simplest to set the business up as a C corporation. But such a decision could be very costly down the road if you subsequently sell the assets of the business at a substantial gain because you may be faced with paying tax first at the corporate level on the entire gain, and then once again on your personal income tax return. Even a stock sale will cost you because the buyer will recognize the gain inherent in the assets and adjust the purchase price down to reflect the tax that will be payable upon their sale. One way to avoid this problem is to establish your business as a pass-through tax entity such as an S corporation or a limited liability company. It is important that you, your accountant, and your attorney agree on an appropriate structure with you.

Your choice of entity will also be affected by your need for investment capital. In such an event you will want to be sensitive to the desires of your potential investors. The best way to figure this out is to ask them or to ask the intermediary who is helping you raise the money.

The Next Step

After you have decided on the form your business will take, you should address the organizational documents needed. If you are starting the business with others, you will need an agreement to spell out the relative rights and duties of the parties. Either a partnership agreement, a shareholders agreement or, in the case of a limited liability company, an operating agreement. You should consult with your attorney on the appropriate form, the issues involved, and your own unique circumstances. The issues typically raised are:

Investment	How much and from where?
Duties and obligations	Who does what?
Compensation	How much does each founder receive?
Ownership share	How much does each founder own?
Restrictions on transfer	Rights of first refusal/estate planning?
Control and governance	How are decisions made and who controls them?
Disability	What happens in the event of physical or mental disability?
Disagreement	What happens if the owners are unable to agree?
Death	What happens if one of the owners dies?

After these issues have been resolved, attention should be directed to the creation of appropriate agreements needed for the business, such as software development agreements for customers and work-made-for-hire agreements for employees and independent contractors. An experienced lawyer will know just what you need and will have forms that can be customized for your business without a major investment.

There are two major concerns that should be addressed at this point, both of which relate to your company's ownership and protection of its intellectual property rights.

The Protection of Trade Secrets

First is protection of all proprietary information, or *trade secrets*, that your company develops in the course of its business. Trade secrets consist of that knowledge, information, and know-how that has been developed in the course of your business and is not publicly or generally known. A classic example of a trade secret is the formula for Coca-Cola syrup.

Some companies maintain the source code to their software as a trade secret, refusing to file even a portion of the source code with the Library of Congress, as would be necessary in order to bring an action for copyright infringement.

Contrary to popular belief, however, trade secrets are neither copyrighted nor patented. Historically, protection for trade secrets has been based upon the common law theory of theft or misappropriation. Enforcement has been the province of state courts and legislatures. Congress, however, has recently passed a bill criminalizing the "theft of trade secrets," which would certainly make anyone contemplating this kind of thievery to think again.

What actually constitutes trade secrets can vary remarkably from industry to industry. Many industries maintain that certain types of information, such as a customer list, constitute trade secrets, whereas courts have been hesitant to extend the umbrella to cover anything but the most clearly proprietary information and know-how. Thus, a customer list may not be protectible as a trade secret, which is all the more reason to carefully and jealously guard it. Once in the hands of the wrong person, you've lost all control of it.

To protect your trade secrets, you must demonstrate to the world (and ultimately the court) that you regard them as valuable to your business and that they are, indeed, secret. To do this, you must exercise a combination of continuous and diligent efforts to maintain their secrecy and requiring written non-disclosure or confidentiality agreements from all persons with access to them. Your failure to diligently require such agreements from each person with access to them can be used against you if you ever have to sue. That is why requiring a written non-disclosure agreement from each and every employee is so important. That first employee who doesn't sign the agreement may result in the loss of protection for your trade secrets.

Contracts

The second major intellectual property rights issue that needs to be addressed is ensuring that your company has and maintains all rights with respect to copyrightable and patentable material created by your staff in the course of your business, including both employees and consultants or subcontractors. You should ask your lawyer to provide you with forms of employee and consultant *work-made-for-hire* agreements. These agreements will clearly establish that your company owns all copyrighted material created by your employees, consultants, or subcontractors in the course of their employment or engagement.

In addition, where appropriate, it should also provide that your company owns all inventions made by your staff in the course of their work. When you engage a consultant or subcontractor it is especially important to have a clear written understanding regarding the ownership of the resulting work product before any work is done because your failure to do so will likely result in the consultant's or subcontractor's ownership of the work product and serious problems or additional costs for you.

The phrase *work-made-for-hire* describes:

- A work prepared by an employee within the scope of his or her employment.

- A work prepared in specific categories only (such as contributions to an audio/visual work) or a work prepared by an independent contractor that was ordered specially or commissioned, provided the parties have agreed in writing that the work will be the property of the company. Not all countries have a work-made-for-hire concept in their copyright laws, so you must check with your lawyer before engaging the services of any non-resident artist or author.

As a developer of new media, you will probably render most of your services as work-made-for-hire for your clients. Typically, companies developing Web sites want to own the copyright in the site. Thus, it is especially important to have appropriate agreements with each member of your staff to avoid potential disputes.

Software patents have become an important factor in the development and growth of digital media. With all of the ground-breaking work being done in new media, the Internet, and the Web, you never know when the work you are doing will lead you to develop software that qualifies for patent protection.

You can't wait until then to take care of the rights issues because by that time, members of your staff may realize the value of their invention and decide, whether they have the right or not, to keep it for themselves.

Nothing solves the problem of a reluctant employee or consultant more quickly than a written agreement clearly spelling out who owns the rights to the invention. On the other hand, you may want to motivate your staff for extraordinary creativity by agreeing to share the rewards from their inventions in the form of a royalty.

Intellectual Property Rights

Although the topic of intellectual property rights is not exclusively the province of copyright, copyright is clearly of fundamental importance, and it is the subject most immediately associated with intellectual property rights in most people's minds. The differences between copyright and the other forms of intellectual property rights are subtle, but significant. The purpose of this section is to clearly establish the elements of each type of intellectual property right, the differences between each of them, the respective schemes of legal protection, and how it all fits into your business.

Copyright

The law of copyright has a rich history that is intertwined with some of the most significant historical events of our era—events such as the invention of the VCR and the assassination of JFK (more on that later in this chapter).

A Brief History of Copyright Law

Copyright has been with us for almost 300 years, having been first recognized in England by the adoption of the Statute of Anne in 1710, which granted to authors and their heirs the exclusive right to copy the author's work for a 14-year period. Although copyright law today speaks in terms of protection of the artist or author, the genesis of copyright was to protect the established book publishers and their monopoly over the publishing industry in 18th century England.

In 1787, the U.S. Constitution carried over the English tradition by empowering Congress to adopt laws "To promote the Progress of Science and useful Arts, by securing for limited Times to Authors and Inventors the exclusive Right to their respective Writings and Discoveries." The key word in that phrase is, of course, promote. The concept is that the government wants to encourage the artist and inventor to be productive, and to such end may grant artists and inventors the exclusive rights to exploit their work, for at least some period of time. In consideration of the grant of such exclusive rights, the public has the right to freely exploit such properties thereafter. This led to the first copyright law to be adopted by Congress in 1790.

In 1909, Congress adopted a comprehensive revision of the copyright laws, which remained the basic law until January 1, 1978, the effective date of the Copyright Revision Act of 1976. Under the 1909 Act, copyright lasted from the date of publication (or the date of registration, in the case of unpublished works) for a period of 28 years and could be renewed for an additional 28 years.

The 1976 Act provided that all works fixed in a tangible medium of expression are entitled to federal statutory copyright protection from the moment they are so fixed, regardless of whether they are published or disseminated. In addition, the 1976 Act extended copyright protection to many new types of expression, including recordings, cable and educational television programs, motion picture soundtracks, and computer programs. It also extended the term of copyright protection for works published in the United States prior to January 1, 1978 to 75 years from first publication.

The 1976 Act eliminated the registration requirement as a condition of copyright protection but continued the notice requirement, with provisions for curing the failure to provide notice under certain circumstances. Under the 1976 Act, protection for works created on or after January 1, 1978 begins upon creation of the work and continues for the life of the author plus 50 years. (Actually, the copyright expires on December 31st of the calendar year in which the copyright would otherwise expire. Where the author is an anymous or pseudonymous author, such as a corporation, the copyright term runs for 75 years from the year of first publication, or 100 years from the year of creation, whichever expires first.)

Although registration is no longer a condition of copyright protection, registration is required prior to the commencement of an infringement action with respect to works created by a United States author. Further, registration is encouraged by permitting recovery of attorney's fees and statutory (in lieu of actual) damages for infringement occurring after registration.

On March 1, 1989, the United States became a member of the Berne Convention, the international treaty governing copyright law. One of the requirements imposed by the treaty on its signatories is to conform to certain common legal principles. One of the most important of these is the prohibition of any impediments to copyright protection for authors and artists. In order to conform the U.S. copyright law with the Berne requirements, the notice requirement became optional, rather than mandatory. While the copyright law requires the deposit of copies of copyrighted works with the Library of Congress, such deposit is not a condition to copyright protection. Thus today, the author of a work enjoys copyright protection from the moment such work is fixed in a tangible medium. One of the next challenges for U.S. copyright law will be recognition of the moral rights of artists and authors to prevent the esthetic corruption or destruction of their works. Moral rights has a long history in Europe, particularly in France, but is almost unknown in the United States—more on this later in the chapter.

What is Copyright?

Copyright is the ownership of artistic expression in the form of writing, images, sound, three-dimensional objects, or a computer program— essentially, any medium cognizable by human senses either directly or through the use of mechanical devices, such as phonographs, televisions, or computers.

A few years ago, at the dawn of the multimedia era, rumors began to circulate that copyright was dead, that digital technology would render copyright laws unenforceable, and that the same digital technology would obviate the need for copyright by enabling the evolution of a new paradigm for the encouragement of creative effort. Well, that prediction, as with so many of the digital era, has not yet come to pass, and it doesn't look like it will be any time soon. But there is no denying that digital technology has made copyright infringement an everyday occurrence. In fact, more people are aware of what copyright is today than ever before. So, until another scheme comes along, copyright is what you've got to be familiar with to protect your assets and avoid problems with other people's assets. One of the first lessons you've just learned is that copyright is a double-edged sword for those in the business of creating intellectual property rights. The more restrictive the law, the better protected your intellectual property rights may be, but the more likely you will infringe on other people's intellectual property rights—and the less restrictive, the less well protected, and so on.

It is important to remember that copyright protects only the expression, not ideas, concepts, or facts incorporated therein.

Facts may be protected under theories of commercial misappropriation and unfair trade practice as was the case with respect to the reporting of the play-by-play of an NBA basketball game. In *National Basketball Association v. Sports Team Analysis and Tracking Systems, Inc.*, a federal court granted the NBA's request for a preliminary injunction, holding that the NBA has a property interest in the play-by-play information and that the reporting of that information on a concurrent basis by the defendant through its "SportsTrax" service amounted to commercial misappropriation of the NBA's property: "… the excitement of an NBA game in progress." The difficulty of dealing with the new technology is evidenced by the fact that the court ignored section 301 of the Copyright Act, which was enacted specifically to overrule the misappropriation theory as being superseded by copyright law. The Supreme Court will likely have a final say on this matter.

Under current law, copyright vests in the author at the time the work is created and fixed in a tangible medium. The author is the person who actually creates the work, with two exceptions:

- A work created by an employee within the scope of employment, in which case the employer is deemed the author.

- A work created as a work-made-for-hire pursuant to a written agreement if it falls into one of nine specific categories: contribution to a collective work; part of a motion picture or other audio/visual work; translation; supplementary work; compilation; atlas; instructional text; test; or, answer material, in which case the party that hired the creator is deemed the author for copyright purposes.

Copyright is not just a single right. It is really a bundle of rights that are divisible and can be dealt with separately. Thus, copyright law grants to the author of a work the exclusive right to:

- Reproduce the work

- Prepare derivative works

- Distribute copies of the work

- Perform the work publicly

- Display the work publicly

- Authorize others to do any of the above

In addition, the author has the exclusive right to control the first publication of the work, publication being defined as the distribution of copies by sale or other transfer of ownership.

If two or more persons create a single copyrightable work, they are deemed to be joint copyright holders, and either one has the right (in the absence of an agreement to the contrary) to exploit that work. This is subject only to an obligation to account to the other joint copyright holders for revenue derived from such work. In such cases, a collaboration agreement is needed to control the management and exploitation of the joint work.

The term of copyright protection has varied dramatically over the years. Today, copyright protection runs for the life of the author plus 50 years, or in the case of an anonymous or pseudonymous author, such as a corporation, 75 years from publication, but not more than 100 years from creation.

In the case of an author who is an identifiable natural person (and not anonymous or pseudonymous), copyright is automatically renewed after 28 years; but, if a voluntary renewal registration is filed timely, then all derivative uses pursuant to pre-existing licenses will terminate unless the author's successors approve such use.

Derivative works includes translations, dramatizations, fictionalizations, motion picture versions, condensations, abridgements, and other forms in which a work may be, "recast, transformed, or adapted." It also includes works consisting of editorial revisions, annotations, elaborations, or other modifications to an original work.

A derivative work need not be in the same medium as the original. Indeed, some of the most noteworthy examples of derivative works include theatrical and made for television motion pictures base on the popular works of novelists Herman Wouk, Stephen King, and Danielle Steele. Because a derivative work involves additional creative work, it is frequently copyrightable independently of the original work.

Compilations are collections of other materials, whether copyrighted (such as an anthology of poems), in the public domain (such as a collection of Shakespeare's plays), or just non-protectable facts (such as a white pages telephone directory). A compilation is entitled to copyright protection as a separate work, provided it meets the minimal requirement of originality in its "selection, coordination, and arrangement." What is protected by a *compilation copyright* is the totality of the work, rather than its individual elements and regardless of whether or not such elements are entitled to copyright protection.

Computer Software: Intersection of Intellectual Property Rights

Computer software is a unique type of intellectual property right, because it qualifies for protection under both copyright and patent law.

Copyright protection for computer software came in 1978. But the nature of computer software (instructions to the microprocessor to perform certain functions, including creation of the display or interface as a visual image) is so different from a book or poem, that the Supreme Court, in 1982, accepted the notion that software, when combined with hardware, also can constitute an *invention* that can be protected under patent law.

Because copyright protects the expression, not the underlying facts or ideas, what is being "expressed" and therefore entitled to copyright protection? Well, it is clearly settled that the lines of text comprising the source code, or the higher level computer language used to compile the machine or object code, consisting of the "0s" and "1s" of binary instructions on which our computers are based, qualify for copyright protection as a literary work. So does the machine or object code. Indeed, some photo archives have taken the position that digitized versions of public domain images are separately copyrightable. Now if the bits and bytes comprising the digital image are copyrightable, then the image displayed on a computer screen would also be copyrightable as a derivative work. Is this logical or appropriate? This issue, amongst many, remains unresolved. (Don't we feel special being at the forefront of the industry?)

Computer Interfaces

What about computer interfaces, such as a command structures or graphical user interfaces (GUIs or *gooey*)? Always eager to improve the protection of their intellectual property rights, software publishers have pushed the envelope to extend copyright protection beyond the computer code itself. One result of these efforts was the recognition a number of years ago that the interface itself was entitled to protection. Before the popularity of GUIs, the protection was sought in the command structure (the number and combination of keys necessary to evoke each function) almost as a musical composition with the keyboard. Then with the almost universal adoption of windows and icons as the basis for evoking the computer's functions, the images and *look and feel* of the computer screens became the focal point for the extension of copyright protection.

In a series of lawsuits over the past 10 years, the degree of copyright protection available for interfaces has been explored in some detail. In the case of *Lotus v. Borland*, it was finally determined that the command structure of Lotus' spreadsheet program was not protected and could be copied in Borland's competing spreadsheet program in order to make it easier to convert users. In *Apple v. Microsoft*, Apple could not prevent Microsoft from using a trash can icon to evoke the function of erasing a computer file as long as the particular image used by Microsoft was different from that used by Apple. Thus, the degree of copyright protection afforded to interfaces today is relatively thin, requiring a high degree of similarity before an infringement can be found. You cannot own the metaphor itself. Thus, use of an image of a supermarket aisle for an online shopping service, or of the turning pages of a book for a work of interactive fiction, is not protectible, although the particular image used will most likely be protected.

Although the general look and feel may not be protectible, there is reason to believe that your particular expression of that look and feel should be. This theory is based on the success that some restaurant chains have had in protecting their particular formats against competitors who have attempted to copy their entire mode of operation, including the proprietary design of their restaurants.

At the very least, the use of distinctive designs and the generous deployment of registered trademarks will make it harder to mimic your work.

Clearing Rights: The Lore of Copyright

The law and lore that surround each type of media have evolved into varied and unusual concepts and principles. A basic understanding of how these work is essential for anyone dealing with rights issues or having to license content.

The most important word to remember when you're licensing rights is *indemnification*, which means the obligation of one party to reimburse another party for costs or damages incurred as a result of the breach of a representation or warranty. Make sure that each party from whom you have secured any rights has agreed to indemnify you if anyone makes a claim arising from the use of those rights. And even more important, make sure they will be able to indemnify you if the need arises. It makes no sense to get an indemnity from a company that may not be around six months hence.

Here is a brief description of how each industry has structured the owner-ship, use, protection, and licensing of its particular type of intellectual prop-erty rights.

Literary Property

Literary works include works of fiction and non-fiction, such as books, magazine and newspaper articles, and essentially all written or printed works. The reproduction in whole or the excerpting of any portion of a copy-righted literary work requires written permission from the copyright holder. So does the creation of a derivative work based in any substantial part on the copyrighted work, such as a screenplay based on a novel.

Copyright ownership of a book generally resides with the author, usually sub-ject to an agreement with a *publisher*, that often runs for the life of the copy-right in the work. Newspaper and magazine articles can be owned (or controlled) by the author or the *publisher*, and conducting a copyright search may very well be impossible. Even though a third party, such as a publisher, may control the rights to a work in book or periodical format, the author may have retained some or all of the other rights to the works, either because the agreement with the publisher did not contemplate such uses, or because the author negotiated to retain such rights. Sometimes the author has a right to require the publisher to revert certain rights to the work if the publisher has failed to exercise them within some period of time from publication.

A copyright search can resolve questions as to ownership, but probably not with respect to the terms of any publishing agreement. You may need to rely on the author's representation that your rights don't violate the pub-lishing agreement. Ask the author first, of course, and if the author refuses, you may wish to rethink your interest. But you also might want to contact the publisher and ask before you sign an agreement. Of course, if you've started with the publisher, you will probably have to rely on their repre-sentations as to their rights. If they are reputable (and financially solvent), that should be no problem.

Musical Compositions and Sound Recordings

There is an arcane and confusing tangle of rights surrounding the music industry. Rights exist in the *musical composition* (which is the written sequence of musical notes), any *arrangements* thereof, *recorded perfor-mances* and *live performances* thereof. Licenses for the use of each of these rights will vary depending upon the type of use, such as the right to incorporate a musical performance into an audio/visual work, such as a theatrical motion picture or a multimedia CD-ROM.

Copyright in *musical compositions* is owned by the *music publisher*, typically a corporation formed by the *composer*. Copyright in the sound recording of a *musical performance* is typically owned by the recording label that maintains the master recordings.

Mechanical licenses are required to manufacture and distribute physical objects (such as CD-ROMs) incorporating a musical composition. They are usually obtained from music industry's well-known Harry Fox Agency.

Synchronization licenses are required to synchronize a musical composition with visual images, such as a motion picture. They are obtained from the *music publisher*.

Public performance licenses are required to perform the *musical composition* publicly. They are obtained from the *music publisher*, and they may be necessary for use of music on an on-line area. These licenses are typically administered by performing rights societies (ASCAP or BMI). It was only recently that the copyright law was amended to grant to the performer a public performance right in their recordings.

Master recording licenses are required to reproduce and distribute the sound recording of a particular *musical performance*. They are obtained from the record company or the owner of the *master recording*.

Of course, figuring out which permissions you need requires a mastery of these intersecting rights—not a job for the faint of heart. A Web site, for example, that incorporates an existing recording may require a mechanical license, a synchronization (or synch) license, a master recording license, and a public performance license. Better leave this one to the experts.

Photography and Graphic Artists

Photographs and visual images are given a high degree of copyright protection. Although the idea behind each picture may not be protectible, commissioning a work to mimic another specific work could result in a claim of infringement.

Of course, the use of a copyrighted photograph or graphic image requires permission from the copyright owner. Because photographers frequently work freelance, they usually retain copyright ownership of their photographs. Frequently a *photographer* will be represented by an agent or a *stock photo house*. It is important to obtain appropriate indemnifications from a reputable *stock photo house*.

When using a photograph for commercial or non-editorial purposes, releases must also be secured from identifiable persons and the owners of trademarks that are identifiable in the photograph. A reputable stock photo house will know the release status of each of its photos.

Graphic artists are often represented by syndication houses or agents. Appropriate permissions should be obtained.

Motion Picture Clips

The use of an excerpt from a motion picture requires permission, typically a *clip license*. You can see clips from current movies on the Web or on commercial on-line services. Such clips are secured from interactive press kits distributed by studios to promote the film. The use of these clips by on-line publishers is often based on an implied license. That is, that the submission by the studio of its interactive press kit to the on-line publisher is an implicit license to put the clips contained in the interactive press kit on-line. An implied license, if one exists at all, is subject to revocation at any time by the studio.

By their nature, movies and videos are inherently collaborative, involving at least one writer, one director, actors, camerapersons, technicians, stunt doubles, and so on. The use of clips may require additional clearances and payments for music rights (if the clip contains music) or for residuals (to unions or guilds, such as The Screen Actors Guild) if it contains the voice or image of a member. This makes the process of clearing rights quite complex and expensive, and best left to experienced clearance agents.

Appropriate clips sometimes can be obtained from a stock film house or library. Be sure to deal only with reputable companies that can stand behind their clips and who are willing to give you an appropriate indemnity.

News Footage

The use of copyrighted news footage for any purpose requires permission from the copyright owner. Normally, the copyright holder is the news division of the station or network, but sometimes an amateur takes the footage. Footage of the assassination of JFK, for example, which was shot on a home movie camera by Mr. Zapruder, is currently licensed by a company that acquired the copyright to the footage.

Many news organizations have made arrangements for the licensing of their footage either through an agent or an affiliate. Copyright could also be in the hands of a freelancer. Releases must be secured from identifiable persons and trademark owners in the footage. Because of the inherently collaborative nature of such endeavors, there are frequently unresolvable rights questions with respect to older footage.

Databases

Many computerized databases are compilations of statistics or other facts. The Supreme Court has ruled that such compilations are protected by compilation copyright depending upon whether there was at least a minimum of creativity, in terms of selecting and organizing the subject facts, involved in the creation of the database.

But, as the Supreme Court indicated in *Feist Publications v. Rural Telephone Service Co.*, it is hard to find any creativity in a database of facts, which by its very nature is supposed to be exhaustively complete and alphabetically organized. It may be even more difficult to meet the minimum requirements of Feist when you consider that a computer database, in fact, has no organization, but consists of bytes of data that are organized only when searched by a database user.

Because databases are subject to copyright protection, permission may be necessary to use them, but even if the database qualifies for compilation copyright protection, facts, or other unprotected content are not protected. Anyone with access can copy facts from the database. The wholesale copying, however, of an entire or substantial portion of a database may subject the copier to a claim of copyright infringement, based on the compilation copyright.

Many database owners have resorted to contractual restrictions (which are in the nature of state trade secret law) whereby access to the *database* is conditioned on the user's written agreement to use the database only for limited specified purposes and not to copy or otherwise use the database or any portion thereof. Frequently, databases are protected by shrink wrap licenses (either on CD-ROM or on-line), which are presumptively enforceable. If a database is protected by compilation copyright, a license is required to copy and republish it.

To License or Not to License: When Can I Use Copyrighted Material Without Permission?

This is really a trick question. There are *no* circumstances in which you have the right to use anyone else's copyrighted material without their permission. But when considering the use of existing material, there are two circumstances in which you may use that content without permission: First, you may use the content if it is not protected by copyright (such material is considered to be *in the public domain*). Second, you may use the content if it falls into the category of those limited cases permitted under the First Amendment, which guarantees freedom of expression, and embodied in the doctrine of *fair use*.

The complexities of rights clearance has resulted in the development of what are known as rights clearance agents. These individuals specialize in clearing rights to using copyrighted material and frequently have extensive contacts in the relevant industries. You would be well advised to consider using one of these services if you have any kind of sophisticated rights clearance issues. Again, be cautious when using this information and do so only in conjunction with your lawyer. A mistake in this area could subject you to substantial damages and attorney's fees.

Public Domain

Works considered to be in the public domain include:

- Works where copyright protection has either expired or been lost for some reason

- Works prepared by an officer or employee of the United States government as part of that person's official duties

Under current copyright law, an author does not need to do anything to claim copyright in his or her work. The mere act of putting the work into tangible form vests the author with copyright ownership. Prior to 1989, however, a work could have come into the *public domain* in the following ways:

- For works first published in the United States prior to January 1, 1978, failure to place proper copyright notice on the work and failure to comply with the registration and deposit requirements

- For works first published in the United States prior to between January 1, 1978 and February 28, 1989, failure to place proper copyright notice on the work that was not properly cured

- For works first published in the United States prior to January 1, 1964, failure to renew the copyright at the expiration of the first 28-year term

Determining that a work is not protected by copyright can be quite difficult. For works first published prior to January 1, 1978, the lack of a copyright registration would indicate that the work is in the public domain. For works published after that date, the lack of a copyright registration would not be determinative. You may, however, wish to conduct a copyright search (which can be performed by the copyright office or a private organization). The existence of a copyright registration will determine when the work comes into the public domain.

Even if a work is clearly in the public domain, it does not necessarily mean that you can use the work for any purpose. There are other rights, such as the *right of publicity* (which restricts the use of an individual's persona for commercial purposes) that might restrict the permitted use of such materials. Works that have entered the public domain may also contain elements that are still subject to copyright protection. Although, for example, the motion picture *Rear Window* may be in public domain due to a failure to properly renew a copyright registration, the script on which it was based is still protected by copyright. Thus, the owner of the copyright in the script can control the exploitation of the film as a derivative work. (Paying attention to this level of detail will help keep you from becoming a bad example in someone else's legal chapter.)

As a consequence of certain agreements by the United States under international treaty, the foreign owners of certain foreign works that came into the public domain in the United States due to a failure to comply with some technical requirement of United States copyright law, are entitled to have copyright restored in such works, further complicating the determination of which works are in the public domain.

Fair Use

You may recall that the Constitution provides the mandate and authority for Congress to adopt copyright laws that grant exclusive rights to authors. The First Amendment, however, guarantees freedom of expression. How can we reconcile this freedom of expression with the right of an individual to prevent another from using his copyrighted material? The concept of fair use is an attempt by the courts to reconcile the two. *Fair use* limits the exclusive rights granted to the author and permits the use of copyrighted material without permission in certain extremely limited circumstances, such as satire and parody, critical commentary, and education. There are four factors commonly referred to in fair use cases:

- What is the purpose and character of the use? Is the use of a commercial nature, or is it for non-profit educational purposes?

- What is the nature of the copyrighted work? Is the copyrighted work published or unpublished? Is it fact or fiction? Is it informational or entertainment oriented? Is the work available or out of print?

- What is the amount and substantiality of the portion used in relation to the copyrighted work as a whole?

- What is the effect of the use upon the potential market or value of the copyrighted work?

It may appear that these factors can be used to determine when fair use is available. But the truth is that fair use always turns up as a defense. In other words, having used the material without permission, you've been sued and the only excuse you can come up with is that the First Amendment guarantees you the right to use it. Sounds a bit like kids who shout names at each other, and then when confronted argue that, "It's a free country and I can say anything I want." But it's not and you can't. So, please discuss it with your lawyer before you use it.

The Right of Publicity

The *right of publicity* is the right to protect the use of one's personality or *persona* for commercial purposes. The right of publicity can protect the use of a celebrity's name, voice, signature, photograph, or likeness against unauthorized commercial exploitation. In an increasing number of states, a celebrity's right of publicity is protected even after death.

There have been a number of interesting court battles over the right of publicity. One of the earliest involved the undisclosed use of a Woody Allen lookalike in an advertisement, suggesting the endorsement of the product by him. Both Bette Midler and Tom Waits have won cases involving the use of singers imitating their distinct singing styles. Perhaps the most interesting case involved Vanna White and Samsung. In that case, Samsung had secured the rights to use a futuristic *Wheel of Fortune* game in an advertisement, but did not obtain Ms. White's permission. They probably thought they didn't need her permission, because in the ad Ms. White was replaced by a very mechanical robot (that was admittedly dressed very nicely). But the court thought otherwise, holding that Ms. White's right of publicity had been violated.

Moral Rights

Moral rights are a kind of copyright law. These rights apply generally to literary, visual, or audio/visual works, such as books, paintings, limited edition prints, and motion pictures. Moral rights give the author the right to the physical integrity of a work as a whole, and the right to be identified as the creator of the work (or to disclaim such authorship).

Moral rights have been recognized by federal law under the 1991 Visual Artists Rights Act, applying only to fine art, such as paintings and drawings, or limited edition (up to 200 copies) signed prints. The law protects rights of integrity and attribution. It does not apply to works-made-for-hire. Moral rights can be waived.

Some states, including New York, Massachusetts, and Maine, have moral rights laws. California has a resale royalty law, which grants a royalty on the resale of a work of fine art.

Internationally, the extent of moral rights varies from country to country. In France, for example, *"droit moral"* applies regardless of the country of origin of the work. Moral rights may not be transferred or waived and are perpetual.

Trademarks

A *trademark* is a symbol (words, designs, names, or slogans) used to identify and distinguish the origin of goods or services. Rights are acquired when the trademark is used in commerce or upon filing an *intent to use* (ITU) application with the United States Patent and Trademark Office.

Today, trademarks are amongst the most powerful and valuable types of intellectual property rights. The value of a trademark is a function of the public's perception of that brand, and that perception is based on the quality of the products to which the brand is attached as well as the substantial sums spent on marketing, promoting, and advertising the brand. The placement of a well-known brand on a product and the value of a well-known, international consumer products brand can reach the hundreds of millions, if not billions.

A copyrighted work, such as a fanciful design or a cartoon character, also can serve as a trademark. Thus, even if the copyright on a character or design has expired, it might still be subject to trademark rights. Before you can freely use a cartoon character that has entered the public domain, you must determine whether it is a protected trademark.

The designers of the Internet naming scheme probably did not anticipate the explosion in the use of domain names identical or similar to well-known trademarks. Domain names have become a sort of quasi-trademark, in some cases even more important than the one filed in Washington.

Permission should be obtained where use of a trademark is potentially confusing or implies endorsement. If the use is editorial (such as news reporting) then no permission should be required.

Recent federal law protects the owners of well-known or famous trademarks against *dilution*. If you build enough brand equity in your mark, you are entitled to protect it over a broader range of products and services.

Patents

A *patent* is a government sanctioned monopoly for a limited time on an *invention* or *process*. Ideas are not patentable; inventions or processes are. In order to qualify for *patent* protection, an invention must be reduced to practice and must be new, useful, and non-obvious. A patent application must be filed within one year of *public disclosure* of the invention.

Under our Constitution, patent protection was intended to encourage the sciences. In exchange for a public statement and explanation of an invention, the inventor is entitled to the exclusive exploitation of the invention for a limited period of time which, due to recent amendments to the patent law, is now 20 years from the filing date. This latest change is part of an effort to normalize United States patent law with those of other countries.

The owner of a patent has the right to prevent others from making, using, and/or selling anything which is covered by the claims of the patent. The grant of letters patent by the United States Patent and Trademark Office is not a guarantee of protection. Anyone challenging the patent can claim that it does not qualify for patent protection and introduce evidence to that effect. Patents can be invalidated on this basis.

In 1982, the Supreme Court determined that software/hardware combinations can qualify for patent protection. Since then there has been an explosion of software patent filings. The lack of available precedent with respect to software technology prior to 1982, however, and the lack of familiarity of patent examiners with software, has resulted in some notorious patent grants which have been withdrawn (in the case of Compton's patent on the use of multimedia).

The conflict between the appropriateness of patent versus copyright protection for software continues today. Given the radical difference between the two schemes of protection that controversy is likely to continue.

Clip Libraries

Increasingly, there are more and more clip libraries available from various sources. They can contain, music, sound effects, art, video, and so on. Some of these are available royalty-free and others are for comping purposes only. Be careful of what you are buying—read the fine print and be sure you have the correct permissions and are indemified. If you don't have the time to do all that is needed, hire someone to do it for you.

Sample Contracts

Because the essence of any solid business is solid business agreements, we thought we would include a few standard contracts. On the following pages you will find samples of the following contracts:

- Work Made for Hire Agreement – Employee
- Work Made for Hire Agreement – Independent Contractor
- Subcontractor Agreement

Work Made for Hire Agreement – Employee

This agreement should be signed by each employee to ensure ownership of all intellectual property rights created by the employee in the course of employment. It also contains a confidentiality provision to protect the employer's trade secrets.

_____

Re: Ownership and Non-Disclosure of Proprietary Materials

(Date)

Dear _____ :

This is to confirm the terms and conditions under which _____ ("Employer") will employ you and you agree to be employed by Employer, as follows:

1. You acknowledge and agree that as an employee all material created by you in the course of your employment (the "Material") is a work made for hire under copyright law and all rights therein are the sole and exclusive property of Employer, including the worldwide right to own and register all copyrights in all Material in Employer's name. In the event that any Material is determined not to be a work made for hire for any reason, you hereby irrevocably assign all rights therein to Employer and you agree to execute such additional documents as may be requested by Employer to evidence Employer's ownership of the Material. You also hereby assign to Employer and/or waive any and all claims that you may now or hereafter have in any jurisdiction to so-called "moral rights" or rights of "droit moral" in connection with the Material.

2. To the extent that any of the services performed pursuant to this Agreement produce or include patentable inventions, or other intellectual property, including know-how or trade secrets (collectively, "Inventions"), such Inventions shall be owned exclusively by Employer from the time of conception and/or reduction to practice. This provision shall be construed as and constitute a complete assignment to Employer of any and all right, title, and interest you may have, if any, in this regard. You shall promptly notify Employer of all such developments. You also agree that you will communicate to Employer all facts known to you respecting the same, testify in any legal proceedings when called upon by Employer, sign all lawful papers deemed by Employer as expedient to vest in it the legal title herein sought to be conveyed or to obtain rights therein (including the filing and prosecution of all applications and patents, both United States and foreign), and otherwise aid Employer, its successors and assigns, in obtaining full patent protection on said Inventions and enforcing proper protection under said patents.

3. You agree (i) to hold all proprietary information of Employer in the strictest confidence, and (ii) not to use or exploit any such proprietary information or disclose any proprietary information to any third party other than as necessary in the course of your engagement and as disclosed to and approved by Employer in writing. You acknowledge and agree that all copies, reproductions, or versions of any proprietary information, including but not limited to, any electronic, magnetic or optical versions, and all notes or sketches (whether or not created by you) are the sole and exclusive property of Employer and you agree to return all such copies, reproductions or versions to Employer upon the termination of your employment or at any time upon the request of Employer.

4. Since a breach or threatened breach of the restrictions set forth in this Agreement may irreparably damage Employer, you agree that Employer shall have, in addition to all other rights and remedies, the right to obtain an injunction from a court of competent jurisdiction enjoining your breach or threatened breach of any of the restrictions of this Agreement. In addition, Employer shall not be required to post a bond or security prior to, or in conjunction with, any such relief.

5. Nothing set forth in this Agreement shall require Employer to continue to employ you for any said period of time or cause your employment to be anything other than employment at will or prevent either you or Employer from terminating the employment relationship with or without cause.

6. This Agreement constitutes the entire agreement between the parties with respect to the subject matter hereof. This Agreement shall be governed by the laws of the State of New York and any dispute arising out of or related hereto shall be submitted to the state or federal courts located in the County of New York whose jurisdiction is hereby consented to by you and Employer.

7. This Agreement may be amended only by a writing signed by both you and Employer. The failure of either party to enforce any term or condition of this Agreement shall not be deemed a waiver of any terms or conditions of this Agreement.

EMPLOYER   ACCEPTED AND AGREED:

By: _____   _____
Name: _____ Title: _____   Name: _____

Work-Made-for-Hire Agreement – Independent Contractor

This agreement should be signed by each consultant or independent contractor engaged in the regular course of business. It ensures ownership of all intellectual property rights created by the consultant or independent contractor in the course of the engagement. It also contains a confidentiality provision to protect the company's trade secrets.

_____

Re: Work-Made-for-Hire

(Date)

Dear _____:

This is to confirm the terms and conditions under which _____ ("Company") will engage you to perform the services described on the schedule annexed hereto (the "Schedule") for Company, as follows:

1. You acknowledge and agree that all material created by you in the course of your engagement (the "Material") is a work made for hire under copyright law and all rights therein are the sole and exclusive property of Company, including the worldwide right to own and register all copyrights in all Material in Company's name. In the event that any Material is determined not to be a work made for hire for any reason, you hereby irrevocably assign all rights therein to Company and you agree to execute such additional documents as may be requested by Company to evidence Company's ownership of the Material.

2. In the event that the Material is not copyrightable, you hereby irrevocably assign any and all ownership rights in the Material to Company. You also hereby assign to Company and/or waive any and all claims that you may now or hereafter have in any jurisdiction to so-called "moral rights" or rights of "droit moral" in connection with the Material.

3. To the extent that any of the services performed pursuant to this Agreement produce or include patentable inventions, or other intellectual property, including know-how or trade secrets (collectively, "Inventions"), such Inventions shall be owned exclusively by Company from the time of conception and/or reduction to practice. This provision shall be construed as and constitute a complete assignment to Company of any and all right, title, and interest you may have, if any, in this regard. You shall promptly notify Company of all such developments. You also agree that you will communicate to Company all facts known to you respecting the same, testify in any legal proceedings when called upon by Company, sign all lawful papers deemed by Company as

expedient to vest in it the legal title herein sought to be conveyed or to obtain rights therein (including the filing and prosecution of all applications and patents, both United States and foreign), and otherwise aid Company, its successors and assigns, in obtaining full patent protection on said Inventions and discoveries and enforcing proper protection under said patents.

4. You agree (i) to hold all proprietary information of Company in the strictest confidence, and (ii) not to use or exploit any such proprietary information or disclose any proprietary information to any third party other than as necessary in the course of your engagement and as disclosed to and approved by Company in writing. You acknowledge and agree that all copies, reproductions, or versions of any proprietary information, including but not limited to, any electronic, magnetic, or optical versions, and all notes or sketches (whether or not created by you) are the sole and exclusive property of Company and you agree to return all such copies, reproductions, or versions to Company upon the termination of your engagement or at any time upon the request of Company.

5. This Letter Agreement shall be governed by the laws of the State of New York and any dispute arising out of or related to this Letter Agreement shall be submitted to the state or federal courts located in the County of New York whose jurisdiction is hereby consented to by you and Company.

6. You may not assign or delegate your duties hereunder and any such purported assignment shall be void. This Agreement contains the entire agreement of the parties with respect to the subject matter hereof and may be amended only by a writing signed by both you and Company. The failure of either party to enforce any term or condition of this Agreement shall not be deemed a waiver of any terms or conditions of this Agreement.

COMPANY

ACCEPTED AND AGREED:

By: _____

_____

Name: Title:

Name:

_____

Address:

Subcontractor Agreement

This agreement should be used for specific projects undertaken by a developer for a third-party client, where the work product will be owned by the client. It contains provisions ensuring ownership of all copyrightable material by the client and all inventions by the developer. It also contains a confidentiality clause to protect the developer and the client.

Re: Subcontractor Agreement for (Project)

(Date)

Dear _____ :

This letter agreement sets forth the terms of your agreement with _____ ("Developer") to perform services and/or create materials in connection with _____ (the "Work") for and on behalf of _____ ("Client"), its grantees and licensees.

1. **Materials.** You agree to provide the following services (the "Services") and the following materials (the "Materials") for inclusion in the Work:

   [Insert description of Services and Materials]

2. **Delivery.** You agree to perform the Services and deliver the Materials to Developer on or before _____ , 199_, in content and form satisfactory to Developer. Time is of the essence in connection with your performance hereunder. If you fail to perform the Services or deliver the Materials, or any portion thereof, in accordance with the above date or such later deadline as Developer may in its discretion fix in writing, Developer may terminate this Agreement without any further obligation to you.

3. **Compensation.** As full compensation for all Services performed and Materials provided by you hereunder, Developer will pay to you $_____ . You acknowledge that Developer bears the responsibility for making such payments and you will not look to or make any claim against Client in connection therewith. Any claim by you against the Developer will not affect Client's rights to or ownership of the Materials. You will be responsible for your own travel and out-of-pocket expenses incurred in connection with the Services and the delivery of the Materials, and you acknowledge that you are not authorized to incur any expenses on behalf of Developer or Client without their prior written consent.

4. **Work-made-for-hire.** You acknowledge and agree that the Services performed and the Materials provided hereunder have been specially ordered or commissioned as a work-made-for-hire for use as a contribution or supplement to the Work and Client shall own all right, title, and interest thereto. You further acknowledge that Client shall be considered the author of the Materials for the purposes of copyright, shall own all rights in and to the copyright of the Materials, and shall have the right to register and renew the copyright in its name or the name of its nominee(s). To the extent that the Materials do not vest in Client as a work-made-for-hire, you hereby irrevocably grant, assign, and transfer all of your right, title and interest in and to the Materials to Client. You shall secure at your sole cost and expense all necessary permissions and releases necessary to enable Developer and Client to use, distribute and exploit the Materials as contemplated by this Agreement and you shall advise Developer in writing of all such necessary permissions and releases and deliver to Developer and Client original copies thereof duly executed by all necessary parties. You also hereby assign to Developer and/or waive any and all claims that you may now or hereafter have in any jurisdiction to so-called "moral rights" or rights of "droit moral" in connection with the Material.

5. **Inventions.** To the extent that any of the services performed pursuant to this Agreement produce or include patentable inventions, or other intellectual property, including know-how or trade secrets (collectively, "Inventions"), such Inventions shall be owned exclusively by Developer from the time of conception and/or reduction to practice. This provision shall be construed as and constitute a complete assignment to Developer of any and all right, title, and interest you may have, if any, in this regard. You shall promptly notify Developer of all such developments. You also agree that you will communicate to Developer all facts known to you respecting the same, testify in any legal proceedings when called upon by Developer, sign all lawful papers deemed by Developer as expedient to vest in it the legal title herein sought to be conveyed or to obtain rights therein (including the filing and prosecution of all applications and patents, both United States and foreign), and otherwise aid Developer, its successors and assigns, in obtaining full patent protection on said Inventions and enforcing proper protection under said patents.

6. **Advertising/Promotion.** You authorize the use of your name, biographical material, and likeness in connection with the Work and the advertising and promotion thereof, but Client has no obligation to acknowledge your contribution to the Work.

7. **Confidentiality.** You shall treat all information provided to you in connection with this Letter Agreement, and the Services performed and the Materials created hereunder, as proprietary and confidential, whether or not so identified, and shall not disclose the whole, or any part thereof, to any third parties, without the prior written consent of Developer.

8. **Editing/Approvals.** You acknowledge and agree that the Services performed and the Materials prepared hereunder shall be in form and content satisfactory to Developer, and Developer and Client have the right to edit, change, add to or delete from the Materials. You understand that Developer will withhold final approval and acceptance of the Materials until Client approves and

accepts the Materials. In the event that Client does not approve and accept the Materials, or any portion thereof, the Developer may either (i) have you revise such Materials, at your expense, and deliver such revised Materials to Developer in accordance with delivery dates determined by Developer, or (ii) terminate this Letter Agreement without any obligation to you.

9. **Termination.** This Letter Agreement shall continue in effect, unless terminated sooner pursuant to this Letter Agreement, until you complete the Services and Materials described hereunder and Developer has notified you that Client has given its final approval and acceptance of the Materials. If Developer terminates this Letter Agreement prior to the completion of the Services and Materials, Developer's sole obligation will be to pay you, pro rata, the amount due for the Services acceptably performed and the Materials approved and accepted by Client.

10. **Independent Contractor.** You hereby acknowledge that you are an independent contractor and not an employee of Developer or Client. You understand and agree that you are not entitled to any benefits provided to any employee of the Developer or Client. You acknowledge that it is your sole responsibility to report as income any compensation received hereunder and to make requisite tax filings and payments to the appropriate federal, state or local tax authority.

11. **Compliance.** You agree that you will personally be responsible for compliance with all federal, state and local laws, regulations and orders in connection with taxes, unemployment insurance, social security, worker's compensation, disability or like matters.

12. **Warranties and Representations; Indemnity.** You warrant and represent that you have full right and power to enter into this Agreement; that the Materials will be original and that all necessary permissions and releases have been obtained by you prior to their use; that the Materials will not contain any libelous or otherwise unlawful material or violate any copyright or personal or proprietary right of any person or entity. You will defend any claim of breach of warranty and, if it is determined that you breached the warranties set forth herein, you will indemnify Developer and Client for any loss they may suffer as a result of such a breach. You acknowledge that the warranties and representations herein shall survive the termination of this agreement.

13. **Miscellaneous.** This Agreement sets forth the entire agreement and understanding between you and Developer, and supersedes any prior agreements or understanding, whether oral or in writing. This Agreement and the rights and obligations of the parties shall be governed and construed under the laws of the State of New York as if executed and fully performed therein. You may not assign or delegate your duties hereunder and any such purported assignment shall be void.

DEVELOPER

By: _____
Name: _____ Title: _____

SUBCONTRACTOR

Agreed and accepted this

_____ day of _____ , 199__

By: _____
Name: _____ Title: _____

_____
Address:

_____
Social Security Number:

In Summary

This chapter is meant as a stepping stone to helping you understand the legal issues of new media. Because of new media's rapid growth, it is wise for you to speak with an attorney who is familiar with the industry and can advise you appropriately.

Case Study: 3D

You will find that the format of this case study differs a bit from the others. This is because the interview with this company started out as a sidebar interview for Chapter 3, "Designing for New Media." (You will also find some of Heller's comments about design in that chapter.) As the interview evolved, the makings for an interesting case study surfaced as well—one that is relevent to the freelance and small studio population. Many times, these people are asked to be part of a larger team and contribute only one or two areas of expertise—other times they are expected to handle an entire project. This case study shows two typical project scenarios that these professionals are likely to encounter.

Company

Donald N. Heller
The Big Cheese, Interface Designer, Animator, Musician, Teacher
Magik Lantern Productions
Danbury, Connecticut

Employees

One

Freelance

As needed

Romeo and Juliet CD-ROM

The *Romeo and Juliet* CD-ROM was created for Sunburst Communications, a long-time leader in educational software. This case study will discuss the art/animation created for this project which consisted of:

- An aerial fly-in sequence over the town, which was never used in the final piece

- A 360° scene of a courtyard, which had to include four main buildings

- One interior room for each main building

The aerial fly-in sequence had to include the courtyard and the tops of the town's buildings with enough detail to be believable in the animation. So, Heller decided that he really only needed to detail the roofs and a few key elements. Once you were in the courtyard, you didn't see the surrounding town. Frames were rendered at 320×240 pixels at 15 frames per second.

The courtyard (see Figures 7.1 and 7.2) was a 360° scene created in Specular's Infini-D. When using the CD-ROM, it appears that this was done with QuickTime VR, but in fact, was completely animated in Director (part of the programmer's job). "QuickTime VR was still in its infancy, and we were concerned about compatibility." A lot of attention was given to the detail of the surfaces to give them a rich, as well as rustic, look of the times. A total of 72 frames were rendered every 5°.

Figure 7.1
A View of the Romeo and Juliet Courtyard

Figure 7.2
Another View of the Romeo and Juliet Courtyard

Each of the four main buildings' interior rooms had a small animation that was created in Photoshop after the final rendering was complete (see Figure 7.3). It was quicker than rendering all the extra frames in 3D. Later, the frames were animated in Director. All of this animation was included in the final fee. All in all, the project was pretty simple from a production point of view, but it took quite some time to create the look that was needed from an artistic point of view.

Figure 7.3
An Animation Created in Photoshop after
the Original Scene was Rendered

Cost

$9,000

This cost included $2,000 for the introductory sequence that was never used. The client had a budget that Heller felt he could work with. Additionally, the client knew what was needed for the scenes, and Heller simply had to bring his vision to the project.

Color versions of this CD-ROM can be seen in Color Plate #1.

Esto Photographics

The Esto Photographics Web site was the first Web site done by Heller. It was simple and straightforward. Although the site consisted of 40 pages, they all had essentially the same layout requirements except for the home page. This made it very easy to produce the HTML. Also, there were no complicated graphics (the client was to supply all of the photos), no CGI programming, no frame layout, no content creation (the client did all that), no navigational organization (the client did that, too)—everything was pretty simple.

Heller created the overall look and worked with a student intern to create the HTML. The entire project consisted of three or four client meetings, the design look and feel, the HTML, and three three-hour sessions to train the client in how to update their own pages.

Cost

$4,000

$3,000 for the site and $1,000 for the training.

Heller decided to give this client a lower price than usual. The site was very simple and the client was very specific in their needs. Heller didn't feel a need to second-guess their content and navigation.

Color versions of this Web site can be seen in Color Plate #2.

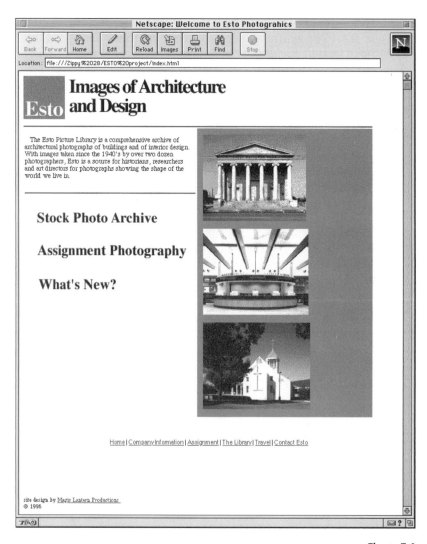

Figure 7.4
A Typical Example
of a Well-Respected Company Creating
its Presence on the Web for a Nominal Fee

Figure 7.5

In Summary

These projects are typical of those encountered by the freelancer or small design studio. Oftentimes, freelancers are asked to join a group and bring specific expertise to a project, or they are asked to work on a complete, but often smaller, project, such as these. That is not to say, however, that the small studio cannot gear up to produce a large-scale project. With the right people, it doesn't matter whether the people are on staff or freelance; the project can be just as successful.

Case Study: Enhanced CD

Project Overview

LIFEbeat, the Music Industry Fights AIDS, is a non-profit organization that promotes AIDS awareness as well as raises funds to help teenagers with AIDS who cannot afford treatment for their disease.

The organization's Board AID Super CD Plus was created with the purpose of promoting LIFEbeat's annual snowboard/skateboard fundraising event, which features live performances by popular bands and public service announcements promoting AIDS education. The CD Plus also provides viewers with information about the mission of LIFEbeat, as well as a contest sponsored by MTV.

A CD Plus, or more commonly referred to as an Enhanced CD, is a product that users can put in their CD player to listen to music, or put in their computer and interact with multimedia.

Size of Market

When the Enhanced CD first made its entry into the marketplace, it brought with it the hope that it might serve as a sort of new media Trojan horse. Setting aside the complicated technical issues regarding sound standards, an Enhanced CD is generally presented on EPs, or three to five song releases that have ample room remaining for multimedia content. Because recorded music is a billion dollar industry, it was hoped that people purchasing regular CDs would purchase Enhanced EPs, find them appealing, and warm up to multimedia.

Early titles included popular releases from The Cranberries, Moby, and Regina Joseph's inventive sample SPEW+ title produced by REV Entertainment in conjunction with Atlantic Records. This year, the German art-band Einsturzende Neubauten added its limited edition *Ende Neu* to the field with material including videoclips and sounds.

Thus far, sales of Enhanced CDs have paralleled those of new media—there have been a few hits, but reaction has not been overwhelming. Part of the problem is intrinsic to the Enhanced CD itself. Although consumers tend to want more than simple electronic versions of liner notes, they aren't willing to pay for the price point that would be necessary to make it possible to produce more robust titles.

At Tower Records, the average four-song EP ranges in price from $6 to $9. As one manager at the giant retailer pointed out, "These disks cost $12 to $15." When asked why sales have been slow, the manager reported, "Why pay $15 bucks for a few songs and a 30-second video of the band, when you can get the whole album on sale for $12.98!"

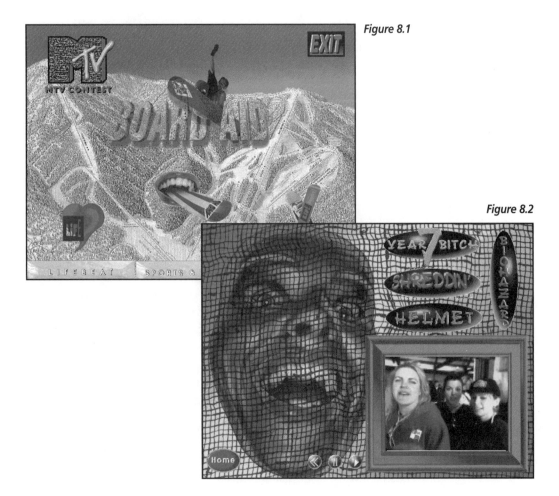

Figure 8.1

Figure 8.2

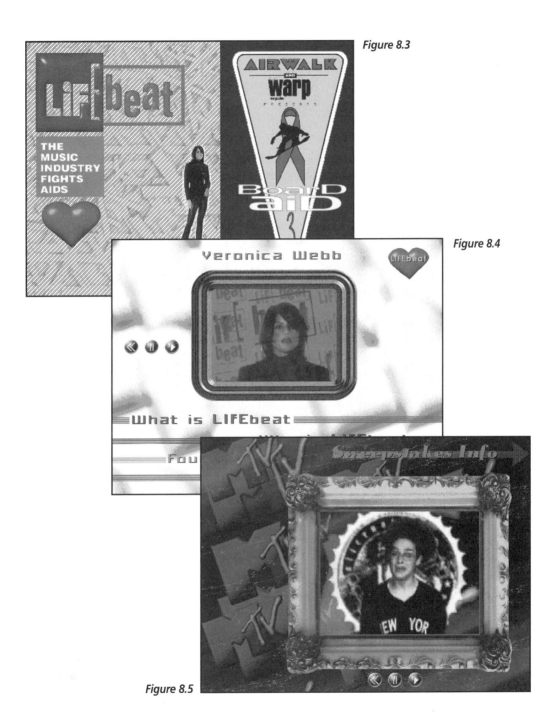

Figure 8.3

Figure 8.4

Figure 8.5

Company Profile

Wild Kind
New York, NY
http://www.wildkind.com
wildkind@bigmagic.com

Clients

Music clients include the Water Lilies, Orbital, Warner Brothers, and Todd Rundgren. Fashion clients include Bergdorf Goodman, Nieman Marcus, Issey Miyake, Vogue, Jordache, and Ralph Lauren. Additional clients include Disney, Carnival Cruise Lines, MTV/VH1, NYNEX-Bell Atlantic, Canon, UNUM, Carnegie Hall, Columbia Pictures, and more.

Company's Mission

Says Mordecon: "We created Wild Kind to be a self-contained, start-to-finish production company specializing in producing affordable high-quality video and multimedia projects in a uniquely creative environment."

Key Projects

Wild Kind has recently been contracted to provide video and multimedia work for a new production of playwright Sam Shepard's *Tooth of Crome*.

Employees

Three

Freelance

From time to time, the company brings in videographers and programmers.

Equipment List

Macintosh Quadra 900 and two Power Macintosh 8100s (80 and 110 megahertz). Each of the 8100s is equipped with Radius Telecast, Video Vision Studio cards, and FWB Hammer disk arrays. Two scanners, a UMAX Powerleaf scanner and a Nikon slide scanner. The company also has a Canon Digital Video Camera and assorted other cameras.

Company Profile

Richie Williamson, Dean Janoff, and Rick Mordecon came to new media from non-traditional backgrounds, to say the least. Williamson graduated from the University of Texas, Austin, as an artist and illustrator. Dean Janoff went to college to study pharmacy, but found himself cutting class while he sat in his dorm room drawing pictures.

The two met working in the Bronx when they were designing everything from shirt patterns and towels to glassware. "One day the company promoted this guy who didn't know anything about the work, let alone managing us," Williamson remembers, "We convinced him to fire us, and with the $4,000 we got from unemployment, we started our own studio." The upstart company got its first job producing the background set for a Lola Falana commercial that was nominated for a Clio. "At the time, no one knew who we were, and all of a sudden we are being nominated for an award," reflects Janoff.

Work continued to come in and Williamson and Janoff eventually designed the now-legendary stage at New York's trendsetting Studio 54. That set made them celebrities, and the team soon found itself designing sets for such music industry giants as Kiss, Grace Jones, Foreigner, Hall and Oates, The Cars, and Elton John. There was also the Copacabana set they designed for Barry Manilow.

Tiring of theatrical set design, Williamson started tinkering with photography. His interest landed him a job as one of Bloomingdale's mainstay fashion photographers for more than a decade. He also became an editor-at-large for Andy Warhol's *Details* magazine. After several photo spreads and articles, his interest waned when Warhol died. "Andy never tried to control anything," he explains, "but he was magical. By the sheer nature of his presence, the magazine came together and embodied his artistic vision. When he was gone, *Details* unraveled. It was no longer Andy. It was just another magazine."

In 1987, Williamson and Janoff bought their first computer. "It was a Mac II with a 13-inch monitor and a 60 MB hard drive," notes Janoff. "We also added a black-and-white scanner and printer, Quark, Letraset's Image Studio, Illustrator, and Graphis Paint. The whole thing cost us $16,000."

As Williamson and Janoff worked at pioneering digital imaging (they were featured in a film series produced by the Rochester Institute of Technology), they became friends with Mordecon, a playwright, who by then had already written several plays and had one work optioned for a film.

"We come from a theatrical perspective," explains Mordecon. "Ritchie and Dean produced sets and I wrote plays. We bring that background and sensitivity to our projects."

Project Details

Description and Goals

The goal of the project was to produce a cross-platform, Enhanced CD for teenagers that would work on the lowest common denominator—machines equipped with 4 MB of RAM and 256K 13-inch monitors.

Client

LIFEbeat, the Music Industry Fights AIDS.

How Did the Company Get the Job?

A friend introduced Wild Kind to Tim Rosta, executive director of LIFEbeat. The company initially presented a proposal to build the LIFEbeat Web site, but the project fell through. A short time later, Wild Kind pitched the idea of an Enhanced CD, which tied in more closely with the organization's music industry orientation.

How Many People Worked on the Project ?

In addition to the three members of the Wild Kind team, there was a freelance artist, a composer who did the music for the project, and one programmer.

Challenges

The first challenge had to do with budget. The second challenge had to do with budget and the third challenge had to do with budget. As a non-profit organization, LIFEbeat could not afford to underwrite the full cost of the project—much of that cost was underwritten by Wild Kind. "In short, we worked for free," comments Mordecon.

Second, the project represented the first time that Wild Kind had produced a CD product for a real client. "We had produced CD-ROMs for ourselves to send out as promotion, but we never produced one for a client before. That represented a challenge with a certain pressure attached to it," says Mordecon.

"One of the other challenges we had was dealing with poor-quality video," adds Janoff. "What we essentially had was a lot of half-inch tape that had been shot with hand-held cameras as people interviewed bands backstage or in their hotel rooms. We had to spend a lot of time coming up with creative ways to present what most people would have rejected as poor-quality video."

The Proposal

Budgeted versus Actual Numbers

The Wild Kind team charged LIFEbeat $7,500 to produce the entire project from start to finish, which took about four months to produce. The pricing partly had to do with the fact that LIFEbeat was a non-profit organization. It also had to do with the fact that the company wanted to contribute its considerable talents to a cause it believed in. However, the company did prepare an actual budget based on what it would have charged for the entire project. The budget would have been as follows:

Concept and Storyboarding (including development of the treatment and flow charts): $5,000

Hunter-Gathering (a process Wild Kind describes as buying footage, scanning images, searching for relevant content, and "getting all of the information into the computer so that we can massage it"): $5,000

Video Production (including buying necessary footage, shooting any short video footage, digitizing all video material, and editing it for the Enhanced CD): $7,500

Art Creation and Production (including scanning, creating artwork, interface design, and screen animations): $8,000

Programming: $7,500

Testing and Final Output (LIFEbeat, with ties to the music industry, had the disc gold mastered and duplicated): $5,000

Client Revisions and Changes: $3,000

Total: $41,000

Final Analysis

Reaction to the product was strong. According to Wild Kind, MTV got involved in the project because of its satisfaction with the final product. Similarly, Atlantic Records is said to be interested in the product and plans to produce and distribute 25,000 of the benefit discs to be sold in stores.

Artistically, Williamson is pleased with the interface. "We succeeded in our goal of creating a fast interface that works well," he says. "The average CD enables what I perceive as an inordinate amount of options. You sit in front of it and wonder what to do. We took all of the uncertainty out of the navigation. We reduced choice because we wanted to make people have to read the information on AIDS education. That message is not hidden, it is up front and clear.

While that sort of navigation might sound confining, on this CD it works. "The product had to be simple," Williamson continues. "It was designed to educate young kids. We compensated for the so-called forced navigation by making the product as fast as possible," he continues. "The product has a fast pace. Something happens and happens quickly. We have something to say, boom we say it, you move on. It's upbeat and electric," he concludes. "Short attention span theater at its finest," adds Janoff.

In the end, LIFEbeat was pleased. "They were so great to work with," says Mordecon. "This whole thing was new to them but they promised us that we would have their complete cooperation and they gave it to us. As the project proceeded we both started to get the feeling that we were making something special. They were special to work with and that helped us produce our best work," he concludes.

Despite the limited budget, most of the problems were technical.

"If I had to pick the one bummer on the project," says Williamson, "it would be Director. Don't get me wrong, Director is a wonderful program and it is the industry standard, but it has some inherent weaknesses." Janoff elaborates: "Director does not enable enough motion. You can move one thing on the screen, maybe two, but if you try to get more than a few things going at once, everything starts to slow down."

"And Lingo is so difficult. We are artists and we need to be able to use Director to implement our artistic vision, but with Director you need to be a serious programmer to get something simple done. Why? The tool should be more enabling." "Plus," explains Williamson, "in the middle of the project Macromedia released Director 5, not an upgrade, but a complete overhaul. While the product has more features overall, it takes others away. For example, Director 5 makes it possible to kern text. That's great. But it used to be so easy to put a shadow on text and now it is far more involved. Why is it that those of us who are using a product for three years are forced to practically relearn the entire tool from scratch just because the company releases an upgrade? It makes no sense."

Being a theater-oriented company with an expertise in video, Wild Kind also felt a little constrained by the limits of CD-ROM technology. "You can't do full screen video yet and the rate of data transfer—desktop bandwidth—isn't there yet," comments Janoff.

Sums up Williamson: "These aren't complaints. It was our pleasure to work with LIFEbeat to produce this project for a great cause, but every once in a while you have to stand back and look at the computer and ask yourself why is it like this? It could be better. We need more artists developing these tools."

In Summary

The Enhanced CD went a long way to boost Wild Kind's confidence. "It galvanized us as a team," says Mordecon. "We know we can pull together and produce great work." Music industry executives have begun to take notice and Wild Kind has started to get calls for more work from high-profile clients.

But most of all, the team at Wild Kind is moving into the future and feeling good about itself.

"At one point, when we were working on the project we thought 'Are we crazy?'" says Williamson, smiling. "But the fact of the matter is we wanted to do this job. We wanted to do our best work on the project and we went for it." "With the Enhanced CD, we used all of our company's skills—writing, editing, designing, video production, artistic creation, programming—everything," says Mordecon. "Most importantly, this gave us a way to reach out and help other people," explains Mordecon. "Non-profit organizations can benefit from multimedia. While some of them are afraid of it, they need to realize that this technology can be a great way to communicate important messages to people who need it. We also believe that if you give to a good cause, only good things can come back to you."

Not only does the company report that the LIFEbeat Enhanced CD is a powerful promotion tool, it has been so well received by the company's current clients that it has made current projects the company is working on develop more smoothly. "Our clients look at the Enhanced CD and they trust us more. They know we set high standards and we can deliver. They give us their basic ideas and give us more freedom to do what we do best—communicate those ideas in a creative fashion," says Mordecon.

That freedom has also affected the company in one other way. "Working on this project we started to develop the sense that as we mature as a company, we are moving from service and production towards more creative content—whether for our clients or for products that we develop in-house and market ourselves. That is an important transition. Without the experience we had on the Enhanced CD, we might not have started down that path," Williamson concludes.

Color versions of this Enhanced CD can be seen in Color Plates #4 and 5.

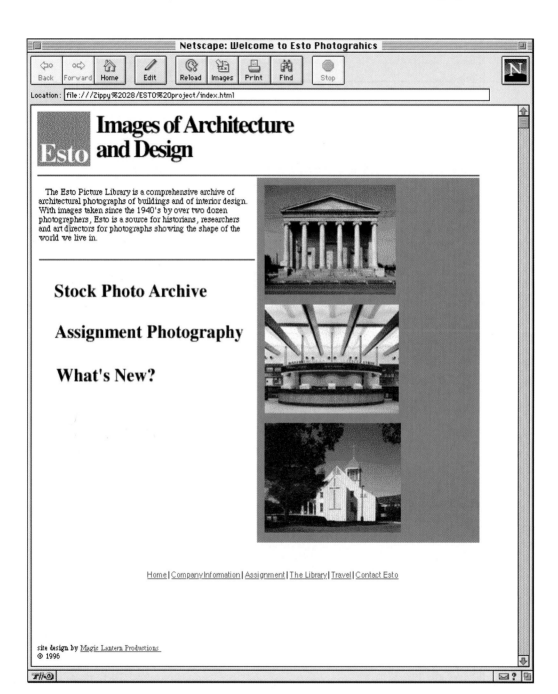

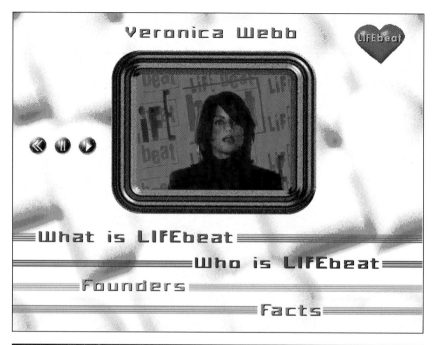

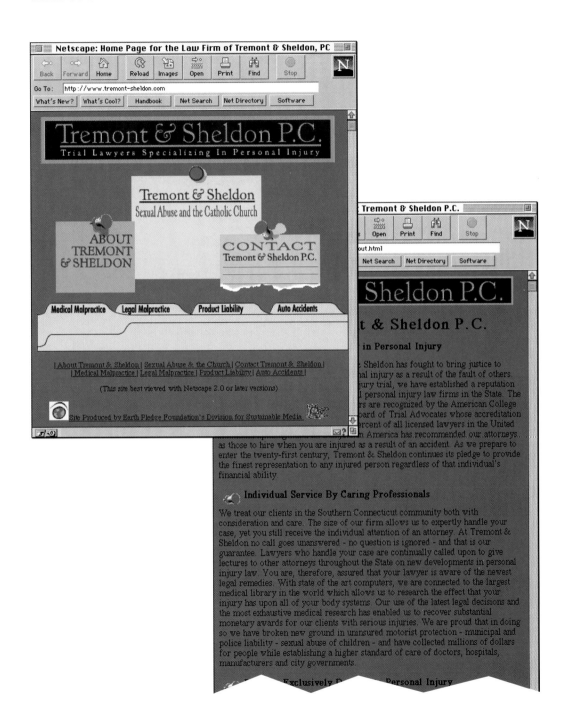

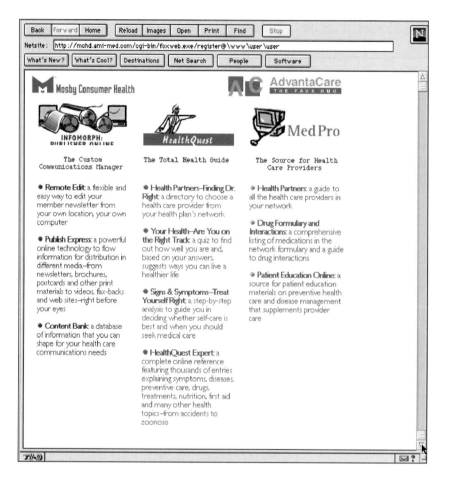

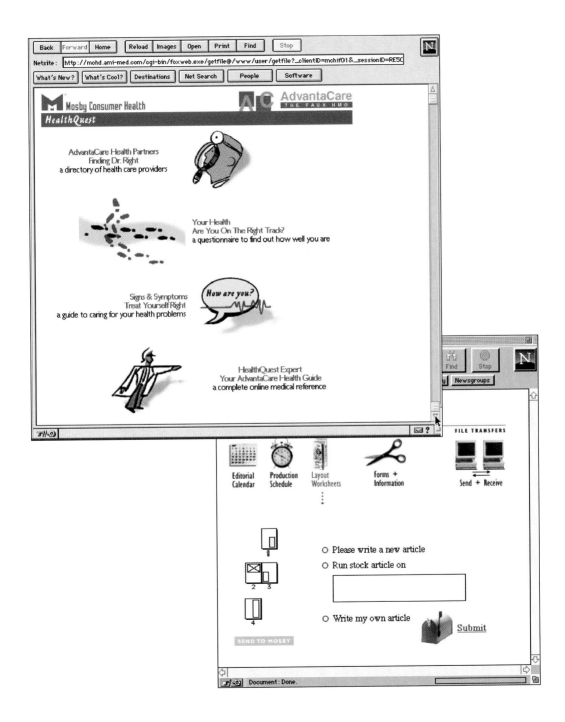

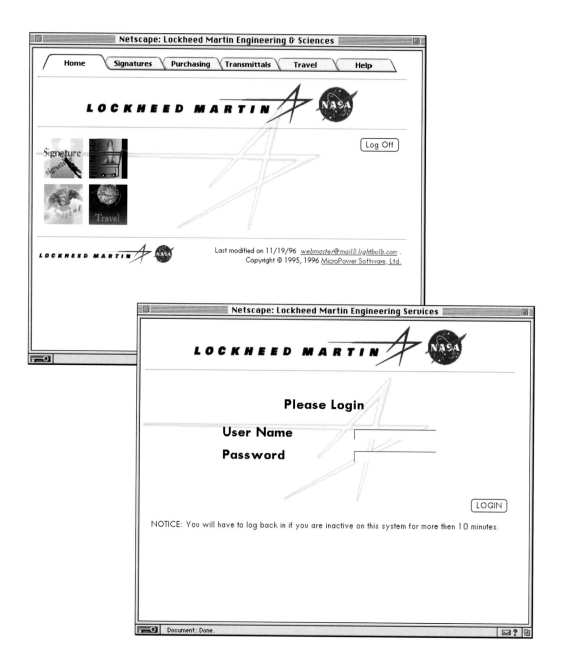

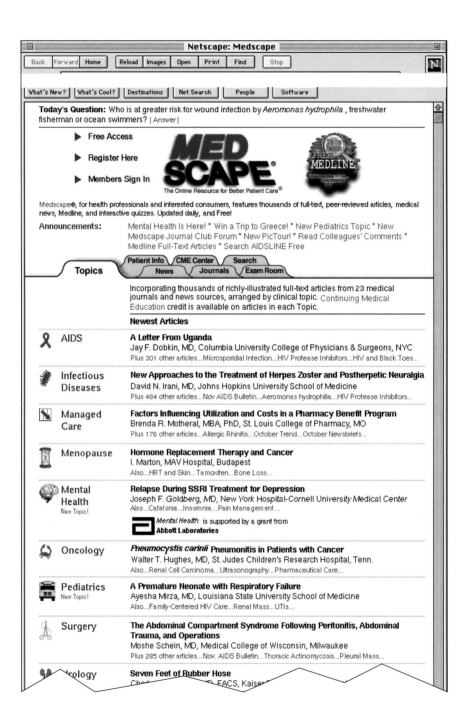

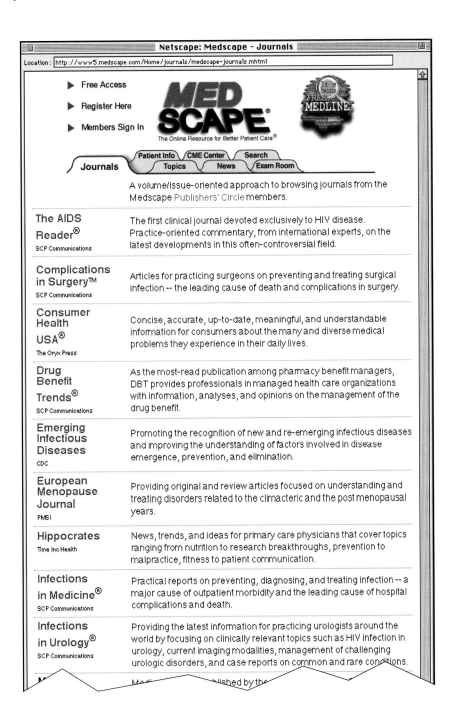

Netscape: Medscape – Journals

Location: http://www5.medscape.com/Home/journals/medscape-journals.mhtml

► Free Access

► Register Here

► Members Sign In

MEDSCAPE®
The Online Resource for Better Patient Care®

FREE MEDLINE

Patient Info \ CME Center \ Search
Journals   Topics \ News \ Exam Room

A volume/issue-oriented approach to browsing journals from the Medscape Publishers' Circle members.

The AIDS Reader®
SCP Communications

The first clinical journal devoted exclusively to HIV disease. Practice-oriented commentary, from international experts, on the latest developments in this often-controversial field.

Complications in Surgery™
SCP Communications

Articles for practicing surgeons on preventing and treating surgical infection -- the leading cause of death and complications in surgery.

Consumer Health USA®
The Oryx Press

Concise, accurate, up-to-date, meaningful, and understandable information for consumers about the many and diverse medical problems they experience in their daily lives.

Drug Benefit Trends®
SCP Communications

As the most-read publication among pharmacy benefit managers, DBT provides professionals in managed health care organizations with information, analyses, and opinions on the management of the drug benefit.

Emerging Infectious Diseases
CDC

Promoting the recognition of new and re-emerging infectious diseases and improving the understanding of factors involved in disease emergence, prevention, and elimination.

European Menopause Journal
PMSI

Providing original and review articles focused on understanding and treating disorders related to the climacteric and the post menopausal years.

Hippocrates
Time Inc Health

News, trends, and ideas for primary care physicians that cover topics ranging from nutrition to research breakthroughs, prevention to malpractice, fitness to patient communication.

Infections in Medicine®
SCP Communications

Practical reports on preventing, diagnosing, and treating infection -- a major cause of outpatient morbidity and the leading cause of hospital complications and death.

Infections in Urology®
SCP Communications

Providing the latest information for practicing urologists around the world by focusing on clinically relevant topics such as HIV infection in urology, current imaging modalities, management of challenging urologic disorders, and case reports on common and rare conditions.

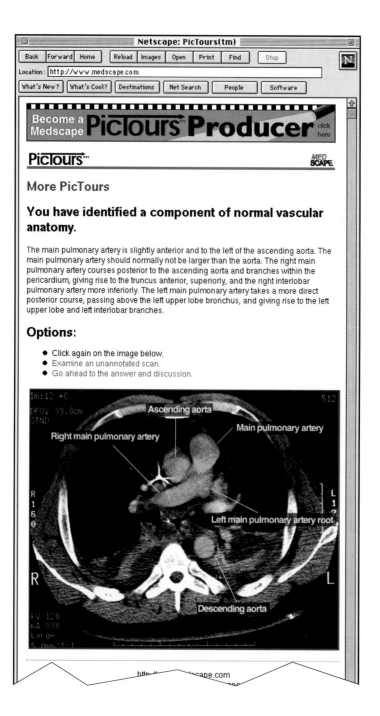

Netscape: PicTours(tm)

Back | Forward | Home | Reload | Images | Open | Print | Find | Stop

Location: http://www.medscape.com

What's New? | What's Cool? | Destinations | Net Search | People | Software

Become a Medscape **PicTours Producer** click here

PicTours™   MEDSCAPE

More PicTours

You have identified a component of normal vascular anatomy.

The main pulmonary artery is slightly anterior and to the left of the ascending aorta. The main pulmonary artery should normally not be larger than the aorta. The right main pulmonary artery courses posterior to the ascending aorta and branches within the pericardium, giving rise to the truncus anterior, superiorly, and the right interlobar pulmonary artery more inferiorly. The left main pulmonary artery takes a more direct posterior course, passing above the left upper lobe bronchus, and giving rise to the left upper lobe and left interlobar branches.

Options:

- Click again on the image below.
- Examine an unannotated scan.
- Go ahead to the answer and discussion.

Im:12 +0   512
DFOV 33.0cm
STND
                                        Ascending aorta
                                                                    Main pulmonary artery
        Right main pulmonary artery

R
1
6   L
0   1
                                                            Left main pulmonary artery root

R   L

                                        Descending aorta

kV 120
mA 330
Large
5.0mm

http://www.medscape.com

Case Study: Interactive Entertainment

Project Overview

In an industry where much attention is lavished on games targeted for the teenage market, EPG Multimedia's project *The Cypher* is an anomaly. True, *The Cypher* is an interactive entertainment product, but it is also far more than that. *The Cypher* is one of the most original creations presenting interactive fiction on CD-ROM. "We aren't sure there is anything quite like it," says Paul Gregutt. He might be right.

First, *The Cypher* is serialized. One chapter of it appears as a section on Launch, a Bimonthly Entertainment CD-ROM published by 2Way Media, Inc. Featuring multimedia content on music, movies, games, and animation, Launch (along with Blender, the slightly more avant-garde CD-ROMzine) is one of the pioneers, and survivors, in the commercial CD-ROM marketplace.

Second, *The Cypher* is a cross-media phenomenon that starts out on the Launch CD-ROM and continues on the Web.

"Starting with Chapter 7, *The Cypher* became a piece of hybrid fiction," explains Ted Evans. "There are keys on the CD-ROM that you unlock as you search for clues, then it takes you to a secret section of a Web site where additional threads in the story continue."

At the heart of *The Cypher*'s uniqueness is old-fashioned storytelling. Says Gregutt, "It's a cliffhanger that spans the Middle Ages, 1900, and late 1999, in the tradition of Dickens, H.G. Wells, and the Saturday Afternoon Movie Series. At the end of each chapter, a shoe drops, something happens. That something is played out in the next chapter."

Unlike some multimedia products, which are often built around and showcase certain technologies, *The Cypher*'s focus is on what the three principles of EPG define as "plot and character, plot and character with multimedia fiction, and plot and character thrown in for good measure."

Size of the Market for the Product

With the excitement of the Internet and the World Wide Web, the new media press has been quick to point out the demise of the commercial CD-ROM. The popular refrain is that "you can't make money selling 25,000 CD-ROMs...but if you sell 25,000 CD-ROMs, you've got a blockbuster."

The truth is that the hype of multimedia was over-exaggerated and so is the death. "I would say multimedia is not dying, but changing," says Evans. "The Web has been the focus of everyone's attention, yet machines still keep shipping with CD-ROM drives in them. Our experience has been that there are a lot of titles out and it is hard for a consumer to differentiate between what is good and what is not. The market is becoming more mature, and people are becoming more discerning consumers."

One direction the CD-ROM industry is rapidly moving into is the hybrid CD-ROM category demonstrated by titles such as *The Cypher*, which link CD-ROMs to an on-line communication forum including the Internet or a major on-line service.

According to market research presented in the Digital Periscope, a section of the Web site for MultiMedia Merchandising (http://www.m3mag.com), titles with on-line communications, links to expanded content, or network game-play are expected to increase from 311 titles at the end of 1995 to 3,500 in 1997—nearly 10 percent of all CD-ROM titles in print worldwide.

The MultiMedia Merchandising report cites "The Hybrid CD-ROM/On-line Assessment," a study by the market research firm InfoTech, which states that common types of hybrid CD-ROM/on-line titles include games with dial-up network multiplayer capabilities; reference titles and directories with online updates; entertainment and lifestyle titles with hooks to on-line forums and Web sites; and applications software, including more than 50 different Internet-specific programs offering built-in connectivity, on-line upgrades, or remote technical support.

General Introduction to the Project

The Cypher began as Ted Evans' idea. "I've always had this desire to write a book, do a movie—basically create a work of fiction that blends history and science fiction," he says.

While at the creative agency Watt-Silverstein, Evans met partners Vince Peddle and Paul Gregutt. "I started telling them about this wacky idea that I had, this crazy story in my head. We all figured that we should try to do something about it, so the three of us sat down and cooked up this story we call *The Cypher*," a story the *Financial Times* called "part Sir Walter Scott, part H.G. Wells, part William Gibson."

The trio started taking an informal poll and came to the conclusion that what they wanted to make was a work of fiction for adults, an engaging story that didn't involve puzzles or games—in short, a story that people could interact with.

"Many people are talking about the death of the CD-ROM," says Gregutt. "What they overlook is the fact that people love engaging a good story and an environment that they can immerse themselves in. *Myst* is still selling, which proves there is a market for smart, well thought-out, old-fashioned story-telling," he adds. "Prior to *Myst*, most multimedia was geared at 18-year-old boys. The adult market had been untapped. How many Hollywood movies flop? That doesn't mean people aren't going to the movies. It means they are going to certain kinds of movies and they are going in droves. The same can be said for the CD-ROM."

The Cypher has won Best of Show 1996 honors at the Association for Multi-Image Awards (AMI), was the 1995 Merit Award Winner at the IICS Summit Awards, and captured the Bronze Medal in the 1996 INVISION Awards in the Entertainment Category from *New Media* magazine.

AND RELATIVELY MODEST IN PROPORTION. THE ROOM EXISTS DIRECTLY BEYOND THE DOOR WITH NO ENTRYWAY. NONETHELESS, THE ENGINEERS SHOULD HAVE BROKEN DIRECTLY INTO THE CHAMBER FROM ABOVE GROUND! WE HAVE MEASURED, DOUBLE-CHECKED OUR MEASUREMENTS AT LEAST 50 TIMES, ALWAYS WITH THE SAME RESULT; THE ABOVE GROUND EXCAVATION SHOULD HAVE PIERCED THIS CHAMBER ALMOST DIRECTLY CENTRE!! THE ENGINEERS AND DRS. RAMESEY AND PROGMIRE ARE DECIDELY BAFFLED.

THE CHAMBER WHICH WE ARE CALLING "THE GALLERY" IS TOTALLY EMPTY, SAVE ONE ORNATELY CARVED STONE SEAT OR THRONE AND SIX UNDESCIBABLY BEAUTIFUL FRESCOES. THERE ARE TWO OF THESE FRESCOES ON EACH OF THE 3 WALLS FACING THE DOOR. THEY CAN ALL BE VIEWED FROM THE SEAT OR THRONE EASILY. WE BELIEVE THIS ROOM WAS USED FOR PRECISELY THAT.

THE WORKS THEM-
SELVES, ARE UNLIKE
ANY ARTWORK OR
PAINTING I HAVE
SEEN FROM THIS
ERA OR EVEN FROM
THE RENAISSANCE.
THEY ARE SIMPLY
UNLIKE ANY PAINTING
I HAVE EVER SEEN.

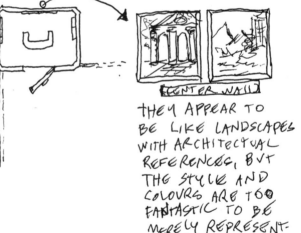

CENTER WALL

THEY APPEAR TO
BE LIKE LANDSCAPES
WITH ARCHITECTUAL
REFERENCES, BUT
THE STYLE AND
COLOURS ARE TOO
FANTASTIC TO BE
MERELY REPRESENT-
ATIONS OF A REAL
SETTING.

Figure 9.1
A Page from Ted Evans' Original Treatment of "The Cypher"

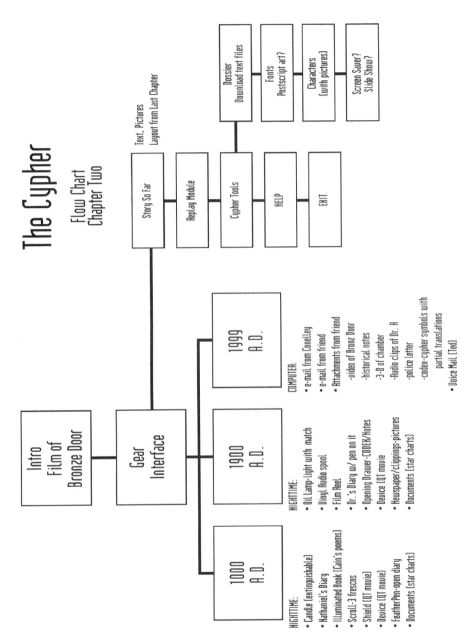

The Cypher

Flow Chart
Chapter Two

Intro
Film of
Bronze Door

Gear
Interface

1000
A.D.

NIGHTTIME:
- Candle (extinguishable)
- Nathaniel's Diary
- Illuminated Book (Cain's poems)
- Scroll-3 frescos
- Shield (QT movie)
- Device (QT movie)
- Feather/Pen-open diary
- Documents (star charts)

1900
A.D.

NIGHTTIME:
- Oil Lamp-light w/ match
- Vinyl Audio spool
- Film Reel
- Dr.'s Diary w/ pen on it
- Opening Drawer-CODEX/Notes
- Device (QT movie)
- Newspaper/clippings-pictures
- Documents (star charts)

1999
A.D.

COMPUTER:
- e-mail from ConeLley
- e-mail from friend
- Attachments from friend
  - video of Bronz Door
  - historical notes
  - 3-D of chamber
  - Audio clips of Dr. R
  - police Letter
  - codex-cypher symbols with partial translations
- Voice Mail (Ted)

Story So Far
Text, Pictures
Layout from Last Chapter

ReplayModule

CypherTools

HELP

EXIT

Dossier
Download text files

Fonts
Postscript art?

Characters
(with pictures)

Screen Saver?
Slide Show?

Figure 9.2
Flow Chart for Chapter 2

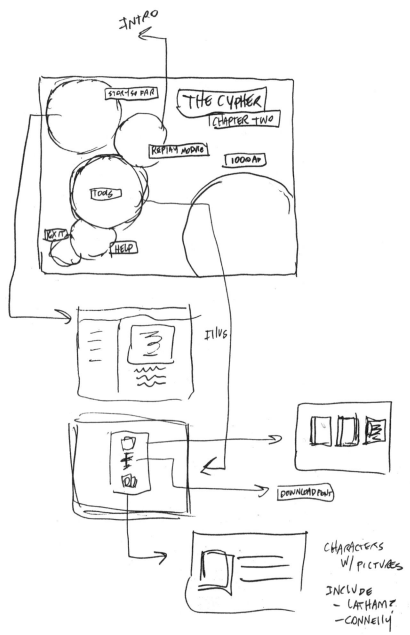

Figure 9.3
"The Cypher's" Main Interface Storyboard Rough Outline

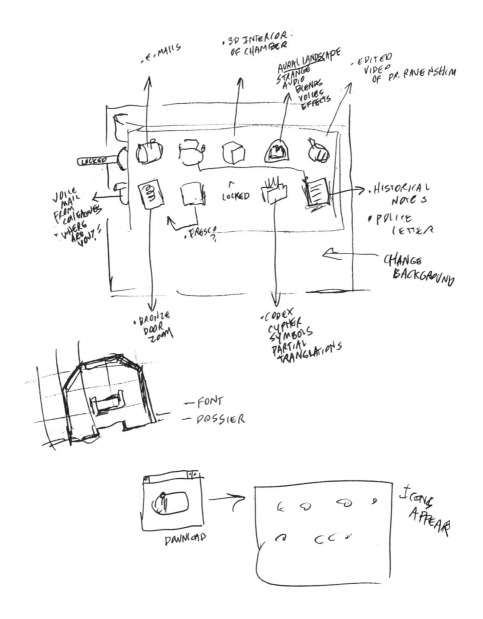

• E-MAILS

• 3-D INTERIOR OF CHAMBER

AURAL LANDSCAPE
STRANGE
AUDIO
BLENDS
VOICES
EFFECTS

• EDITED VIDEO OF DR. RAVENSHIM

LOCKED

VOICE
MAIL
FROM
COLLEAGUES
• WHERE ARE YOU?!

LOCKED

• HISTORICAL NOTES

• POLICE LETTER

CHANGE BACKGROUND

• FRESCO?

• BRONZE DOOR ZOOM

• CODEX
CYPHER
SYMBOLS
PARTIAL
TRANSLATIONS

— FONT
— DOSSIER

DOWNLOAD

ICONS APPEAR

Figure 9.4
A Rough Outline for the Year 1999 Interface

209

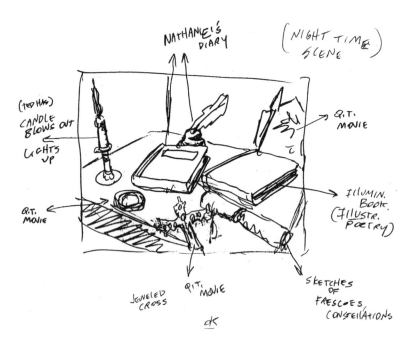

Figure 9.5
Year 1000 Interface Rough Outline with Links Noted

Company Profile

EPG Multimedia Inc.
Seattle, WA
http://www.epgmedia.com
epgmedia@halycon.com

Clients

Aldus, Apple Computer, Inc., *Better Homes and Gardens*, Corbis Publishing, Disney Vacation Club, Intel, iTravel, Microsoft, Nintendo of America, The Paramount Theater, Softimage, StarPress Publishing, US West Communications, Wall Data, *The Washington Post*

Company's Mission

"For the three of us," says Ted Evans, "it all comes down to telling stories. Our focus is telling stories creatively and interactively, whether it is for the

Web, for our fiction works, or our clients, we employ design, writing, images, and audio to create a sense of theater for the mind."

Key Projects

EPG's principals provided creative direction, design, and scripting for the highly acclaimed *Material World*, a CD-ROM offering an inspiring and surprising look at how average families live in 30 countries around the world. *Material World* is currently being translated into several foreign languages.

Corbis Publishing's *A Passion for Art*, a look at the world's greatest collection of Impressionist and post-Impressionist art, has been named one of the best CD-ROMs of 1995. EPG worked with Corbis to write, design, and produce the opening and "newsreel" style biography of eccentric collector Dr. Albert C. Barnes, the focal point of the disc.

Employees

Seven

Freelance

Two or three

Equipment List

"We don't focus much on that. We tend not to have the latest bells and whistles. We are still a start-up, and in that regard, every penny still counts," Evans says. "We have six Macintoshes, three IBMs."

Company Strategy

Before building a detailed production schedule and budget for a multimedia project, the company creates a detailed creative treatment (a design document). The treatment includes an overview of the project with specific interface design ideas and a screen-by-screen flowchart of the project.

The company's treatment answers the following questions:

- Who is the intended audience?
- What is the delivery platform (CD-ROM, kiosk, Internet)?
- What are the platform requirements/system standards?
- What specific questions must the presentation answer?

- What specific information must the presentation include?
- What level of interactivity will it incorporate?
- What options must the main interface design include?
- What pathways will branch from the main interface?
- Where will each of those pathways lead and how will they connect?
- What existing content (text, graphics, video, audio, or photos) can be used?
- What new content must be acquired?
- What is the timeline for approval of creative, design and production, testing, installation, and final delivery of the finished presentation?
- What are the budget parameters for this project?

How Does the Company Handle the Issue of Cost?

The first meeting with the client is free. Samples of work and a needs analysis is discussed. EPG then proposes a "concept and creative" fee, which ranges from $7,500 to $10,000. The fee enables EPG to thoroughly research and brainstorm the project, write a creative treatment, design a full set of storyboards, and put together a complete production schedule and budget for a project.

Project Profile

Description and Goals

The Cypher is a CD-ROM–based serialized work of fiction that also contains a link to the Web. The goal of the project for EPG was to create a work of non-fiction that took intrinsic advantage of the visually rich, interactive format of multimedia.

Client

Launch, a CD-ROM bimonthly entertainment magazine.

How Did the Company Get the Job?

EPG created a concept and prototype that was then mailed to several publishers. Launch agreed to present the project in serial form. EPG currently has a "month-by-month" contract with Launch to produce *The Cypher*.

How Many People Worked on the Project (internal, external)?

Five. Gregutt wrote the script. Evans served as the creative director and illustrator for the project. Peddle assisted in the illustration and handled production. Kim Sajn wrote the music and did all the programming for *The Cypher* in Macromedia Director. Gregutt and Peddle shared audio and production duties. EPG also had a voice-over actor and artist who charged the company on a session-by-session basis.

Hardware and Software

The Cypher was produced on a Macintosh Quadra 840 AV and a Macintosh IIci. Additional work was done on a 486/Compaq.

Challenges

The first challenge concerned price point.

The average CD-ROM can cost anywhere from $15 to $75. EPG's goal was to keep the cost low. The company overcame the challenge by breaking its story into chapters, serializing it into smaller segments that could be sold separately at a lower cost. This approach also gave the company the opportunity to shape and wind the rest of *The Cypher*'s plot over a period of time, rather than feel the production pressure to create the entire plot at once. Ultimately, serialization had the effect of enabling the company to focus on plot development with maximum flexibility.

The second challenge concerned marketing and distribution costs—typically two to three times larger than the development costs associated with the project.

"One of the biggest problems in the multimedia industry concerns shelf space," says Gregutt. "We could have gone the route of looking for investors, raising a few million dollars, setting up shop, and throwing money at our problems. But we have friends who have already gone that route, and in most cases the company goes out of business, or worse, the investors take over the company," he adds.

EPG felt that it had developed the content and that the best option for overcoming the marketing and distribution challenge was to team up with a publisher in a way that would not mean having to give up creative and editorial control—not to mention ownership.

"We shopped the proposal around to several of the CD-ROM magazines including Launch, Media, which is now defunct, and Blender. All were interested, but Launch eventually bought the project."

The win-win partnership between content creator and publisher worked. "Launch is reaching an audience of some 250,000 people. We didn't have the resources to even begin to think about that type of audience for the CD-ROM," says Evans.

Evans explains that "Launch is positioned as an impulse buy at stores such as Tower Records, where it typically costs about $6. It has the right price point and reaches the general audience interested in what's new in music and film. Having us piggy-back onto that product was critical to our getting *The Cypher* into as large an audience as possible as cost-effectively as possible."

In addition to price point, marketing, and distribution challenges, another concern became the technical challenge. *The Cypher* is limited to 15 to 20 MB of disk space on Launch. It must also function on both Macintosh and Windows machines with less than 2.5 MB of RAM.

While such technical challenges might be considered daunting, the EPG team was intrigued by the limitations. "If we had $5 million to make the project, and everyone viewing it had the most advanced multimedia machine, *The Cypher* wouldn't be much fun," says Gregutt. "What makes it interesting for us is deciding what the limitations are—be it price point, distribution, size, memory—and not only working within those limitations, but using those limits to our advantage in creating the best product we possibly can."

The Proposal

Budgeted versus Actual Numbers

Each issue of *The Cypher* cost EPG Multimedia $25,000 to produce. Each issue took the staff approximately eight weeks including creative, design, programming, and music. Although Evans points out that "one chapter was done from start to finish in three full days...they were long days, but strangely it was our best chapter."

The company breaks down the costs into the following budget categories:

Creative: $10,000

This includes developing creative concepts, creating all of the illustrations for one chapter, including icons and interfaces, as well as complete page designs.

Editorial: $5,000

This includes a budget of approximately 45 to 60 hours necessary to develop the story line and write the complete chapter.

Programming: $5,000

This includes programming entirely in Macromedia Director.

Music and Sound: $3,000

EPG composes its own music. Music and sound costs include paying voice-over talent, as well as studio editing time, and the purchase of miscellaneous sound clips. More and more, the company is bringing its music and sound production in house and managing it on the desktop.

Miscellaneous Expenses: $2,000

Includes various expenses such as additional time that runs over for various production and testing components, photography, miscellaneous software, and so on.

Total Cost of Production: $25,000

Total Number of Chapters Produced: 8

Total Investment in *The Cypher*: $200,000

Total Amount of Revenues: $5,000 per issue, total of $40,000.

Net: $160,000

EPG produces each issue of *The Cypher* on a contract-by-contract basis with Launch.

Figure 9.6
The Cover and Two Screens
from the Interface of Launch

Figure 9.7
A Prototype Screen

Figure 9.8
A Prototype Screen

Figure 9.9
A Final Introductory Interface Screen

Figure 9.10
A Final Interface Screen
for the Year 1000

In Summary

What Went Right?

In terms of accounting, EPG billed its time and expenses for *The Cypher* as a marketing expense. "Developing multimedia projects is a competitive environment," explains Evans. "We view *The Cypher* as our calling card. It has opened a lot of doors for our company. Essentially, we have been paid to do marketing for our company," he adds noting that the company's goal is to make *The Cypher* a profitable stand-alone product.

Evans notes that *The Cypher* has garnered several major multimedia industry awards, has led to the company being invited to speak at several national conferences and special events, and meeting people who liked the project. In several cases, companies who have seen *The Cypher* have contracted EPG for other corporate multimedia projects both on CD-ROM and the Web.

Not only has *The Cypher* been an outstanding calling card and marketing piece, but it has also enabled the company to develop its internal creative and production process. "What *The Cypher* helped us to do is build a technology model for our other projects. We honed our creative style with *The Cypher*—blending still images and illustrations with audio to create a mood and environment. We have leveraged the process and the style in our other projects and it has made them more profitable for us as a company," Evans explains.

In short, *The Cypher* put EPG on the multimedia map, enabled the company to develop a core technology and develop and test EPG's creative ideas.

What Went Wrong?

"Nothing catastrophic," says Gregutt, "there were some long hours and sometimes an overwhelming sense that we might tap out, that when we sat down to create the next chapter we just couldn't top what we did in the previous chapter. Fortunately, we pushed ourselves and were able to produce better work," he concludes.

EPG did not create *The Cypher* as a marketing device. They created it to develop a commercially successful and financially lucrative extension of the company's creative desires. While *The Cypher* has been a terrific marketing device, there is a sense of frustration at the company that it has taken far longer to get to the point where it is now a finished piece; *The Cypher* now contains eight complete chapters, although the story may continue.

"We wanted to make a major product in small steps," says Evans. "But we still wanted to make a major product, and it has taken us quite a long time to do it."

Where is the Company Now?

EPG views its opportunities in two ways: first pertaining to *The Cypher* and second pertaining to the company's rapidly expanding corporate CD-ROM and Web development business.

In terms of *The Cypher*, EPG is discussing the option of producing a complete CD-ROM containing all eight chapters of *The Cypher* as a stand-alone title. The company is also in the beginning stages of discussing the possibility of producing an Internet-enriched version of *The Cypher* for a cable modem company seeking to develop content to showcase its technology. There has also been discussion with a publisher interested in publishing *The Cypher* on paper without the bells and whistles as a fiction work. And the most recent offer comes from a producer interested in taking *The Cypher* from the computer screen to the silver screen.

The Cypher has had an impact on EPG's business development. Based on the work, the company recently entered into a strategic partnership with Crosswater Multimedia, a company based in London. "Crosswater has been a successful British firm for a number of years producing large-scale corporate shows and events as well as sales and marketing films," explains Evans. "They had started an interactive branch but it has struggled to get off the ground. In our partnership, we provide the multimedia development for Crosswater, and Crosswater is developing *The Cypher* for the European market with plans to expand, first into France and then across Europe."

Business is booming and the company is also focused on its plans to develop an interactive fiction mission for the Web, as well as servicing its major corporate clients in both business-to-business CD-ROM markets and Web sites.

Says Evans: "The corporate use of multimedia is huge. While many people are shying away from the commercial CD-ROM market, many businesses recognize that the CD-ROM is still a great way to hand a customer a marketing message. It is still one of the best ways to sell a product."

Color versions of this Web site can be seen in Color Plates #6 and 7.

Case Study:
Children's CD-ROM

Type of Product Being Profiled

Rodney Alan Greenblat is an artist. He has real paintings, real sculptures, and has had real gallery shows. In fact, in the downtown New York art scene he is *known*. Prints of his work can be purchased in some art stores in SoHo, the heart of Manhattan's art world.

His product, *Dazzeloids*, is a CD-ROM that, above all else, represents a window into the mind of its creator—Rodney himself. *Dazzeloids* is a carefully woven tale that creates an interactive storybook falling somewhere between a Red Grooms work, an episode of the Simpson's, and Dr. Seuss. In describing his own work, Greenblat says, "It's like folk art from another planet."

"I had seen all of the so-called storybooks," says Greenblat, "and with *Dazzeloids* I wanted to try to create something completely original, something that not only improved upon the model for existing interactive story books, but smashed it by creating an entirely new way of doing things."

By all accounts, he succeeded. *Dazzeloids*, which features "superheroes on a binge against boredom," tells the tale of how Stinkabod Lame (daredevil prankster and slamdancer), Yendor Talbneerg (technoid supreme and the creator's name spelled backward), and Titan Rose (muscleman and poet) work under the direction of commander Anne Dilly Whim to battle the Mediogre, head of the Blando Corporation. While the characters, sounds, and animations appeal to children, *Dazzeloids'* message has struck a chord with new media enthusiasts and the general public for its intelligence and creativity.

Size of Market

How big is the market for children's CD-ROMs? It's hard to say actually. One minute the multimedia industry is the next biggest thing since motion pictures, the next, it is the Edsel of entertainment media.

What is known is that more and more consumers are purchasing CD-ROMs—either separately or included in the home computer systems they are buying.

The CD-ROM Market

According to "Facts on Doing Business in Today's CD-ROM Market," presented on the Web site of the Interactive Multimedia Association (http://www.ima.org), the number of retail CD-ROM units sold translates to 32.9 million in 1996, or $1.4 billion in retail value.

The same source refers to data that suggest there are in excess of 11,000 CD-ROM and multimedia titles commercially available worldwide; annual title growth is estimated at more than 50%, and profits for CD-ROM software publishers could top $8.8 billion in 1997.

Still, according to the Stamford, Connecticut-based SIMBA, a unit of Cowles Business Media (http://www.simbanet.com), only 6% of the titles offered for sale in 1994 turned a profit.

General Introduction to the Project

"I really wanted to do a kids' project," says Greenblat. "My earlier project, *Rodney's Wonder World*, was a strange product with a demographic of one—me," he says. "But with *Dazzeloids* I wanted to do a storybook like *Grandma and Me*. I liked the interaction in that product, but in some ways, *Grandma and Me* was better as a book. My story was created specifically for CD-ROM. The real intent was to crumple up all the rules and start fresh."

Company Profile

The Center for Advanced Whimsy
http://www.whimsyload.com
rodney@whimsyload.com

Located in New York City, The Center for Advanced Whimsy specializes in creating original worlds in a variety of formats. We have created CD-ROM productions, digital paintings, children's books, music, animation, and a line of consumer products distributed in Japan.

Officially incorporated in 1996, founding member Rodney Alan Greenblat has been creating successful paintings, sculpture, furniture, and children's books since 1982.

The Mission of the Center For Advanced Whimsy

- To revel in imagination and remind the world how valuable fun, wonder, and play really are

- Integrate children's books, consumer products, CD-ROM, television and video games in new and exciting ways

- Create an independent multi-million-dollar company

- Have fun

Key Projects

Rodney's Wonder Window, Rodney's Fun Screen, Dazzeloids, Clickamajigs (for Nickelodeon).

Employees

Four, in addition to Rodney. Dina, his wife is the company manager; Jenny Horn, talented illustrator and animator, and programmer David Anderson.

Freelance

From time to time freelancers are used.

Equipment List

A Macintosh Powerbook 540C, a PowerMac 8500, a Quadra 950, a Macintosh IIci, and a Rodney original—a fully functional, hot pink Macintosh LC. There's also an assortment of digital and analog keyboards.

Project Profile

Publisher

The Voyager Company

How Did the Company Get the Job?

Rodney sent the company a prototype for what he wanted to do and Voyager purchased it.

Challenges

First there were the budget constraints (more on that later).

Second, time constraints. The entire project had to be created entirely from scratch—including story lines, character drawings, animations, and sound—and on the shelf in less than one year.

Figure 10.1
Center Screen
Interface

Figure 10.2
Hamster Becomes Ill
With the Dreadful
Fuzzy Rodent Flu

Figure 10.3
Jeremy's Shriveled Brain Needs Help!

Figure 10.4
The Bad Guys Plot Their Reign of Boredom

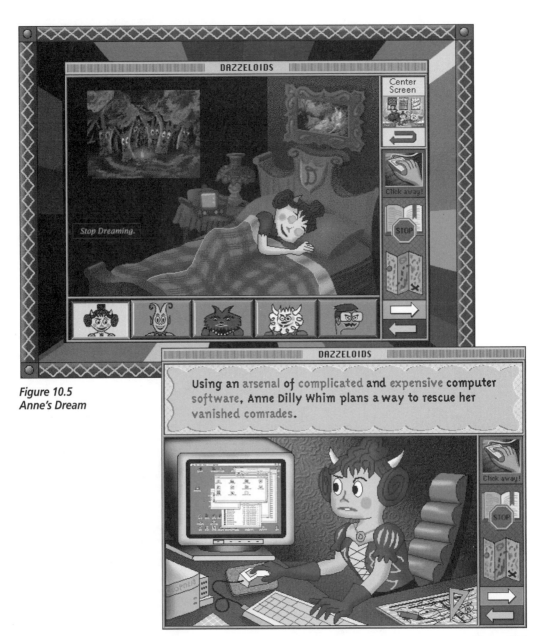

Figure 10.5
Anne's Dream

Figure 10.6
Anne Works on Saving Her Friends with Sophisticated Software

"In order to do that, I chose a simple form to follow," says Greenblat. "I wasn't branching into hypertextual infinity land. I had a basic story and I kept it simple."

Greenblat also says that technology was not important. "I didn't want to have to jump over hurdles, technologically speaking," he says. "I wanted to tell funny stories, through great characters, with good sound. There was no interest in over-technologizing the project. I wanted it to work." The strategy was to create the entire CD-ROM in Macromedia's Director, keep it basic, and reduce the amount of technical problems by not doing anything challenging. In short, keep the focus on the art.

Budgeted versus Actual Numbers

The story of the budget process for *Dazzeloids* is almost as intriguing as *Dazzeloids* itself.

"It wasn't exactly science," describes Greenblat. "I added up my overhead, a salary for Jenny, a salary for the freelancer and programmer, and came to some sort of a crazy number," he recalls. "What I forgot was to double the amount—that would be called profit," he laughs. "And, then double it again, that would have covered the actual time it really takes to produce a CD-ROM. It would have covered the fact that no matter how simple you keep it, everything can go wrong."

Rodney Greenblat, as decent and honest as he is creative and talented, cringes when it comes to floating out how much he got paid by Voyager to create and produce *Dazzeloids*.

"It's too embarrassing," he says, "I can tell you it wasn't less than $50,000 and it wasn't more than $100,000. The rest is too painful," he says kidding in his good-natured way. "Looking back on it, it should have been a $350,000 budget. That would have accounted for all of our time, we would have made a profit, and had some left over."

As it stands, Greenblat estimates that with 7,000 copies sold, *Dazzeloids* has, at the very least, *barely* broken even for all his work. A shockingly low figure when you consider that nearly every publication that reviewed the product rated it among the best CD-ROMs ever made. That critical success puts *Dazzeloids* into Mark Twain's definition of a classic—a book that everybody talks about, but no one has read. "I know a lot of people who love *Dazzeloids*, they heard about it, they rave about it, but I don't know many people who have actually bought it," says Greenblat.

In Summary

By all accounts *Dazzeloids* was a critical success. It won *New Media* magazine's INVISION Award for the Best Children's Piece, Consumer Category. It also won the IMAGIC award for the best product in the home category, an outstanding design in the interactive category from *ID* magazine, and additional honors from *Newsweek* magazine.

More important to Rodney Greenblat the artist, the project was an aesthetic success. "It really is me," he explains. "I made some critical points with the project, communicated some ideas using humor, and also managed to provide some depth without being boring."

He acknowledges and thanks his publisher, The Voyager Company, for giving him full artistic license. "I was happy to work with Voyager. Not many other publishers would have the guts to let me be me."

Greenblat readily admits that the way he structured his deal with Voyager did not take into account the unique nature of the new media creation process.

"In my contract, I set up benchmarks that I had to meet in order to get my checks," he explains. "For example, the first storyboards were to be done by this time, the first story with sound by that time, and the animation by another date."

But, as he points out, the new media production process doesn't quite lend itself to that type of linear contract progression. "I wasn't prepared and didn't realize the chaos involved in doing the sound. It threw off the whole schedule. I ultimately found myself in a position where I needed the capital to pay for the project, but I had not made my goal. My benchmarks didn't make sense."

More important, one gets the sense that Greenblat is disappointed with the sales for his products. Compared to the rave reviews and critical acclaim it received, *Dazzeloids* was not a blockbuster success. "I don't think Voyager was disappointed in *Dazzeloids*, but I wished that it could have done better," he admits.

Another problem concerned marketing. "There's a balance between artistic freedom on the one hand and sales on the other," comments Greenblat, "it is axiomatic that the more artistic freedom you allow, the less commercially viable the product will be."

Says Greenblat: "As a publisher, The Voyager Company doesn't focus on the CompUSA or the Egghead Software stores. They tend not to understand how important the retail market is to a product's success."

Voyager's strategy, it appears, is to sell its CD-ROMs in bookstores because they regard it as pure content rather than technology or software. "Unfortunately," says Greenblat, "we both learned that you tend not to sell a lot of software in bookstores."

Not only does Greenblat feel that distribution was a problem, but that *Dazzeloids* also lacked marketing muscle. "There simply wasn't any advertising money," he claims. "In some ways, it was depressing. The biggest lesson I learned was that you have to do more than create the best product, you need to market it and make sure that people know about it. Not enough people know about *Dazzeloids*."

Where is the Company Now?

Greenblat says he learned a lot about marketing and distribution from *Dazzeloids*. "I learned more with that product than you learn in business school," has says. "I also learned the medium and I am not afraid of it," he says of how *Dazzeloids* affected its business. "But I will not do another CD-ROM and there will not be a *Dazzeloids II*," he adds. "I have moved on."

What's Next for the Artist?

"There is no question that *Dazzeloids* opened a lot of doors for my work. We are working with Sony on a Play Station game for kids. It's called *PaRappa The Rapper*," says Greenblat. That product will be out in Japan by the end of 1996. "The Japanese are so much more accepting of my work," he says. "In the United States, there is a tendency to categorize things. In Japan, there are no boundaries, they just accept what I do."

As a result of his acceptance in Japan, Greenblat is working with Fuji TV on a one-minute animated segment for a children's show that will tie into a paint program.

In the meantime, he is still hard at work on his *Clickamajigs* animated series for Nickelodeon and is now turning to the Web. "I find the Web is a total artistic experience," he says. "We are going to go nuts and do some totally crazy stuff on the Web." Look for his non-profit Web site showcase to appear at http://www.reallygood.com.

Color versions of this CD-ROM can be seen in Color Plate #3.

Case Study: Educational CD-ROM

Type of Product Being Profiled

Where would you expect to find one of the first, and certainly one of the most significant, documentaries ever produced on the Vietnam War Memorial? An arts theater? A museum? On public television?

What if that documentary was produced entirely on CD-ROM? Where would it be sold? In computer stores where people expect to purchase software? In record stores where consumers expect to find music? Or in bookstores where people traditionally shop for works on paper? More important, what would you call such an important product that provides insight into one of the most turbulent events in American history?

In a consumer society where everything has to fit in categories, Magnet Interactive Studios' *Beyond the Wall: Stories behind the Vietnam War* defies categorization and transcends every notion of what interactive technology is all about.

The product enables viewers to take a vivid three-dimensional journey to the Vietnam Veterans Memorial in Washington, DC. Along the way, viewers discover a forgotten side to the war: the jarring memories and reflections by the family members of the 58,000 Americans who died in the Vietnam War, soldiers who have their names inscribed on Maya Lin's architectural testimony.

"It's the only CD-ROM that ever made me cry," reported one *New Media* magazine INVISION Award judge. *Beyond the Wall* was honored with an Award of Excellence in the Information and Reference category as well as overall best of show for new media CD-ROMs.

But does categorizing *Beyond the Wall* as a reference product do it justice? "It's difficult to fit this product into a neat category with space on a shelf. It's an interactive documentary of the highest quality, a history product with meticulous attention to detail, and it's also very engaging," comments John Gamba, Director of Marketing and Business Affairs at Magnet Interactive Studios, producer and publisher of *Beyond the Wall*.

Size of Market

It is difficult to determine the size of the market for a product such as *Beyond the Wall* because you can slice the pie in so many ways. You could come at it from the perspective of the families involved in the war and decide that the potential market might be the number of people who were affected by the war, or the general public interested in the war itself—after all, movies such as *The Deer Hunter*, *Platoon*, *Hamburger Hill*, and *Born on the Fourth of July* have been well-received by the general public at the box office.

Then there's the educational software market believed to range in the billions of dollars of sales annual. "We examined the educational software market," says Gamba, "looking at the unit sales in five or six subcategories within that market, and based on industry trends, we felt we could create a quality-driven product that could rival the unit sales of other competing products in the marketplace. We felt that if we could sell anywhere from 25,000 to 30,000 units we would be in good shape as far as profitability."

Figure 11.1
Artifacts

Figure 11.2
A Personal Story

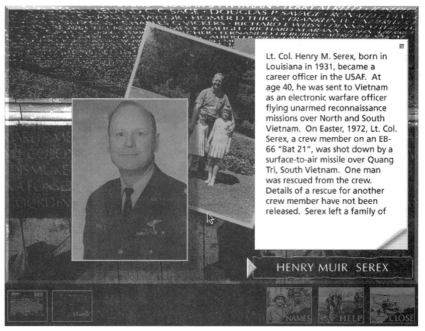

Lt. Col. Henry M. Serex, born in Louisiana in 1931, became a career officer in the USAF. At age 40, he was sent to Vietnam as an electronic warfare officer flying unarmed reconnaissance missions over North and South Vietnam. On Easter, 1972, Lt. Col. Serex, a crew member on an EB-66 "Bat 21", was shot down by a surface-to-air missile over Quang Tri, South Vietnam. One man was rescued from the crew. Details of a rescue for another crew member have not been released. Serex left a family of

HENRY MUIR SEREX

Figure 11.3
Another Personal Story

General Introduction to the Project

The concept for creating a documentary about the Vietnam War Memorial originated as a project in school. "I was working on my master's thesis at New York University's Interactive Telecommunications Program," says Joe Feffer, the creator and driving force behind the project.

"I was looking to tell a story using new media. I was trying to break the boundaries associated with reference products and inject an emotional and human element into new media," he reflects. "I had been to the Wall on several occasions and one day, when I was doing research for my thesis topic, I went down there to see what was going on. As I got closer to the Wall and I could see the names of the soldiers killed in battle engraved on it, I started to listen. There were people telling stories about family members who had died. There were people selling stuff. I was watching what people were doing at the Wall and it clicked. It was an important and powerful subject and the right message for a new medium."

Company Profile

Magnet Interactive Communications, LLC
Washington, DC
http://www.magnet.com

Clients

Twentieth Century Fox Home Entertainment, Microsoft Corporation, Dow Jones, Inc., J. Walter Thompson, and Time Life, among others.

About the Company

Magnet Interactive Group (MIG), headquartered in Washington, DC, is the holding company of two subsidiaries—Magnet Interactive Communications (MIC) and Magnet Interactive Studios (MIS). Founded in 1989 as a progressive print and three-dimensional design firm, Magnet saw the potential for interactive multimedia and dedicated itself to becoming a leading, full-service interactive development studio.

MIC is an interactive agency positioned at the convergence point of marketing, technology, and entertainment. MIC weaves business interests with cutting-edge technology and an exciting creative perspective. MIC fills a void that advertising agencies, production houses, PR firms, and consultants cannot. Interactive communication—including on-line, CD-ROM, diskette, and network applications—is a new discipline that requires study and experience to apply elegantly. As a developer who started on the ground level, MIC has not only assimilated the vast and burgeoning information on these media, but originates model methods of using them skillfully.

MIS is a well-renowned interactive entertainment and edutainment developer and publisher of award-winning CD-ROM titles including *Beyond the Wall: Stories Behind the Vietnam Wall*, *Comedians*, *Chop Suey*, and *ICE-BREAKER*. Twentieth Century Fox Home Entertainment is MIS' distribution partner for self-published titles. MIS has also developed successful CD-ROM titles for third-party publishers including Time Life, Virgin Sound & Vision, and American Softworks.

Company Background

Magnet Interactive opened its doors in 1989. Since that time, the company has navigated the often treacherous business waters of new media by evolving with technology. "Starting as a progressive print and 3D design company, we have evolved to become a full-service producer of high-end business applications for Fortune 500 companies," explains Gamba.

"Our heritage in design enabled us to develop a strong core competency in the production of interactive applications, which means the company has developed expertise in using technology to create workable solutions to the needs of the corporate community. As the technology market moved to entertainment, we shifted our focus to becoming publishers and developers of high-quality entertainment products with Twentieth Century Fox as our distributors," he explains.

While Magnet was in the process of becoming a full-service producer and publisher, the company saw the rapid emergence of the CD-ROM market, and its quick demise. "We saw it as an enormous opportunity," comments Gamba. "But the window of opportunity was short-lived." As the market seemed to bottom out, Magnet was successfully able to shift its expertise to developing Internet-based business applications.

"We've become a full-service turnkey interactive agency," says Gamba. "We partner with advertising agencies to deliver interactive applications to Fortune 500 companies via the Web, including work for Mercedes Benz, National Geographic, Kellogg's, Pain Webber, Dow Jones, Nissan, Federal Express, Citibank, and others."

The key factor in Magnet's capability to continue to adapt and evolve has been the company's approach to creating new media. "Over time we have developed a stringent design methodology," explains Gamba. "We have honed and perfected the notion of shaping interactive strategies by partnering with our clients and their agencies to ensure that their brands are extended to the World Wide Web in a powerful and meaningful manner."

Employees

With 140 people presently on staff, Magnet is one of the largest interactive developers in the United States.

Freelance

Magnet uses freelancers on rare occasions; as a full-service company, Magnet tends to use staff members for all of its projects.

Equipment List

"We are platform indifferent," says Gamba, "meaning we can develop for any delivery and distribution mechanism: the Web, LAN, WAN, CD-ROM, diskette, game platform, and so on."

Project Profile

Description and Goals

"We began with one goal—to create as high a quality product as possible," comments Gamba. "The focus was to create a visually engaging and fully interactive title that would elicit an emotional response to the Vietnam War in general and the Vietnam wall in particular," he says.

Despite the potentially volatile subject, Magnet's goal, as envisioned by Joe Feffer, was to take an apolitical approach by focusing on the families affected by the war. "Outside of creating the best product we could, we really wanted to focus on the people whose lives were touched by the war," remarks Gamba.

How Many People Worked on the Project?

The number of people working on the project fluctuated. At any given time, there were as few as five people working on *Beyond the Wall* or as many as 20, depending on where the project was in the production process. Team members included programmers, designers, producers, production assistants, quality assurance, videographers, audio engineers, and composers.

Hardware and Software

Macintosh, Windows, and Silicon Graphics

Challenges

At the time, Magnet was a newcomer to the publishing market. "We knew there were three or four publishers that dominated the market," comments Gamba. "Since *Beyond the Wall* was one of our first edutainment titles, we wanted it to be groundbreaking. It was important that we set a standard of quality for the company as well as for the industry. That was the prime challenge—it was our first effort, and we knew there would be no second chances."

Once the project began, there were other questions. "Could this happen?" wondered Feffer. "The enormity of the project started to hang over the project. We started to question whether or not we could pull all of the content together to create the rich experience we desired."

In doing so, Feffer first had to enlist the support of the organization that created the wall, the Vietnam Veterans' Memorial Fund, which had financed the monument through a combination of private donations and a grant of government land. "We approached them in stages," reflects Feffer. "We made a pitch to them and the key in doing so was stressing our sincerity in making a quality-driven project. Fortunately, they understood our intentions and they were also very supportive of our efforts to educate the public about the wall."

With the support of the creators of the wall behind them, Feffer's team started approaching the families whose relatives had died in the war and had their names inscribed on the memorial.

"We were wondering if those family members would want to relive the sadness of thinking about the war," says Feffer. "Then the Federal Express packages started coming in...there were birthday cards that soldiers had sent home to their families from the front which detailed life during the war, audio taped messages from soldiers and photos—all of it so compelling. Maya Lin, the architect who won the 1981 national design competition to design the wall, was wonderful. She pointed us to information on the design of the wall and her work. Our efforts to collect content were overwhelmingly accepted."

Feffer says that in addition to resources provided by the Library of Congress, what emerged was a grassroots network of people all connected by the Vietnam Veterans Memorial Fund. "A friend told a friend and everyone wanted to contribute. What developed was a close-knit group of people who wanted to get involved," says Feffer.

That support created another challenge for the project: Sifting through very personal information about a very charged war and dealing with the emotionality of weaving that information into a story. "For me, that was the definitive creative challenge," comments Feffer. "I started down a path and made a commitment to fulfilling the goals of the project as if it were my own child. I and every member of the team took the project to heart, we all raised it," he adds. "More than anything else," Feffer concludes, "our team was fortunate to get the financial and emotional support of Magnet's management to make the project work. We made a commitment to the families who were on the wall and Magnet made the commitment to us."

Budgeted versus Actual Numbers

Budgets are traditionally determined by the level of technology and interactivity the product contains. On the other hand, both the technical and interactive requirements are determined by the market. If the market will not bear the cost of the project, its efforts must be scaled back. *Beyond the Wall* represents a nice balance. The CD-ROM contains intricate 3D graphics and an interactive database that contains every name engraved on the wall.

The initial budget for *Beyond the Wall* ranged from $550,000 to $650,000, which included the total cost to produce both the Macintosh and PC version of the product. The product was developed on the Macintosh with Silicon Graphics and ported to the Windows platform.

In that budget, programming was the most expensive aspect, in particular, building the database of names.

The second largest aspect of the budget was the animation. The project contains a large amount of 3D animation including a virtual walk along the wall. That animation had to be created on an SGI machine using Alias Wavefront and SoftImage animation software and required using advanced and experienced animators.

When asked if *Beyond the Wall* was a break-even project, Gamba says "No. Our break-even was just under 20,000 units. To date we have sold about 10,000 units.

In Summary

"In production, the team started to really rely on each other. They had a mission and through their dedication the team heard a calling," comments Gamba. "They were committed to telling an interactive story of the families who had the names of the relatives on the Wall. We succeeded in portraying the human side of the War."

Feffer agrees. "An amazing product came out and we were proud to have our names attached to it. It was quite a team effort. Regardless of the issue of sales, everyone received the product with the highest regards."

Because the product did not hit its break-even target, however, it might be said the business side of the project went wrong. When asked to point to why, Gamba cites two key factors. "First, we had misjudged the learning curve on distributing the product. We were not as successful as other larger publishers in marketing those kinds of niche products. Second, we clearly experienced an unfortunate circumstance where the market went south. People thought the market would be a blockbuster, but at the time we started *Beyond the Wall*, the CD-ROM market was in its embryonic state. By the time the product was finished, the Web exploded and the CD-ROM market went soft."

Still, the financial facts don't detract from the creation of the final product. "It was really a labor of love," comments Feffer. "We pulled together a team of artists who believed in something. We believed in doing something different in a medium that was different. We encouraged each other to push the envelope, make a commitment and create our best work. In the end, that is the standard by which true creativity is judged. In the end, regardless of the financials, people are remembered for their creative work."

Where is the Company Now?

Today, Magnet no longer considers itself a publisher of entertainment titles on CD-ROM. It has, however, successfully, shifted its focus to create award-winning Web sites for some of the largest commercial product corporations in the world.

After producing *Beyond the Wall* and another Magnet title, *Comedians*, Feffer served as the company's senior producer of *National Geographic* on-line. Feffer recently left Magnet and moved to Walt Disney where he works in creative development for the Edutainment Group.

As for Gamba, he hasn't given up yet. He presently splits his time trying to sell *Beyond the Wall* directly to consumers (http://www.magnet.com/wall) and the other half developing interactive strategies for Magnet's roster of Fortune 500 companies.

Color versions of this CD-ROM can be seen in Color Plate #8.

Case Study: Small Web Site

Type of Product Being Profiled

This case study presents a simple example of a corporate Web site constructed for a law firm. This type of Web site is indicative of the types of projects that many small to mid-sized design firms and Web developers are likely to produce as they move into the marketplace.

Law firms make excellent candidates for the Web. Depending on the state the firm is practicing in, restrictions may preclude soliciting clients and the issue of advertising is particularly sensitive. On the Internet, a law firm can establish an identity, provide information on the types of law practiced by the firm, as well as offer legal information of interest to consumers—all within accepted standards of conduct. The enormous potential for law firms moving onto the Internet has spawned a number of special conferences specifically addressing the issue. Notes the flyer for one conference, "For a law firm, a World Wide Web address is becoming as important as properly designed letterhead." A very informal Web search reveals that there are, at the very least, some 600 firms on the Internet.

Obviously, the Tremont & Sheldon Web site is not of the same magnitude as www.cnn.com. In most cases, small to mid-sized design shops are likely to enter into Web design by working with their current print clients as they establish an on-line presence. Some may not feel the need to pitch Web business separately, but choose instead to make it a component of the range of services it offers. Others, after they have developed a portfolio of sites, will then actively seek Web work exclusively. In either case, their efforts are likely to start small and grow.

Most of the attention in the Web development industry concerns the emerging Web developers. And with good reason: in many cases, these developers are pioneers now shaping the Internet with creative and technological solutions.

Still, there are others—from freelance designers to design firms with a staff of less than half a dozen, to a small creative department—working in a small to mid-sized business. This case study is for these types of small businesses.

Size of Market

The New York Times reports that the number of sites on the rapidly expanding Web—the highly graphics portion of the Internet—range from 90,000 to 265,000. *The Times* quotes Rick Spence, an on-line analyst at Dataquest (a research firm) estimating that at the very least "tens of millions" of dollars are spent on Web site development annually.

As many small businesses as there are...there is a potential client.

General Introduction to the Project

Although the size of this project is small and manageable, the background and significance is anything but basic. The law firm of Tremont & Sheldon has been involved in a case against the Bridgeport Diocese of the Catholic Church. The case concerns allegations of sexual abuse by priests at the Church. Collaboration regarding the charges is key to Tremont & Sheldon's case.

In what some have suggested is a "historic gesture in terms of the medium," the firm turned to the Internet to communicate the details of the case and seek individuals with information pertaining to the suit to come forward. The Web site had to reach out to those individuals while also remaining sensitive to the nature of the circumstances regarding the claim.

Company Profile

Sustainable Media
New York, NY
http://www.earthpledge.org
jpfrenza@earthpledge.org

Clients

Apple Computer, AT&T, Open Text Corporation, the United Nations, Joe Breeze Cycles, IZM, and more

Company's Mission

Sustainable Media recognizes that computers and communications technology can convert information into knowledge, and connectivity into cooperation promoting sustainable solutions to the challenges we face.

A full-service Internet agency, Sustainable Media raises funds from the private sector to support the development of World Wide Web (WWW) sites for non-profit organizations. It also produces World Wide Web sites for businesses practicing the principles of sustainable development.

The firm believes sustainable media use technology to promote sustainable development by:

- Focusing on programs that minimize the impact of the communications process on the environment
- Fostering greater dialog on environmental, social, and economic needs
- Showcasing innovative solutions and fostering relationships that integrate economic growth, equity, and the environment in public policy

Employees

Four

Freelance

Two

Equipment List

Macintosh platform: Quadra 650, Power Macintosh 7100, Power Macintosh 8100/110, Power Macintosh 7500/100, Powerbook Duo 280c, Powerbook 540c.

Project Profile

Description and Goals

The goal of the project is to provide the client with an Internet presence that discusses information about the firm's case against the Bridgeport, Connecticut, Diocese of the Catholic Church and provides for individuals involved in the case a mechanism to contact the firm with more information.

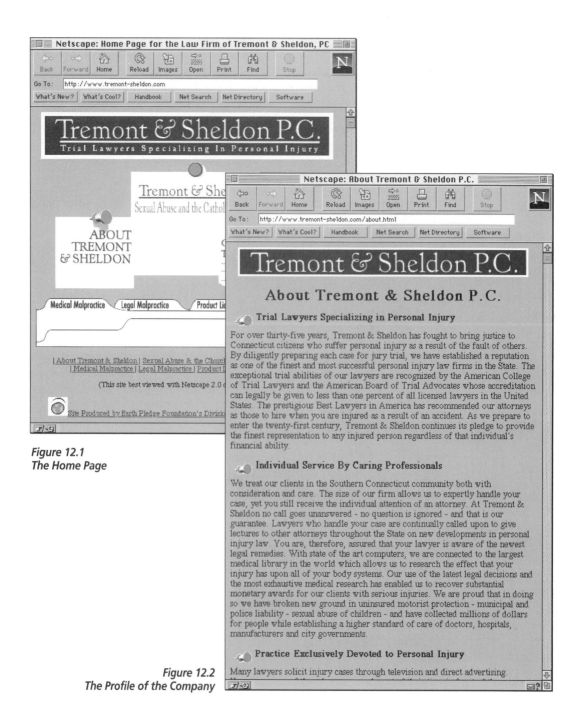

Figure 12.1
The Home Page

Figure 12.2
The Profile of the Company

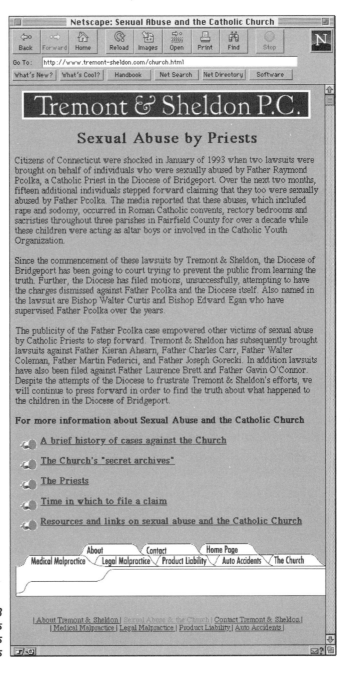

Figure 12.3
This Page on the Site has
Generated Large Amounts
of Attention from the Press

Content Determines Hierarchy

Many larger commercial Web sites are designed to offer viewers a unique on-line experience. They seek to provide a context, or an environment in which the viewer becomes totally immersed. A good example of this is Apple Computer's promotion for the movie *Mission Impossible*. You enter into an environment when you log into *Mission Impossible* (http://www.mission.apple.com). You are now in the world in which spies operate. You see an attaché case and the types of icons that you would expect to encounter if you were operating in the world of international espionage.

This approach is entirely appropriate and effective when the context of the site is really the content. For *Mission Impossible*, the whole point is the environment that Apple has created. In terms of CD-ROMs, *Myst* is another great example where "the environment is the message," to borrow from McLuhan. We like to call this the "electronic texture."

Client

The Law Firm of Tremont & Sheldon

How Did the Company Get the Job?

One of Tremont & Sheldon's clients suggested the firm contact "a friend who built Internet Web sites"—Sustainable Media.

How Many People Worked on the Project?

Two. One individual who served as client contact, project manager, and server administrator, and one individual who designed the site, as well as handled all production and HTML.

Hardware and Software

All of the design, production, and HTML was produced on a Macintosh 8100/110 with 64 MB of RAM. The site is housed on a Macintosh Work Group Server 6150 connected to the Internet with a 56k line.

As a client, Tremont & Sheldon was flexible when it came to the design of the site. The client contacts, Jason Tremont and Doug Mahoney (both attorneys at the firm), immediately approved of the Web site's design, which adapted the traditional law office motif—the legal pad background, the "Post it" memos, push pins, and folders.

The Web site's home page was structured so that visitors to the site could immediately be directed to answer three important questions:

1. What is Tremont & Sheldon?

2. What is the firm's case against the Catholic Church?

3. How do I contact the firm?

The answers to all three questions can be found by clicking the three notes prominently displayed at the top of the home page—About Tremont & Sheldon, Tremont & Sheldon: Sexual Abuse and the Catholic Church, and Contact Tremont and Sheldon.

Since the firm's case against the church was the raison d'être for the project, the structure of the site was built accordingly. At the bottom of the page, the firm provides links that take viewers to other sections of the site that describe the firm's practice. These pages are not heavily trafficked. When viewers click on the section "Sexual Abuse and the Catholic Church," they see a paragraph that provides immediate information regarding details pertaining to the case. Immediately visible is the headline "Sexual Abuse by Priests."

Following that headline is the sentence: "Citizens of Connecticut were shocked in January of 1993 when two lawsuits were brought on behalf of individuals who were sexually abused by Father Raymond Pcolka, a Catholic Priest in the Diocese of Bridgeport." The paragraph continues with specific allegations. All of the other information on this page, highlighted by push pins and titles, provides supplemental evidence and information pertaining to the case.

During the phase of the project where Sustainable Media was determining the structure of the site (a process we call "site architecture"), everyone, including the client, felt that it could take no more than two "clicks" to find all of the details pertaining to the case against the church. The information had to be immediately accessible. With this site, visitors hit the home page (one click) where they see the section "Sexual Abuse and the Catholic Church" prominently displayed. Then they click (the second time)—and are immediately engaged by details about the case.

During the creation of the site architecture the question of putting the background of the case directly on the home page was reviewed as an option. Should there be a statement on the home page about the details of the case? It was finally decided that due to the sensitive nature of the topic, it was best to provide visitors with at least one "buffer page"—the home page—before the details appeared.

This site is a good example of how a Web site's content can determine its structure. That is, the axiom works, "content determines hierarchy." See the sidebar.

Web sites such as Tremont & Sheldon exist exclusively to provide specific information. Unless you are doing work for large entertainment companies, or high-tech businesses that are showcasing a particular product, you are likely to be building sites where your clients have a message and want to communicate that message. They are not likely to have the budget or the desire to engage in designing environments. They are more likely to echo the sentiments of one shoe company that, on having their Web site designed said, "It's simple. We make shoes. Here's a picture of our shoes. Go here to buy our shoes."

That said, the presentation of information has its own challenges and rewards and is not an argument for dismissing sound design principles altogether. There are information-oriented Web sites that are well done, others that are poorly done. The same can be said for sites with an "entertainment" focus.

Challenges

Since the Tremont & Sheldon Web site was small, simple, and straightforward, it did not pose a graphical or programming challenge. There were no forms, no animated GIFs, and no Java. The greatest potential challenge that the Web site posed concerned the content—the specific presentation of it and its language. Fortunately, all of the creation of the content was handled by the law firm, which paid careful attention to the language it used to describe the case.

The Proposal

Here's a look at a few pages from the actual proposal that was presented to the firm.

Initial Budget and Development Areas

Here are the initial budget categories presented to the client for the site:

Server Set Up: $700 (one-time charge)

Including:

- Domain Name Registration

- DNS for one year
- Server hosting for one year

Content Development and Site Architecture: $3,500

- Review content
- Create concept, site organization, section
- Sketch out site architecture (in words)
- Create final site blueprint (navigational map)
- Client revisions on site structure

Design: $4,000

- Create initial sketches (one design concept was given with the design applied to 3 different types of pages that would appear on the site: the home page, a section page, and a data page)
- Create assets (logos, icons)
- Create final designs
- Client approval

Production: $2,500

- Convert artwork (indexing, and so on)
- HTML of all 18 pages
- Test links and navigation
- Test on server

Marketing: $1,500

- Research links and establish contact with resources on the Internet related to the case
- Register with approximately 20 search engines
- Develop two-page press release on the site

Site Maintenance and Management: $1,500 (one-time charge)

- Server management

- Content corrections and updates until the site went "live"

Client Management/Liaison: $1,500

- Client meetings and additional approval
- Cost of sales (developing proposal, and so on)

Total Cost to Client: $15,200

Budgeted versus Actual Numbers

Total Cost to Client: $15,200

Total Cost to Produce: $6,000 (all out-of-pocket and labor expenses)

Total Contribution: $9,200

Contribution Margin Ratio: 60%

Budget Category Analysis

Server Set Up: $700

Over budget. Pertaining to DNS problems. More on this later.

Content Development and Site Architecture: $3,500

Substantially under budget based on the fact that the content was provided by the law firm. The information was clear and well-organized which made sketching out the site a relatively simple task. More important, all of the content was provided on disk and needed no editing or alterations. The majority of the profitability related to this site had to do with the fact that the initial budget anticipated that far more editorial work would be needed.

Design: $4,000

On budget. This had to do with the rates that were set with the designer. Rather than opt for an hourly, the designer agreed to a set project fee. This meant that the design changes and adjustments were all included in the project fee. Design became a fixed, rather than variable, cost.

Production: $2,500

On budget. Included in the same package with the designer who also served as production artist and HTMLer on this project.

Marketing: $1,550

Over budget. Searching the Internet for appropriate links ultimately became a time consuming task that took a long time to yield qualified links. While many search engines returned thousands of results pertaining to the subject matter (Sexual abuse and the Catholic Church), few were approved by the law firm which was understandably sensitive to the types of Web sites that it was providing links to. In addition, the press release took much longer to write than anticipated, causing Sustainable Media to conclude that it is harder to summarize the work than actually do it. On the other hand, a lesson learned concerned the fact that despite search engines, links, and other Web marketing, nothing draws traffic to a Web site more than an old-fashioned article in print!

Site Maintenance and Management: $1,500

On budget. In fact, many last-minute additions to the Web site's case detail were added to the site free of charge. This included additional information pertaining to the legal logistics of the case.

Client Management/Liaison: $1,500

Over budget. Trouble with the client's Internet connection increased costs as separate trips to the client had to be made. More on this later.

In Summary

Overall this was a terrific project advancing a worthy cause—using the Internet to reach out to victims of sexual abuse, an exhilarating use of the Internet as a medium to make a powerful impact on people's lives. This impact concerns our social fabric—one far more intriguing than whether Netscape Navigator is superior to Microsoft's Internet Explorer. After all, what are we looking at through those browsers anyway?

From the client's perspective, the project was a success. Along the way, Tremont & Sheldon, which had never been on the Internet before, started to get a solid handle on the medium. Toward the end of producing the site, they were even surfing the Web and suggesting we add links to some of the sites that they found. There was a real sense of partnership in building this site. In many ways, Sustainable Media became a part of the Tremont & Sheldon team, concerned with the details of the case and its potential outcome. Business was conducted; at the same time friendships were built.

How the Client Felt About the Project

Douglas Mahoney
Attorney
Tremont & Sheldon, PC
Bridgeport, CT
http://www.tremont-sheldon.com
lawfirm@tremont-sheldon.com

Had you heard about the Internet before you started your project?

Yes.

What had you heard?

We had heard that the Internet was a new way to communicate and find information but assumed that it was reserved for "computer types" and not for lawyers.

What was the one deciding factor that made your firm decide to build a Web site?

We were frustrated by the restrictions which the courts put on us and our ability to obtain "discovery" through the normal judicial process. We had to go extra-judicial to obtain the information we needed to win our case against the Catholic Church. For years, lawyers have used private investigators; this is just a new method.

How has being on the Internet affected your firm?

It has generated exposure in the legal community as a result of what is perceived as a very creative way to conduct discovery.

Now that you are there, what are your thoughts?

We are very happy that we did it, and I think that we would like to expand our presence some time in the future.

How do you see the Internet affecting your business as a law firm?

It has really improved our image in the legal community and hopefully increased our referral work. After registration on the search engines, we hope to see a bigger impact in this area.

The site also worked. While we can't go into details (that's for the courts to decide), several individuals who saw the site contacted the firm and are coming forward with additional evidence in the case.

Is this the first time that the Internet has played such a key role in a case of this nature? We are not sure. But the situation bodes well for the medium. It confirms the Sustainable Media notion that the Internet can be an incredibly powerful force for social change, as well as commerce.

For the uninitiated, setting up DNS can be a tricky proposition. This was the first time that Sustainable Media was serving more than one URL off a Macintosh Server. In the past, technical restrictions precluded Macintosh Web Servers from serving multiple domain names. Then came a software product called Home Door, which offered a solution. The product works fine if, and a big if, you fully understand the intricacies of how the Internet uses DNS. We didn't, and going down that path led to some confusing dead ends, mistakes, and budget overruns. Hard lessons learned.

Second, we came to realize that the most important first step in working with clients that are not on the Internet is to get them on-line. In the beginning of the project we set the client up with an Internet Service Provider. The provider was unable to provide the resources to help the client set up their PPP account on a machine running Windows. The project got off to a shaky start because the client did not know the medium and was not set up properly to explore it. This also included having email services.

About a month into the project, we were forced to visit the client's offices (they are in Bridgeport, we are in Manhattan—about an hour and a half commute) and help them set up their machine. Fortunately, after switching Internet service providers and finding one with excellent customer service, even the Macintosh-only Sustainable Media team was able to get the connection up and the client's email functioning.

This enabled the client to be an active participant in the process. They began to send email daily asking "Can we do this?" "Have you seen that?" "Could we adjust this?" All in all, it was this learning process that made the project a success and allowed us to get to know the client personally and professionally.

Lesson learned: make sure the client understands enough to be an active participant in the process.

The Web developer knows the Web; the client knows the project. Working as a team is ultimately what made this project a success.

Where is the Company Now?

The Tremont & Sheldon Web site will grow slowly as the case against the Church continues, and more and more content will be presented on the Web site. The law firm, one of the few in Connecticut with a Web site, will also slowly expand the content in its other sections providing not only information about the firm's activities, but also important information that Connecticut consumers need to know.

Sustainable Media will help the firm grow its site. The company is also now working with several other law firms to help build their Web sites.

Color versions of this CD-ROM can be seen in Color Plate #9.

Case Study: Medium Web Site

General Introduction to the Project

The Interactive Factory's project for Mosby, a medical communication firm, was a prototype for a Web site that the company paid the Interactive Factory to develop. The goal was to determine how the Web site would function and whether the concept warranted development as a major project.

The database-driven Web site featured a public component, which a general audience could interact with, as well as a private component, which was intended for physicians and health-care providers to access.

Company Profile

Interactive Factory
Boston, MA
http://www.ifactory.com

Clients

In addition to the projects it has worked on, the company works with the following clients: Apple Computer; Addison Wesley, Bolt, Beranek & Newman; Boston Museum of Fine Arts; Boston Museum of Science; Cambridge Rindge Latin School; Chicago Museum of Science and Industry; EF Education; Kentucky Educational Television; Lotus; Math Soft; the MIT Media-Lab; Paramount Interactive; PWS Publishing Company; Silver Burdett & Ginn; University of Wisconsin Medical School; and the New Engand Medical Center.

Company Mission

Interactive Factory offers expertise in all aspects of new media design and development. The company has a strong history of forging compelling material into imaginative new products, combining superior design skills, educational theory, and the most recent advances in technology. Interactive Factory takes full advantage of the expanding capabilities of the new medium while at the same time keeping human sensibilities at the center of its work.

Building successful interactive media requires an extremely broad set of skills and talents. The company team includes people expert in interface design, software engineering, educational design, project management, graphic design, illustration, video production, and sound composition. The company takes a project from conception to completion, on time and on budget.

Because the advent of interactive media and the Internet allows people to experience, create, and share ideas and information in new ways, we are experiementing with and designing new narrative architectures, online simulations, and learning environments that allow people to interact with each other, share their thoughts, compare perspectives, and collaborate.

Through its work, the company hopes to expand the horizons of communication, education, work, and creativity.

Employees

10

Freelancers

Nearly a third of the company's work is allocated to freelancers.

Equipment List

Unix, Macintosh, Windows, and Windows NT

Description and Goals of the Project

The goal of the project was to develop a prototype for a consumer health informational site. "The sexy part of the site," explains Rose, "is a health risk analysis where you answer questions about your lifestyle and the site produces a list of areas where you need to change habits in order to improve your health."

The ambitious project, which while still in its infancy in many ways anticipates using the Internet to increase health-care delivery, offers a "symptom analysis" section where people log in and answer questions about a particular symptom they have. Says Rose, "If you have a fever or a cough, you type in an answer to a question. Based on continued feedback, the system will ask the next important question, the types of things a doctor would ask.

Inevitably, you get direction on what to do next up to the point of calling your doctor."

The other side of the project is a custom publishing side designed to foster business-to-business communication between the client, Mosby, and its clients in the health-care industry. Included in the prototype is a custom-publishing system for business-to-business communication, what Rose describes as "a workflow management system."

The system works as follows: Suppose Mosby is producing an informational magazine for the public or its customers called *You & Your Health* for a major health-care company such as Aetna. Each party—Mosby and Aetna—work on the periodical together. The Interactive Factory's prototype allows an individual from Aetna to search an object-oriented database and plan an upcoming issue. "Say you search for articles and pictures, and you can remotely slot articles into a template for viewing. The database loads your query onto a machine in Quark, generates a Portable Document Format (PDF) for you to view directly into your browser," explains Rose. "That way the client can look at the article and the images and approve it. You can even place notes and comments on the article and have it pass back and forth for additional approval."

Client

Mosby, a respected medical publisher of medical information.

How Did the Company Get the Job?

"There were four or five groups in Boston bidding on the development of the prototype," says Rose. "Ultimately, we put forth a solid proposal that clearly communicated our design philosophy for working in this media. The client appreciated our desire to produce value and integrity."

How Many People Worked on the Project?

A producer, a designer, a creative director, and three programmers.

Hardware

All graphics were done on a Macintosh and the database was created on a Linux box.

Challenges

Rose outlines a common problem faced by companies working on the prototype for a particular project: how much will work and how much will not.

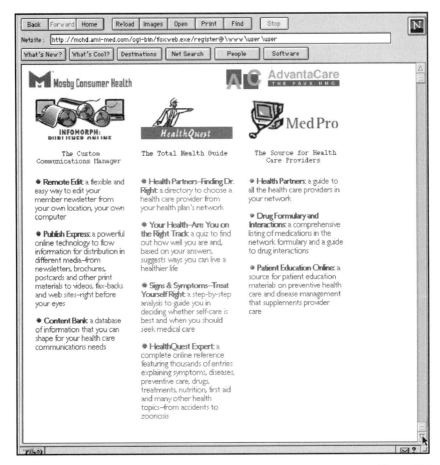

Figure 13.1
The Main Menu from the Mosby Web Site

"During the concept phase of the project, the criteria kept shifting when it came to how functional the prototype would be," he explains. "As we were reviewing the concept, there were some aspects of the project that we said would be nailed down later. What eventually happened was that the client perceived that meant those elements would become working aspects of the prototype. There was a miscommunication, and we ended up having to make more things work in the prototype than we originally estimated. It wasn't a problem, but it certainly presented a challenge."

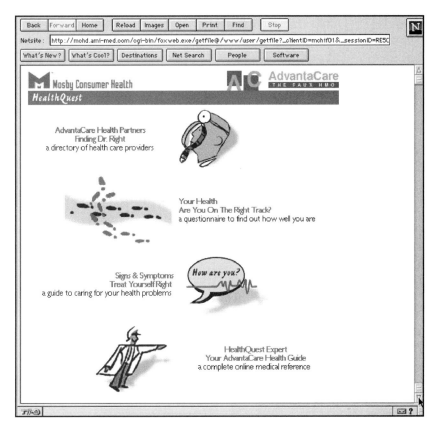

Back | Forward | Home | Reload | Images | Open | Print | Find | Stop

Netsite: http://mohd.ami-med.com/cgi-bin/foxweb.exe/getfile@/www/user/getfile?_clientID=mchif01&_sessionID=RE5C

What's New? | What's Cool? | Destinations | Net Search | People | Software

Mosby Consumer Health

AdvantaCare
THE FAUX HMO

HealthQuest

AdvantaCare Health Partners
Finding Dr. Right
a directory of health care providers

Your Health
Are You On The Right Track?
a questionnaire to find out how well you are

How are you?

Signs & Symptoms
Treat Yourself Right
a guide to caring for your health problems

HealthQuest Expert
Your AdvantaCare Health Guide
a complete online medical reference

Figure 13.2
A Consumer Page

There was also the challenge that many new media and Internet firms face—understanding the inner workings of their clients' business so that they can really help them accomplish their goals. "We got a solid briefing, and we were fortunate that our client spent a lot of time teaching us his business," comments Rose. "But ultimately we had some difficulty understanding the client's lingo." "For us to be successful," he concludes, "we had to understand how our client worked. We went the extra mile in that regard because it was important for us to deliver something that made sense to them." In addition to understanding their client's general business operations, the Interactive Factory also faced the task of structuring the object-oriented database. "We had literally thousands of articles that we had to review and make decisions about in terms of how to structure them," says Rose. "That is a huge challenge as anyone who builds databases knows. The structure has to support the goal." All in all, building the project prototype took 10 weeks from start to finish.

Budget

For its work, the Interactive Factory was paid approximately $100,000, which broke down according to the various sections of the database, which included:

Design:	$18,000
Remote Editing Module:	$7,000
Database:	$8,000
Publishing Creation Aspect:	$18,000
Health-Care Provider Directory:	$3,000
Health Risk Assessment Component:	$7,000
Symptom Analysis:	$7,000
Encyclopedia:	$12,000
Integration:	$4,000
Project Management:	$10,000

Rose felt that presenting a budget for each aspect of the prototype was a better way to communicate how the prototype would come together for the client. The goal, in short, was to make sure that the client was fully aware of how the project would be built and its corresponding costs. "Our clients hire us because of our reputation and the quality of our work," comments Rose. "They trust us to put together the right team to produce our best work in their interests. Because they trust us, it is not really that important that they know how many hours we spend on doing something and at what rate we pay various members of our team, such as designers."

"The downside to that approach," he concedes, "is that you aren't presenting information in such a way that if you billed the client for say, three days of illustration, and you ended up taking five, you can't go back and ask for the difference since that is not how you presented the budget to begin with."

Based on the results of the project, however, Rose's approach was on target. "The project was definitely profitable," he comments. "We did spend more time on learning and engineering a new way to deliver information, but we still hit a 20 to 30% margin, excluding some of the time we spent as a unit learning."

In Summary

"The way we spent time understanding our client and applying our philosophy of design to a complex project was a success for us," says Rose. "We had a great synergy with our client. We successfully melded their ideas and our background. That in the end produced a valuable prototype."

"Perhaps we were a little too optimistic about the performance of the database," says Rose. "The performance speed of the prototype is a little slow. Overall, the experience would have been richer if we invested more in the technology side of the project. Of course, that's because we were really focused on creating a workable and reliable indicator of a project so that it could be thoroughly evaluated. The rest is not really the job of the prototype. The prototype is merely a proof of concept that something should be done. And we proved that it should."

Where is the Company Now?

The project, which by all accounts was a successful one for the Interactive Factory as well as for Mosby, launched the company into the notion of database-driven Web site. "Visualizing what could be done and seeing our team pull together, we now know that we want to do more interactive sites, not just design a few pages on the Web," says Rose.

"What really excites us about the use of such database-driven Web sites is the idea of creating real-time, multi-user environments where people can talk and hear each other. Sites that, while they are mediated by technology, happen in real time," he says.

Toward that end, the Interactive Factory, is in the alpha phase of a project for distance learning called Chalk, which enables professors to lecture to remote audiences while simulating real-time educational environments, even for remote audiences.

"We don't think it will replace the classroom," concedes Rose, who at heart is as much an educator as he is the head of a new media company. "But what you can do is leverage the use of the computer as a resource to put people in contact with professors who they would not ordinarly have access to whether its a result of distance or the fact that the professor is a respected authority on the subject that is generally not available. In that case, Chalk gives people access to information and education they would not ordinarily have."

Color versions of this CD-ROM can be seen in Color Plates #10 and 11.

Case Study:
Large Intranet

Type of Product Being Profiled

Almost as soon as the Internet was "in" and corporate America was rushing to establish a presence on the Web, it was "out." Replacing it was the Intranet, networks where companies communicate internally, share documents and connect to their suppliers and customers to share information and sales. Every year businesses spend millions of dollars preparing paperwork and establishing the processes that enable them to conduct business-to-business communication.

The National Aeronautics and Space Administration (NASA) is no exception. Each year NASA contracts with corporations to provide the organization with technology development and technical support. Each of those contractors, along with NASA's own employees, must follow established procedures in requesting everything from overtime to extra parts. The ability to automate those procedures using the Internet as a network—an Intranet—was the focus of the Lightbulb Factory's project for NASA.

Size of Market

It is widely reported that 80% of all software is purchased by businesses. Intranets offer large corporations the capability to cost-effectively connect large and geographically disperse work forces, manage large amounts of data, and reduce administrative costs.

Both the purchasing power of corporate customers and the potential benefits of Intranets caused *The Wall Street Journal* to estimate that the market for Intranets will more than triple this year and the next. Open Text, the makers of Intranet software, post market studies on their Web site that suggest 50% of all businesses are expected to have Intranets by 1998.

General Introduction to the Project

Lockheed was contracted by NASA to provide logistics, support, and maintenance for the space shuttle. The company provides repair services and support for the space agency's experiments, which are typically loaded into research and development bays housed on the station.

As a NASA contractor, Lockheed had to document all of its services using paper-based forms, which covered everything from detailing experiments, travel expense requests, and reimbursements, for both NASA personnel and Lockheed's employees. In many cases, each document required multiple signatures and approvals from several NASA offices. Since many of Lockheed's and NASA's employees are dispersed throughout this country, and some scientists are as far away as Europe, the submission of paperwork and the approval process often had the propensity to take longer than time allowed. NASA is required by federal law to comply with the Paperwork Reduction Act of 1977, but since the act was passed the majority of NASA's administrative processes were still based on paper.

For several years, the Lightbulb Factory had been working with MicroPower Software Ltd., a company formed by Dr. Dennis Grega to provide commercial and custom high-end business software for client/server applications and the World Wide Web. The two companies have jointly developed the Business Operations Support System (BOSS), a high-end accounting software package that enables companies to perform detailed project management and tracking. The goal of the project was to customize MicroPower's application to enable Lockheed and NASA to maximize efficiency and share data across networks.

When MicroPower was awarded the contract, it subcontracted the programming to Lightbulb. The project initially included two components, one 4D-based accounting system based on BOSS, and the second component a Web-based front end that enabled users to access the system. "Originally, we were going to deliver the entire thing using the complete BOSS application, but when we went to the Ames Research Center, we found that NASA had many older machines that were not capable of running the program," explains Cianca. "We had no choice but to turn to the Web to enable underpowered machines to access the system," he explains. "In addition, we found that there were several researchers in Russia that needed to be able to access the system. We didn't want to make the system a dedicated Ethernet connection, so again, the Web really became our only option."

Figure 14.1
The Home Page

Figure 14.2
The Login Page

Company Profile

Lightbulb Factory, Inc.
New York, NY
http://www.lightbulb.com
sales@lightbulb.com

Clients

AT&T, Solomon Brothers, Citibank, Defense Commerce Agency, Morgan Stanley, and other financial organizations

Company's Mission

To use advanced technologies to reduce the cost of client/server development for customers while empowering clients with new technologies years before they are introduced into the marketplace.

Employees

Four

Freelance

Three

Equipment List

2 Sun SPARC servers, 2 smaller Sun workstations, and 20 Macintosh workstations

Project Profile

Description and Goals

The Lockheed-NASA Intranet needed to allow both company and the space organization to place purchase orders, travel and overtime requests, and get approval for such requests quickly and securely.

The business relationship with the parties was not only typical of government-contractor relationships, but is also indicative of the type of working relationships common in the Web development business—client hires company, company hires freelance designer, and so forth.

In this case, NASA hired Lockheed to provide system support for the space station. Lockheed turned to MicroPower, and MicroPower turned to Lightbulb. The relationships were not transparent to the initial client. "It was a partnership right from the beginning in that each of us was excited to work on the project," Cianca explains. "These types of relationships are common in the government. Typically a government agency will contract with a large company and specify that the large company work with smaller businesses. It helps distribute the wealth and is a way the government can help small or minority-owned businesses."

How Many People Worked on the Project (internal, external)?

Lockheed committed 12 people to the project, MicroPower had 11, and Lightbulb had 3.

From start to finish the entire project took a year and a half to build.

Challenges

The technical challenges of developing a secure, multi-user Intranet system were somewhat daunting.

First, the technology itself was evolving so quickly that it made it difficult to design an approach and stick with it. "From the time we started to design the project to the point in which we were almost halfway through with it, we went from no version of Netscape to Netscape 2.0," says Cianca. "Now, imagine trying to build a highly secure system with a lot of advanced features while that was happening."

The evolution of the Web thus had a major impact on the project. "We started in early 1995 and as new features, such as tables in browsers, became possible, we wanted to use them to make a more functional project," he says. "That meant we had to go back and start from scratch again. In the end it made for a better product, but it took a lot of time and energy."

Security became very important as well. The project relies on a proprietary technology and methodology developed by Lightbulb. "We bypassed the built-in security on the browser and enforced a higher level of security on the server side, which prevents lateral entry into the Intranet," Cianca explains. "There's no URL for the user to save, so they can't come back and spend their time trying to get into the server."

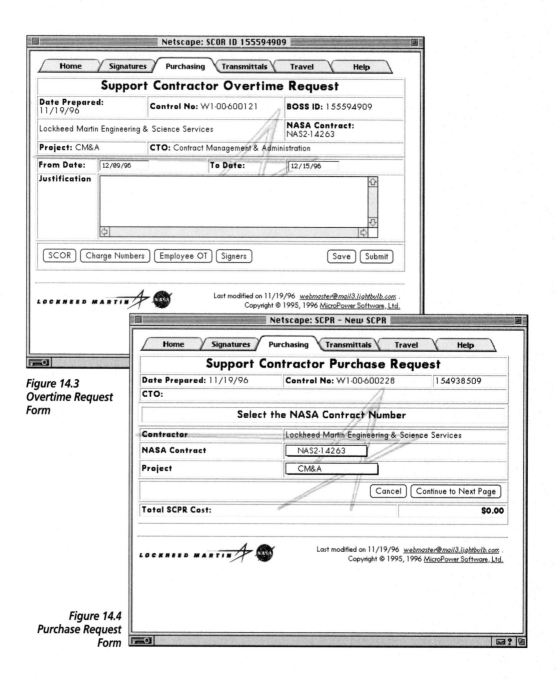

Figure 14.3
Overtime Request
Form

Figure 14.4
Purchase Request
Form

But perhaps the biggest challenge had to do with the fact that not all of the technology needed to make the ambitious project work were fully functional at the time. The entire system is on Macintosh Web servers, one of which serves the accounting package, BOSS, and another which talks to an SQL database. "Our biggest challenge was that Apple's Open Transport and Netscape's Navigator Browser were incompatible," comments Cianca.

Yet while some technology posed challenges, other technology solved them. "We started to write our own Web server since we were working in pre-WebStar Days," says Cianca. "When that product came on the market, we knew we had a good company that had built a solid Web server product, so good we decided to use it. That saved us time," he adds.

In the Macintosh server market, which has seen plenty of new products of late, WebStar is the only commercial grade, industrial strength product for Web serving and securing transactions. "Once we had our WebStar server running, we built custom CGIs to interface with it and we were on our way. That product enabled us to focus our attention on other matters," adds Cianca.

Budgeted versus Actual Numbers

On the project, Lightbulb handled the Web portion of the job. MicroPower handled the implementation of BOSS. The Web elements on the project included development of all of the CGI scripts, HTML, signature routing, and approval technology and security. Cianca estimates that his team of three worked 20-hour days for nearly one year to make the project a success.

For its effort, the company's total budget was $125,000, which included labor and expenses such as an Internet connection, office expenses, and so on. "From a financial standpoint, there is no question that this was really a loss," comments Cianca. "We did a pretty accurate analysis of the project and according to our data, we would have been at a break-even point at $350,000. That's what I would charge to do another project of this type."

Cianca says that $350,000 figure is from the point of view of a traditional 9 to 5 company. "But in our industry, who works from 9 to 5? We had a designer, an HTML person, a CGI programmer, and others working round the clock. At that point, working on this project was a labor of love. It was the challenge that excited us, not the business."

In Summary

Despite Lightbulb's failure on the project at the fiscal level, Cianca remains upbeat and positive. "Yes, the project had a financial downside," he explains, "but despite that fact, far more went right than wrong."

First was NASA's and Lockheed's reaction. "They really are happy with the project," he says. "They were also such great customers to work with. In Lockheed and NASA you have some of the brightest minds in the United States. They understood that we were trying to do something for the first time. At the Ames Research Center, which is NASA's computer center, no one had ever attempted to build a client/server based management system using the Web. We were willing to go the distance for the project and they were willing to go with us," he says.

"These are technology organizations, so they understand technical problems and are very patient," says Cianca with a smile. "They are great at putting up with those days when a few thousand emails go off, and the Director of NASA finds his email box more than a little full one morning."

For NASA, the patience paid off. Cianca says that Lockheed and NASA officials have told him that the system he developed saves each space station research center approximately $1.5 to $4 million per year depending on its size and location.

Lightbulb's partner, MicroPower, is also pleased with the final project. What Cianca's company delivered was the perfect match: MicroPower's highly powerful BOSS system with the capability to deliver a low-cost front end—the Internet. That combination has put the company on the map. And the system that was developed for NASA can be easily sold to any other defense contractor because the forms the system uses are standard acquisition and request forms that are used by any contractor working with NASA or the Department of Defense. "We really have developed a wonderful niche project. There's nothing else like it," says Cianca. "We automated a lot of mandatory paperwork for the government. And now the system has been tested and is fully operational."

For all of the trouble he had on the project, Cianca is remarkably calm and good-natured about it. "It's technology," he says. "Everything doesn't always go as planned, but if you stay at an even pace, you can overcome the technical challenges." Of course, there were plenty. Apple Computer's Open Transport was essential to make the project work, since it enabled the Macintosh servers to handle more transactions and deliver more Web pages than its predecessor, MacTCP. "We had to commit to Open Transport, which was in its infancy," he says. "Unfortunately, it didn't work." Cianca estimates he spent three months working for Apple and Netscape for free debugging Open Transport and Netscape so that the two could work together. "It was unbelievable," he says. "There were some days where I got so frustrated that I was on the verge of tears. I was standing in my office knowing that the technology didn't work. I was losing time and money, and at a certain point, on the verge of going out of business. That was a painful situation to be in."

That wasn't the only problem. 4D could not handle the load required to serve as the database, so halfway through the project Lightbulb had to switch to programming in C. "We eventually moved to Butler for the SQL database," he explains. Butler, made by the Everywhere Development Corporation, is only one of a couple of solid products capable of handling the load. "It was the best product; it was faster and more reliable than anything on the market and going with it really helped" says Cianca. "It's not as fast as Microsoft's SQL or Oracle, but the limitations it comes up against are not in the software but rather constraints of the Macintosh operating system itself."

Lightbulb's lessons learned are applicable to nearly every new media and Web developer. Sometimes the success of the project depends on the software you are using. "It is frustrating that other people's software bugs can delay your project and there isn't much you can do about it. You can report the bugs, but you are really at the mercy of the companies making the tools you are using."

Despite the problems he faced, Cianca has kind words for both Apple and Netscape. "Apple's response on Open Transport was excellent. The engineers there were really trying to create a good product that worked, and they bent over backwards to help us. Other companies, even the old Apple, would not have been so supportive. The same holds true for Netscape. They were incredibly cooperative," he remarks.

Where is the Company Now?

The Lockheed/NASA project enabled Lighbulb to develop a knowledge base for those types of Intranet solutions. "We learned a great deal, the kinds of things you only learn from experience," says Cianca.

For his work, Cianca was elected to the board of the Macintosh Internet Developers Association (MIDAS), a group working to set standards for Macintosh software developers so that their products are more interoperable with each other. His company is also involved in efforts to develop 3D navigation of the Internet. He created the first 3D Internet directory, called X-Space Directory (http//www.xspace.com) to provide an Internet hub where people can find sites ready for the Internet's next biggest interface phase—3D navigation. "Our motto is why type when you can fly," says Cianca.

Color versions of this CD-ROM can be seen in Color Plates #12 and 13.

Case Study: Large Web Site

Type of Product Being Profiled

SCP Communications represents a textbook example of how one small and innovative company can incorporate technology into its culture to compete successfully with larger organizations with much greater resources.

The driving force behind the company's ability to adapt and change in the turbulent health-care market has been its CEO Peter Frishauf. Less well-known than other so-called management visionaries, Frishauf practices what most managers think they can learn at a weekend retreat with high-paid consultants.

His company started in 1982 as a publisher of one title (*Complications in Surgery*) for the physician marketplace. The goal was to provide high-quality medical information that would empower health-care providers, in this case, surgeons. After *Complications in Surgery*, the company went on to create *Infections in Medicine*, a publication that focuses on infection, the number one cause of death in hospitals and the leading condition that brings patients into the primary care physician's office.

Both titles followed SCP's model of providing practice-oriented, peer-reviewed information designed to help clinicians deliver better patient care. In the health care and medical information market, *Infections in Medicine*, with a targeted circulation of 35,000, reaches more high-volume prescribers of oral and injectable antibiotics, antivirals, and antifungals than any other BPA-audited publication. Its emphasis on providing critical, practical information to primary care physicians, oncologists and hematologists, infectious disease specialists, and AIDS-treating physicians has even been expanded to include Continuing Medical Education (CME) for its readers through Tufts University. This means that doctors reading the magazine and responding to the questionnaire printed at the back of the magazine can send in their results and fulfill the ongoing educational requirements as mandated by the American Medical Association.

Additional titles developed for the physician market include the highly respected journal *The AIDS Reader, Complications in Orthopedics, Infections in Urology, Primary Care Review,* and the company's latest, *Drug Benefit Trends.* In addition to its regular publications, SCP also offers custom publishing services such as monographs, newsletters, and special supplements.

The company, which had at the time fewer than 20 employees, was able to produce the depth of material it did by structuring itself along the open and collaborative environment of a newspaper, a model that is not surprising because as a journalist in college Frishauf had already had several page-one stories published in *The New York Times.*

"SCP used computers to conduct its business right from the start," says Frishauf. "In the early days, most of our competitors were using computers as nothing more than fancy typewriters. We built an electronic community at SCP out of necessity. It is built into the culture of who we are. Consequently, the power to share information in a work group environment is an enormous advantage for us. Not many businesses understand that once people are connected to each other via networks, information is organized electronically, and that information is accessible to every member of the company. That is what really matters," he concludes.

Consequently, when the health-care market started to shift its approach to reaching doctors less by traditional print-based publications and more through physician symposia and medical meetings, the company was prepared to make the transition. "We harnessed our energy and infrastructure in a new way. Because we built the organization to function as an open newsroom collaborative environment, we were able to take all of the information we had been working on to produce these publications and change to make lecture programs that could reach doctors not on paper, but face to face at meetings throughout the country," explains Frishauf.

That ability has enabled SCP to manage thousands of medical meetings throughout the country, varying the format, location, and size to make meetings convenient for doctors to attend and keep up on the latest information on advanced patient care. Looking at the health-care and medical information community, you see companies that produce medical publications (magazines, newsletters, and so on) and others that produce medical meetings. SCP is one of the few that does both. "The whole idea is generated from the content. We develop terrific content and then, as an organization, we are able to move that content into whatever communications vehicle makes the most sense, be it print, in person, or electronic," comments Frishauf.

Today, both the traditional publishing business and the symposia business are flourishing and the company is now well on the road to profitability in yet another important market segment—clinical programs, which include Phase III and Phase IV drug research.

About the time that SCP started moving into the clinical trials business, interactive media started to present publishers with an additional communications outlet. The company worked on several video-based teleconferences, slide and audio kits, customized interactive floppy disk programs, and CD-ROMs, all of which are successful product development venues for the company. Again, the same great information, completely different method of delivery.

Then Frishauf started to think about the emerging media of the World Wide Web (WWW). After he figured out what he wanted to do on the Web, Frishauf started to struggle with how, until he remembered a story he had heard one of his college professors at New York University tell.

"John Tebble told a story of how the Associated Press was founded as a result of technology—the telegraph machine," he explains. "During the Civil War there were literally thousands of newspapers in New York City operating what they called the Penny Press. There were wars over the distribution of papers. The telegraph was not designed to transmit text; it was created to transmit banking information, which was why Western Union was one of the first adopters of the technology. During the Civil War, all of the newspapers wanted coverage from the front, but it was impossible. The technology would not enable more than 250 reporters to compete for the bandwidth. The newspaper publishers were forced to come together in agreement and create the Associated Press in a cooperative publishing venture."

Frishauf felt that the same type of venture might make sense for presenting medical information on the Web, although for different reasons. "If you look at it from the perspective of the consumer of medical information—the doctor—the Web could be a mixed blessing. The doctor needs and wants information. If every publisher built its own Web site with its own navigation and its own interface, and there were more than 250 of them, the transfer of information would be inefficient," he comments. "Every publisher wanted to establish its own Web site, with its own brand identity, but that is the worse thing for the doctor. Doctors only care about the quality of the information.

They care less about a structure by magazine title and more about content. In the end, it's the information..."

SCP also recognized that although the company produced an enormous amount of peer-reviewed medical literature, there were still gaps in several therapeutic categories that the company did not cover. Frishauf's plan was to create Medscape, which would serve as one place on the Internet where doctors could come to find the information they needed. By pooling the resources of several publishers, Frishauf believed his company could offer a comprehensive resource of reliable and quality-oriented medical information—what the company calls the *Publisher's Circle.*

Medscape is presently the number one health-care and medical information site on the Web offering full-text clinical journal articles, continuing medical education credits on-line, clinical news updates, interactive self-assessment features, and free access to Medline. The Web site pools information from respected peer-reviewed medical news sources, such as the Food and Drug Administration and the National Institutes of Health.

The Mission of the Site Is to:

- Provide clinicians and other health-care professionals with timely clinical information that is directly applicable to their patients and practice

- Make the clinician's task of information gathering simpler, more fruitful, and less time-consuming

- Make available to a broad medical audience clinical information with depth, breadth, and validity needed to improve the practice of medicine

Highlights and features of the Web site include: thousands of peer-reviewed articles on a variety of topics (including AIDS, cancer, infectious disease, surgery, urology, managed care, women's health and menopause), free access to the National Library of Medicine's Medline biomedical database containing abstracts from 3,800 medical journals, a patient-of-the-month interactive case study, on-line coverage of major medical conferences, late-breaking medical news, and patient information.

According to the company, more than 150,000 members—70% health-care professionals, 30% consumers—have joined Medscape. The site registers a staggering 6,000 new members each week, delivers 800,000 article impressions every month, and serves more than 75,000 visitors monthly.

Because Medscape authenticates every member, the company can pinpoint the types of physicians visiting the site by physician population breakdown. For example, 38.43% of Medscape's registered users come from the general practitioner, family practice, and internal medicine specialties. Approximately 9.44% are surgeons, 5.41% are Ob-Gyns, 5.08% pediatricians, and 4.81% infectious disease specialists.

Medcape's Publisher's Circle

The Medscape Publisher's Circle is a collaborative partnership of leading medical publishers whose content is featured on Medscape. The Publisher's Circle enables content providers to distribute their published material on the Web quickly and cost-effectively, while providing Medscape users with timely information from peer-reviewed articles and quality reference material.

Publishers in the circle supply content to Medscape in the electronic format of their choice. Medscape prepares the content for the Web by formatting it so that it fits into the Medscape look and feel and then uploads the content to the Web site. The effect is to create a true "win-win" partnership that benefits the physician. There's one place on the Web available with great medical information, and each publisher is spared the cost and effort of building and maintaining a Web site as well as the burden of drawing publishers to their site. Publishers join the Publisher's Circle at no cost.

If they code their own material, the publishers keep 70% of the advertising revenue for all of the ads they sell around their articles wherever they appear on Medscape. If Medscape codes the material, the publisher keeps 50% of the advertising revenue. If SCP sells an advertisement near one of the other publisher's articles, it keeps a percentage of the revenue depending on whether SCP or the company coded the article.

Publishers cannot sell advertising around another publisher's content, but they can sell advertising around any of the independent contents that Medscape originally generates for the site.

Current Publisher's Circle participants include *Hippocrates*, *Consumer Health USA*, *Medical Tribune News*, *Family Physician*, *Internist & Cardiologist*, *Obstetrician & Gynecologist*, *European Menopause Journal*, *Emerging Infectious Diseases and Morbidity*, and *Mortality Weekly Report*.

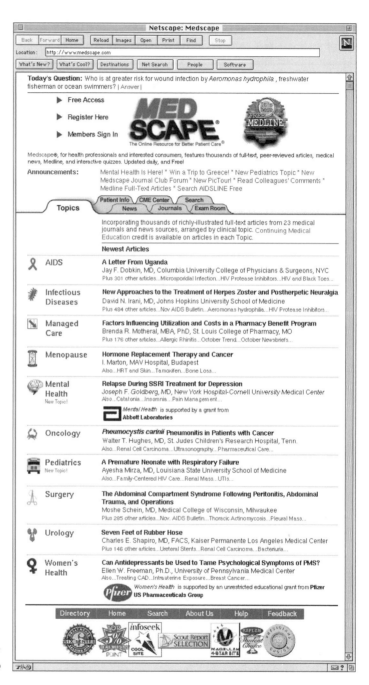

Figure 15.1
The Medscape Home Page

Figure 15.1
The Journals Page

Company Profile

SCP Communications, Inc.
New York, NY
http://ww.scp.com

Client

Medscape, Inc.
New York, NY
http://www.medscape.com
info@medscape.com

Employees

SCP has 75 employees; Medscape has 16.

Freelance

None

Equipment List

The entire company uses Macintosh computers, including Web servers. Medscape is in the process of migrating its Web servers to the Windows NT platform.

Challenges

The company faced three basic challenges.

First, it knew little about the behavior of physicians on the Web. "Who was out there was our biggest initial question," says Frishauf. "In a traditional business model, you could do some basic market research and get a sense. Because all of this was so new we had no idea and no one else did either. It was a tough business decision to gamble on when you are a small publisher that doesn't enjoy the seemingly unlimited resources of larger entities," he comments.

The second challenge concerned design. "Physicians have developed a routine for scanning a wide body of information quickly. We needed to be able to translate that structure successfully on the Web," he says. "Articles needed to be structured simply, but meaningfully to people. Headings needed to be clear, and author affiliations, which are important to physicians, needed to be prominent. In short, we had to replicate the traditional journal model, the way doctors are accustomed to seeing information, yet still make it interesting. For us, the most important thing we had to do was to afford people a way of using computers that provided a familiar look and minimized the risk that doctors could get lost or disoriented on-line. Things such as frames would not be acceptable," says Frishauf.

Finally, the company had to convince other publishers that it was in their best interest to participate. Once convinced they were true partners in Medscape, and that the site was in their best interest, the company had its start.

Budgeted versus Actual Numbers

In operation for a little over one-and-a-half years, SCP has invested $2 million dollars in cash in Medscape, a factor that includes hardware, software, administrative expenses, and salaries.

"We were lucky that while we were a company without debt, we could afford to allocate the resources to start Medscape, which is small when you compare it to the tens of millions invested by other publishers in our field," says Frishauf. But there's a lot of sweat equity in the effort. People such as Stephen Smith, Editorial Director, Bill Seitz, Chief Technology Officer, and the whole Medscape team put a lot of time into the project. How do you put a number on that?"

Against that $2 million investment, Medscape has realized $1.8 million in sales and will recognize $1 million in income in 18 months. Medscape expects to be profitable by 1998. By comparison, there are 162 people working in what *Wired* magazine calls its on-line properties (which includes *HotWired*). In the first six months of 1996, the company has sold $1.1 million in advertising sales.

"We have a three-fold business strategy," says Frishauf. "First, in the tradition of PT Barnum, we have to get people in the tent to see the elephant. The second is when you see who is in the tent. We've done the first two. The final step, which is our goal for 1997, is to make meaningful statements about the people in the tent. That way we can go to the advertisers and say 'these are your customers, let us tell you about their behavior.'"

In Summary

"Ultimately, content wins and because of the Publisher's Circle, Medscape has great content," says Frishauf citing the fact that his product has an undeniable recognition and credibility among a very information-discerning crowd—physicians. SCP has always been one of the primary suppliers of practical medical advice for better patient care. Medscape represents another delivery device for the company's information. Frishauf cites statistics that suggest his site gets 800,000 page views per month as evidence that people don't just come to the Web site, they use the information there—whether to make them more aware physicians or better patients. In many ways, Medscape represents a good example of using the Internet as an information vehicle, not an entertainment medium.

In terms of the big picture, SCP launched a new company that has great potential for the future without spending an enormous amount of capital on new technology. "It's always been the SCP way," says Frishauf. "We try to employ intelligence, ingenuity, and strategy as a substitute for throwing cash at goals."

More than anything, Frishauf cites the fact that the advertising and marketing of the pharmaceutical industry has been slow to embrace the notion of advertising products on the Internet. To gain insight into the process, one has to have a basic understanding of how advertising in the pharmaceutical industry works. A pharmaceutical company might produce several different drugs that are targeted to one or several types of physicians, based on their specialty. For example, you probably wouldn't market AIDS-treating drugs to an orthopedic surgeon, even though they might have an interest in the subject. He or she is not the kind of physician likely to see a large number of AIDS patients. He or she would, instead, see patients who typically need hip or knee replacements. Other physicians would make a better marketing choice, such as general and family practitioners. Each drug might have one senior product manager, or in some cases, a team consisting of product and marketing managers within the pharmaceutical company. That team works with an advertising agency, generally a specialized agency that deals with medical advertising, to develop market strategies, advertising content, and more importantly, to determine in which medical publications to place advertisements to reach the type of doctors who are most likely to need information on the product.

The advertising agency often serves as an "in-between" between the publisher and the product manager. Although this system might have some benefits, it has one particular drawback: the advertising agencies place advertisements in medical publications based on a system. That system includes how many people might see the advertisement, the magazine's print run, price, and so on. Agencies have no system in place to evaluate the placement of advertisements on the Web. "The marketing world did not adopt the Web as fast as we thought it would," says Frishauf. "Advertising agencies typically buy off traditional rate cards," he explains. "But you can't buy the Web like other media and as a result, the advertising agencies have not started to make major advertising budget allocations to this medium."

Most of the advertising sold on Medscape comes directly from the product manager of the drug, not the agency—a surprising fact given that Medscape has drawn the volume and quality of customers that those same advertising agencies would fall over in disbelief if they were for a traditional print publication.

Finally, Frishauf notes that personnel has been a big problem as well. Medscape's success is no doubt due to its core members who have been with the venture since it started. Others have come and gone. "We are not a traditional company," says Frishauf. "We don't hire traditional people. We hire people with a passion for information that will help doctors take care of the sick, help people maintain their health and improve the quality of their lives. If people don't understand how to make medicine interesting, fun, and meaningful, they tend not to make a connection here," he explains. "But it's not enough. They have to understand sales and marketing, technology, design, and the notion that a company has to be an open system where information is shared. There's no turf here. It is a collaborative process. It's very difficult to find people who share all of those visions."

Where is the Company Now?

Medscape has engaged a major Wall Street investment banking firm to find a strategic partner who will provide mezzanine-level financing.

With that project clearly on its way, Frishauf is now turning back to SCP itself and the development of Intranet (a term he dislikes) to empower the company's customers to access information when they need it. "Our clinical trials division will be on our Intranet so that our clients can log in and check on the amount of data we have collected and gain insight into the study as it happens," he comments. "Our symposia group, which holds thousands of medical meetings a year, will also be on the system so that people can log in and immediately check out where the next meeting is, what time it starts, and what the topic will be," he adds. "We want the information that is presently used as part of SCP's electronic community to expand to include our customers as well. Open information has always been our business model and we are now developing the product and the process to make that business model work even more for our customers so that they can get the information they need more conveniently and efficiently in order to make better business decisions. The technology might evolve; that has been our goal since we started the company...and it always will be."

Color versions of this CD-ROM can be seen in Color Plates #14, 15, and 16.

In Closing

Business is not always about time sheets, spreadsheets, hourly rates, business proposals, and plans. Business is not science. There is a human element that defies analysis. In no company is that element more present than in Music Pen. We would be woefully remiss if we ended this book with the last word on a business note. After all, business is as much magic as it is anything else. And Music Pen is as good an example of magic as any we've come across.

An Interview with Yee-Ping Wu, Founder, Music Pen, Inc.

Music Pen founder Yee-Ping Wu wanted to be a classical pianist ever since she was a little girl growing up in China. She left her homeland during Mao's bloody Cultural Revolution and landed at the world-renowned Juilliard, where she met Philip Lui, who was working on his doctorate in composition. Lui, a multi-talented composer, computer technician, and rollerblader, had been working on building a music composition system that could transform the way computers interacted with and created music—what Ping describes as "the ability to use technology to enhance the creative musical experience."

In the middle of her successful concert pianist career, Ping decided she needed to expand her world. She married Lui and the two decided to combine their knowledge and excitement to start a music technology business, which they called Music Pen. That was in 1987.

Today, the company is a highly regarded technology and digital media company, and it has also been one of the few companies to succeed in the somewhat turbulent CD-ROM marketplace. Music Pen released its first CD-ROM in 1993 (the highly acclaimed Lenny's MusicToons), developed its own authoring tools, language, and development environment, and is capable of delivering content not only on CD-ROM and the Internet, but also via cable modems, satellites, and video game platforms as well. With more than 40 products on the market, and clients such as Microsoft and 15 of the largest companies in the world, Music Pen licenses both its own content and proprietary MPen Technology ™ across the major digital platforms. As Wu says, "Music Pen licenses technology and builds content."

We mentioned that it is important to be able to track time and hours in a new media and Internet development business. Music Pen takes a different approach. Why?

When I was a concert pianist, I would practice for hundreds of hours to give a two-hour performance. The audience came to see a product—my performance. They had no idea and no concept how much hard work went into that concert. They only wanted to answer one question: Is the performance enjoyable?

How do you measure enjoyment?

We are in the creativity business. But you can't measure creativity. It's too hard to measure and it cannot be defined. It is almost unfair to measure creativity by the standard of the hourly rate. If we spend five hours producing a product and you love it, that is our talent. And if you don't like the results we have produced, how many hours we spent on the product is irrelevant. That is the nature of our business today. It is something that most business schools do not teach because talent, creativity, and knowledge are difficult to measure, and business models typically don't reflect them. Talent and creativity have immeasurable value and there are no two deals that are the same. You need to define a price based on what you believe your performance is worth, and what you believe its value to the market place is, not only how much time you took to produce it. The value of your product is relative—not absolute. You need to recognize what your final product is worth.

So does talent guarantee success?

Well, I would say that talent alone is not enough, but building on talent is certainly the foundation. There are many other factors, but it is definitely the key. It gives you the chance to compete, but it also takes discipline and practicality to succeed.

How does talent, discipline, and practicality relate to this industry—that of new media and the Internet?

I think there is a huge problem in this industry. No one seems to be willing to tell you what the reality is. I feel very strongly that this industry was started with too much hype and too much money and no practical business planning. As an industry, we have not seen the development of depth and maturity required for long-term success. A shortsightedness dominates and everyone is looking for the quick kill, the quick success. It's supposed to be like a gold mine. This is one of the first industries that simply had too much money right from the beginning.

In some ways it's not about the business but the investment. I have seen so many people put together business plans with salaries that are outrageous while designing no income streams except from the IPO and investors. In fact, we didn't even draw salary for many years. How can you ask others to invest and commit to your business when you aren't? It's very important to have a solid plan, build the business blocks, and earn your own living off of your business, not off of the investors.

Where do you think that "quick kill" mentality comes from?

It is definitely part of the social mentality that is in operation today. It's why gambling is becoming so popular—instant reward, instant gratification.

In the context of this industry, people do not seem to be talking about the process of building a business. There's some focus on the beginning—where a business comes from—and a great deal of attention on the end—that the company's owners went public and made a fortune. But today we're watching those fortunes falter. Many of the businesses were never developed from reality in the first place, and, as a result, could never build into a real business. What happens in the middle is left out of the discussion.

Why is the middle so important?

What happens in the middle concerns the process. The everyday meaning of life. Our plan is to build something meaningful. Yes, the beginning is important because that is where we came from. The end, too, is very important. Our goal is to be successful. But the reality is that in the middle we want to ensure our individual fulfillment. In that way, our business becomes a major part of our life. That is where we derive meaning. And meaning is what makes you get out of bed in the morning. You don't get out of bed in the morning only because you want to go public and make millions of dollars. You get out of bed in the morning...after you worked 18 hours the day before because what you are doing has meaning. Because to you and your life, it makes a difference.

How has focusing on the middle helped you build Music Pen?

It has definitely helped us create a very different kind of company. A company that enables creativity to flourish and fosters collaboration. We don't have walls and office; we work in environments and teams. The focus on a meaningful process has created the kind of environment where we can bring the best people and put them in a position to succeed.

You are also a firm believer in the idea that meaning encourages the pursuit of knowledge...the ultimate resource?

Yes. At Music Pen our philosophy is to "promote knowledge," which goes back to the issue of process. The process is the cultivator of knowledge. And, if your goal is to make money, I suggest you pay close attention to the process. That's where the business planning unfolds. If I believe anything, above all else, it is that knowledge is the fundamental raw material of success.

One last question. So how does the multimedia business compare with the piano?

As hard as this business can be, it is leaps and bounds easier than being a professional classical musician! Classical music is even more competitive than this industry; there's less room for people on top.

But I must say, my drive to grow this business derives a lot from the discipline and motivation classical music has given me. Being a classical musician demands an enormous physical effort, concentration, talent, focus, and intellectual commitment. In short, it demands every aspect of your life.

No one is sitting behind you saying keep practicing. No one places that intense demand on you...if you never get out of bed in the morning and you don't practice, the rest of the world will not care. You and you alone have to be your source of motivation. Sometimes you wake up in the morning and ask yourself "Why am I driving myself so hard?" When you can come up with an answer and still do it...that takes a lot...it means something. Where as running a company you have external demands. You have staff, you have bills, you have consumers. These outside forces are actually refreshing for me.

That's had a direct impact on our company. Music Pen never delays shipping software. When I was a pianist I would never think of delaying my product—the concert. You prepare. You get ready. You deliver. Sometimes people can't believe it, but we deliver. Pianists perform. Software companies ship product. Both should happen on time.

Index

REGISTRATION CARD

Web and New Media Pricing Guide

Hayden
Books

Name _____ Title _____

Company_____Type of business _____

Address _____

City/State/ZIP _____

Have you used these types of books before?   ☐ yes   ☐ no

If yes, which ones? _____

_____

How many computer books do you purchase each year?   ☐ 1–5   ☐ 6 or more

How did you learn about this book?_____

☐ recommended by a friend   ☐ received ad in mail
☐ recommended by store personnel   ☐ read book review
☐ saw in catalog   ☐ saw on bookshelf

Where did you purchase this book? _____

Which applications do you currently use? _____

Which computer magazines do you subscribe to? _____

What trade shows do you attend? _____

Please number the top three factors which most influenced your decision for this book purchase.

☐ cover   ☐ price
☐ approach to content   ☐ author's reputation
☐ logo   ☐ publisher's reputation
☐ layout/design   ☐ other _____

Would you like to be placed on our preferred mailing list?   ☐ yes   ☐ no   e-mail address _____

☐ **I would like to see my name in print!** You may use my name and quote me in future Hayden products and promotions. My daytime phone number is: _____

Comments _____

_____

_____

Hayden Books   Attn: Product Marketing ◆ 201 West 103rd Street ◆ Indianapolis, Indiana 46290 USA

Fax to `317-581-3576`   Visit out Web Page `http://WWW.MCP.com/hayden/`

Fold Here

BUSINESS REPLY MAIL
FIRST-CLASS MAIL PERMIT NO. 9918 INDIANAPOLIS IN

POSTAGE WILL BE PAID BY THE ADDRESSEE

HAYDEN BOOKS
Attn: Product Marketing
201 W 103RD ST
INDIANAPOLIS IN 46290-9058